INJUSTICE
GROUND ZERO

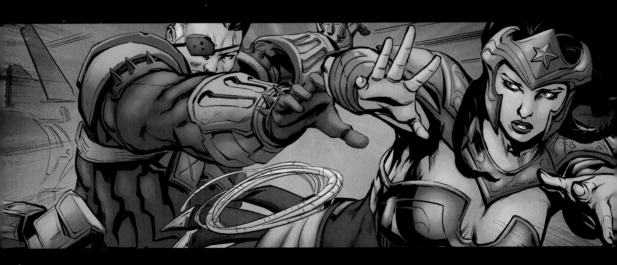

VOLUME 2

INJU

GROUN

CHRISTOPHER SEBELA
Writer

TOM DERENICK   DANIEL SAMPERE   JUAN ALBARRAN
MARCO SANTUCCI   JHEREMY RAAPACK   POP MHAN   DERLIS SANTACRUZ
ANDY OWENS   JUAN ALBARRAN   MIGUEL MENDONCA
Artists

REX LOKUS   J. NANJAN   MARK ROBERTS

STICE
D ZERO

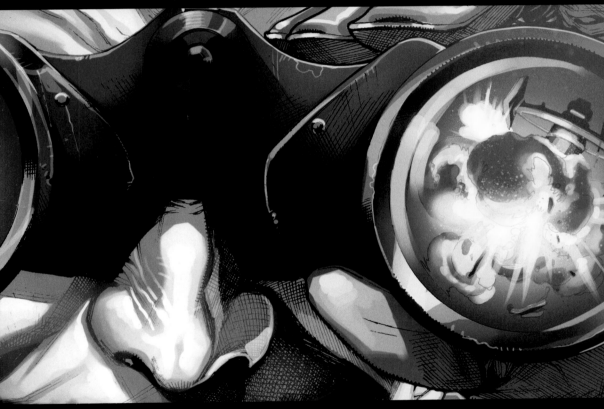

VOLUME 2

SUPERMAN created by JERRY SIEGEL and JOE SHUSTER
By special arrangement with the Jerry Siegel Family

BASED ON THE VIDEO GAME *INJUSTICE: GODS AMONG US*

JIM CHADWICK Editor – Original Series
ROB LEVIN Assistant Editor – Original Series
JEB WOODARD Group Editor – Collected Editions
PAUL SANTOS Editor – Collected Edition
STEVE COOK Design Director – Books
LOUIS PRANDI Publication Design

BOB HARRAS Senior VP – Editor-in-Chief, DC Comics

DIANE NELSON President
DAN DiDIO Publisher
JIM LEE Publisher
GEOFF JOHNS President & Chief Creative Officer
AMIT DESAI Executive VP – Business & Marketing Strategy, Direct to
Consumer & Global Franchise Management
SAM ADES Senior VP – Direct to Consumer
BOBBIE CHASE VP – Talent Development
MARK CHIARELLO Senior VP – Art, Design & Collected Editions
JOHN CUNNINGHAM Senior VP – Sales & Trade Marketing
ANNE DePIES Senior VP – Business Strategy, Finance & Administration
DON FALLETTI VP – Manufacturing Operations
LAWRENCE GANEM VP – Editorial Administration & Talent Relations
ALISON GILL Senior VP – Manufacturing & Operations
HANK KANALZ Senior VP – Editorial Strategy & Administration
JAY KOGAN VP – Legal Affairs
THOMAS LOFTUS VP – Business Affairs
JACK MAHAN VP – Business Affairs
NICK J. NAPOLITANO VP – Manufacturing Administration
EDDIE SCANNELL VP – Consumer Marketing
COURTNEY SIMMONS Senior VP – Publicity & Communications

INJUSTICE: GROUND ZERO VOLUME 2

DC Comics, 2900 West Alameda Ave., Burbank, CA 91505
Printed by LSC Communications, Kendallville, IN, USA. 8/25/17.
First Printing.
ISBN: 978-1-4012-7388-0

Library of Congress Cataloging-in-Publication Data is available.

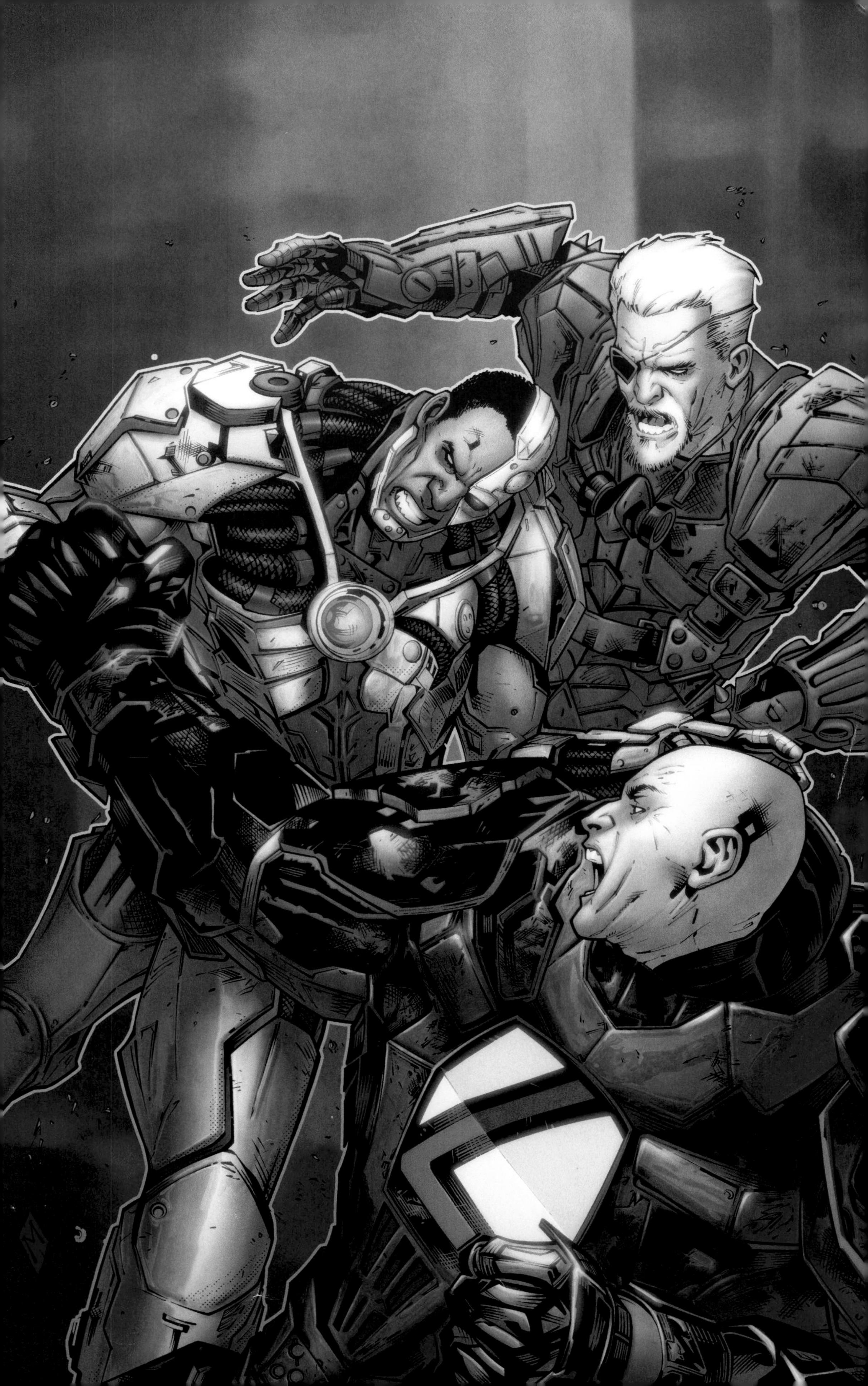

"Let's Have a War" **Tom Derenick** **Pop Mhan** Artists **J. Nanjan** **Mark Roberts** Colorists
Cover art by **Matthew Clark, Sean Parsons** and **Andrew Dalhouse**

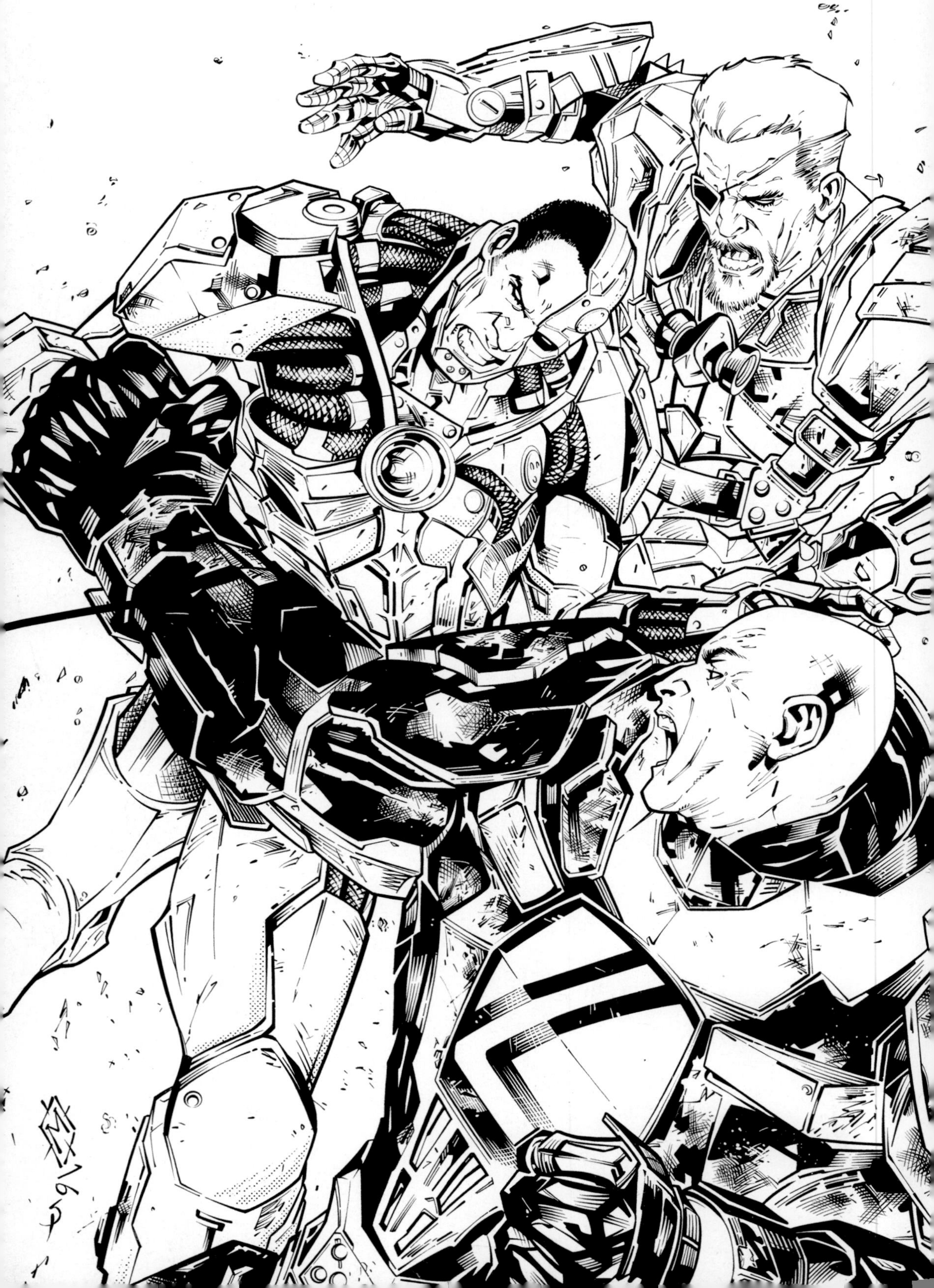

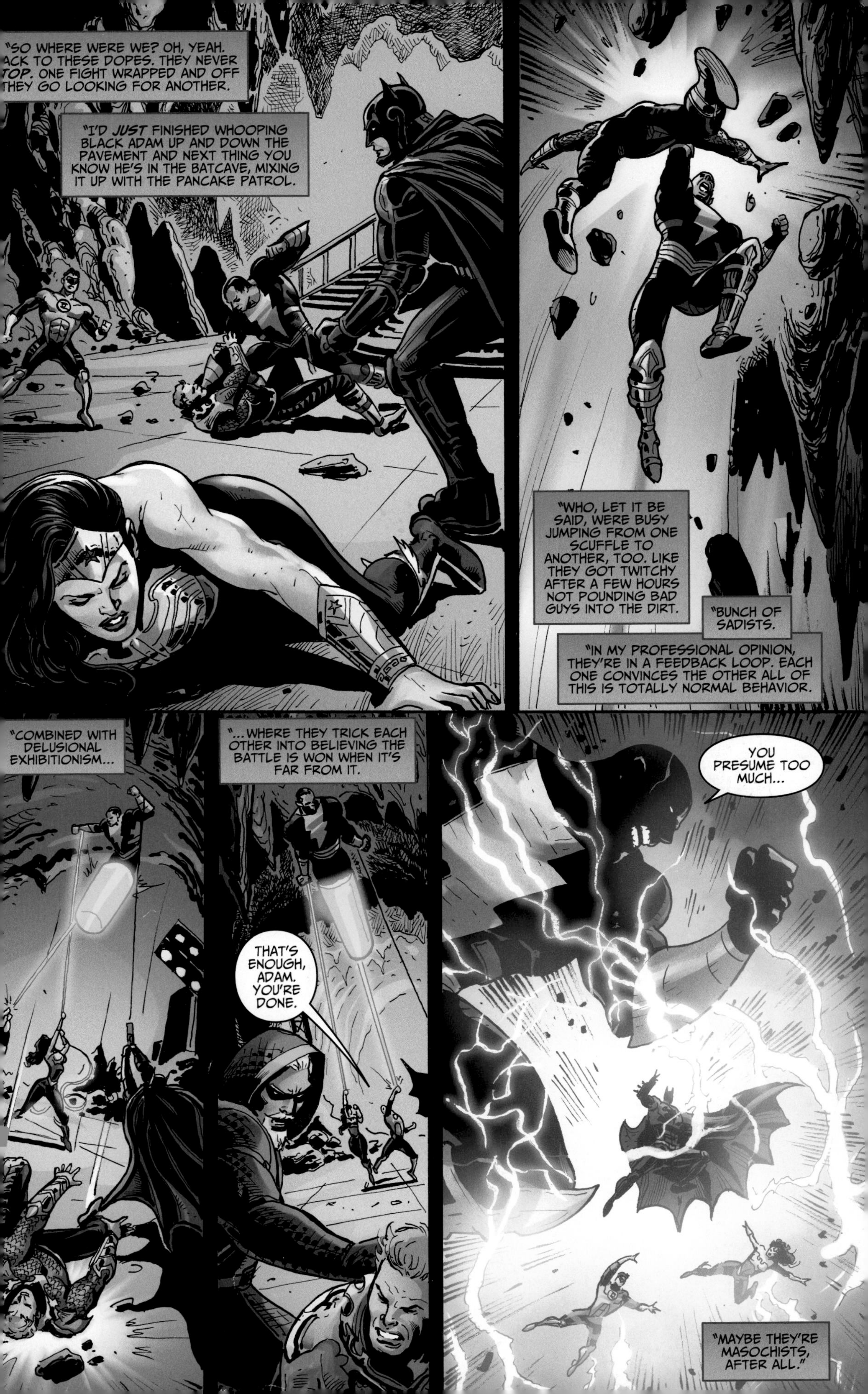

"SO WHERE WERE WE? OH, YEAH. ACK TO THESE DOPES. THEY NEVER TOP. ONE FIGHT WRAPPED AND OFF THEY GO LOOKING FOR ANOTHER.
"I'D JUST FINISHED WHOOPING BLACK ADAM UP AND DOWN THE PAVEMENT AND NEXT THING YOU KNOW HE'S IN THE BATCAVE, MIXING IT UP WITH THE PANCAKE PATROL.
"WHO, LET IT BE SAID, WERE BUSY JUMPING FROM ONE SCUFFLE TO ANOTHER, TOO. LIKE THEY GOT TWITCHY AFTER A FEW HOURS NOT POUNDING BAD GUYS INTO THE DIRT.
"BUNCH OF SADISTS.
"IN MY PROFESSIONAL OPINION, THEY'RE IN A FEEDBACK LOOP. EACH ONE CONVINCES THE OTHER ALL OF THIS IS TOTALLY NORMAL BEHAVIOR.
"COMBINED WITH DELUSIONAL EXHIBITIONISM...
"...WHERE THEY TRICK EACH OTHER INTO BELIEVING THE BATTLE IS WON WHEN IT'S FAR FROM IT.
THAT'S ENOUGH, ADAM. YOU'RE DONE.
YOU PRESUME TOO MUCH...
"MAYBE THEY'RE MASOCHISTS, AFTER ALL."

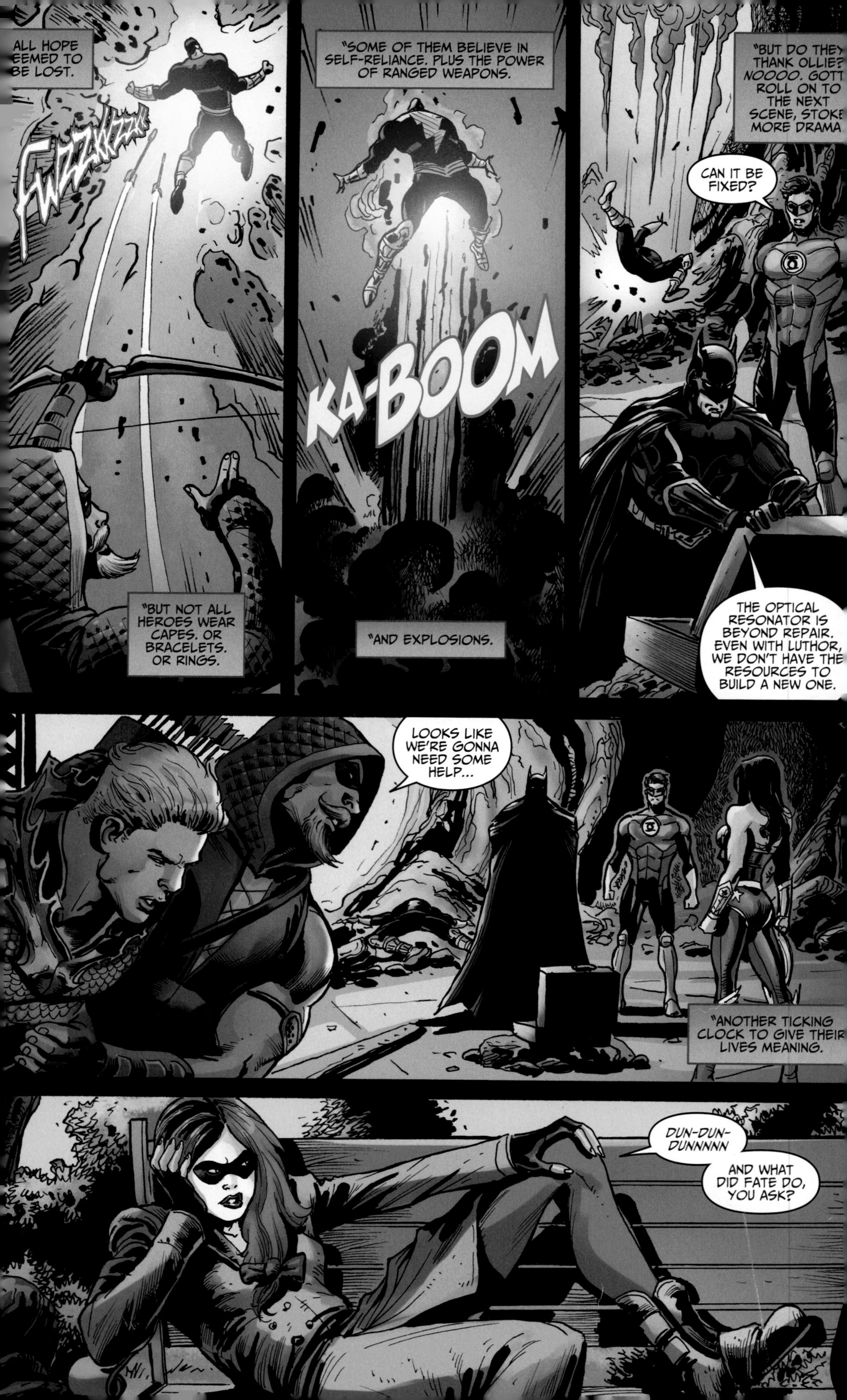
ALL HOPE EEMED TO BE LOST.
FWZZKKZZK
"BUT NOT ALL HEROES WEAR CAPES. OR BRACELETS. OR RINGS.
"SOME OF THEM BELIEVE IN SELF-RELIANCE. PLUS THE POWER OF RANGED WEAPONS.
KA-BOOM
"AND EXPLOSIONS.
"BUT DO THEY THANK OLLIE? NOOOO. GOTT ROLL ON TO THE NEXT SCENE, STOKE MORE DRAMA
CAN IT BE FIXED?
THE OPTICAL RESONATOR IS BEYOND REPAIR. EVEN WITH LUTHOR, WE DON'T HAVE THE RESOURCES TO BUILD A NEW ONE.
LOOKS LIKE WE'RE GONNA NEED SOME HELP...
"ANOTHER TICKING CLOCK TO GIVE THEIR LIVES MEANING.
DUN-DUN-DUNNNNN
AND WHAT DID FATE DO, YOU ASK?

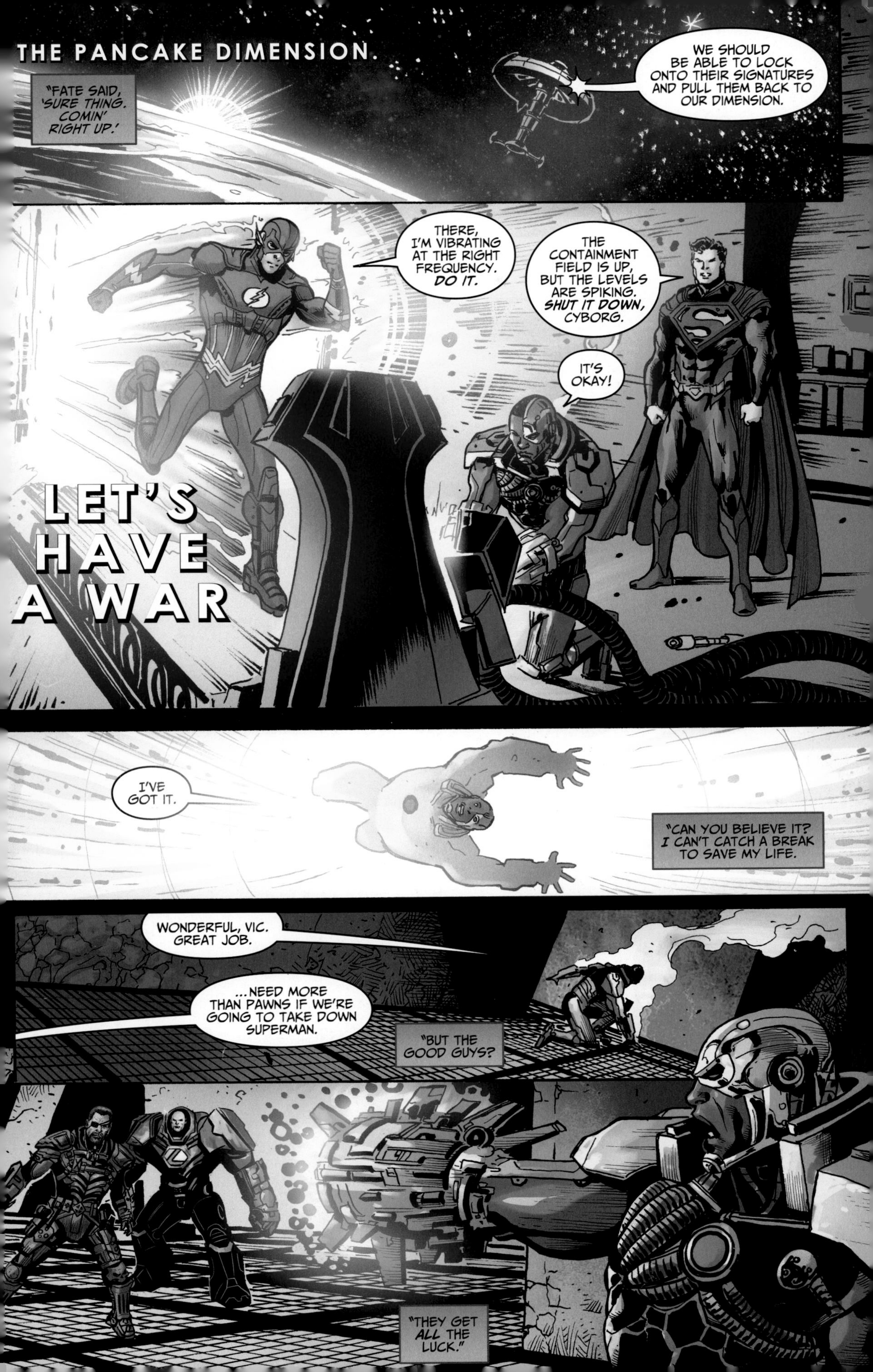
THE PANCAKE DIMENSION.
"FATE SAID, 'SURE THING. COMIN' RIGHT UP.'
WE SHOULD BE ABLE TO LOCK ONTO THEIR SIGNATURES AND PULL THEM BACK TO OUR DIMENSION.
THERE, I'M VIBRATING AT THE RIGHT FREQUENCY. DO IT.
THE CONTAINMENT FIELD IS UP, BUT THE LEVELS ARE SPIKING. SHUT IT DOWN, CYBORG.
IT'S OKAY!
LET'S HAVE A WAR
I'VE GOT IT.
"CAN YOU BELIEVE IT? I CAN'T CATCH A BREAK TO SAVE MY LIFE.
WONDERFUL, VIC. GREAT JOB.
...NEED MORE THAN PAWNS IF WE'RE GOING TO TAKE DOWN SUPERMAN.
"BUT THE GOOD GUYS?
"THEY GET ALL THE LUCK."

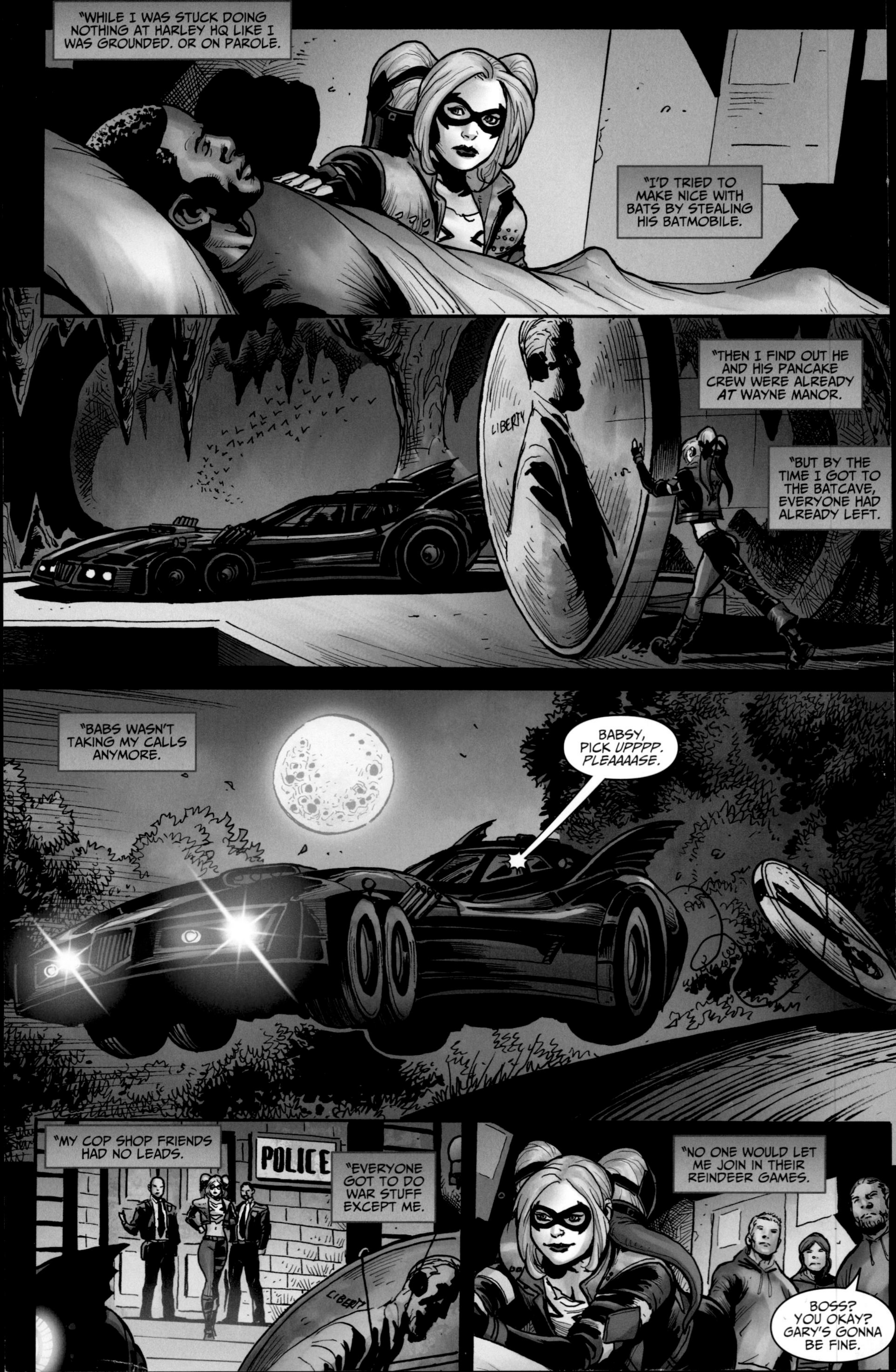
"WHILE I WAS STUCK DOING NOTHING AT HARLEY HQ LIKE I WAS GROUNDED. OR ON PAROLE.
"I'D TRIED TO MAKE NICE WITH BATS BY STEALING HIS BATMOBILE.
"THEN I FIND OUT HE AND HIS PANCAKE CREW WERE ALREADY AT WAYNE MANOR.
LIBERTY
"BUT BY THE TIME I GOT TO THE BATCAVE, EVERYONE HAD ALREADY LEFT.
"BABS WASN'T TAKING MY CALLS ANYMORE.
BABSY, PICK UPPPP. PLEAAAASE.
"MY COP SHOP FRIENDS HAD NO LEADS.
POLICE
"EVERYONE GOT TO DO WAR STUFF EXCEPT ME.
LIBERTY
"NO ONE WOULD LET ME JOIN IN THEIR REINDEER GAMES.
BOSS? YOU OKAY? GARY'S GONNA BE FINE.

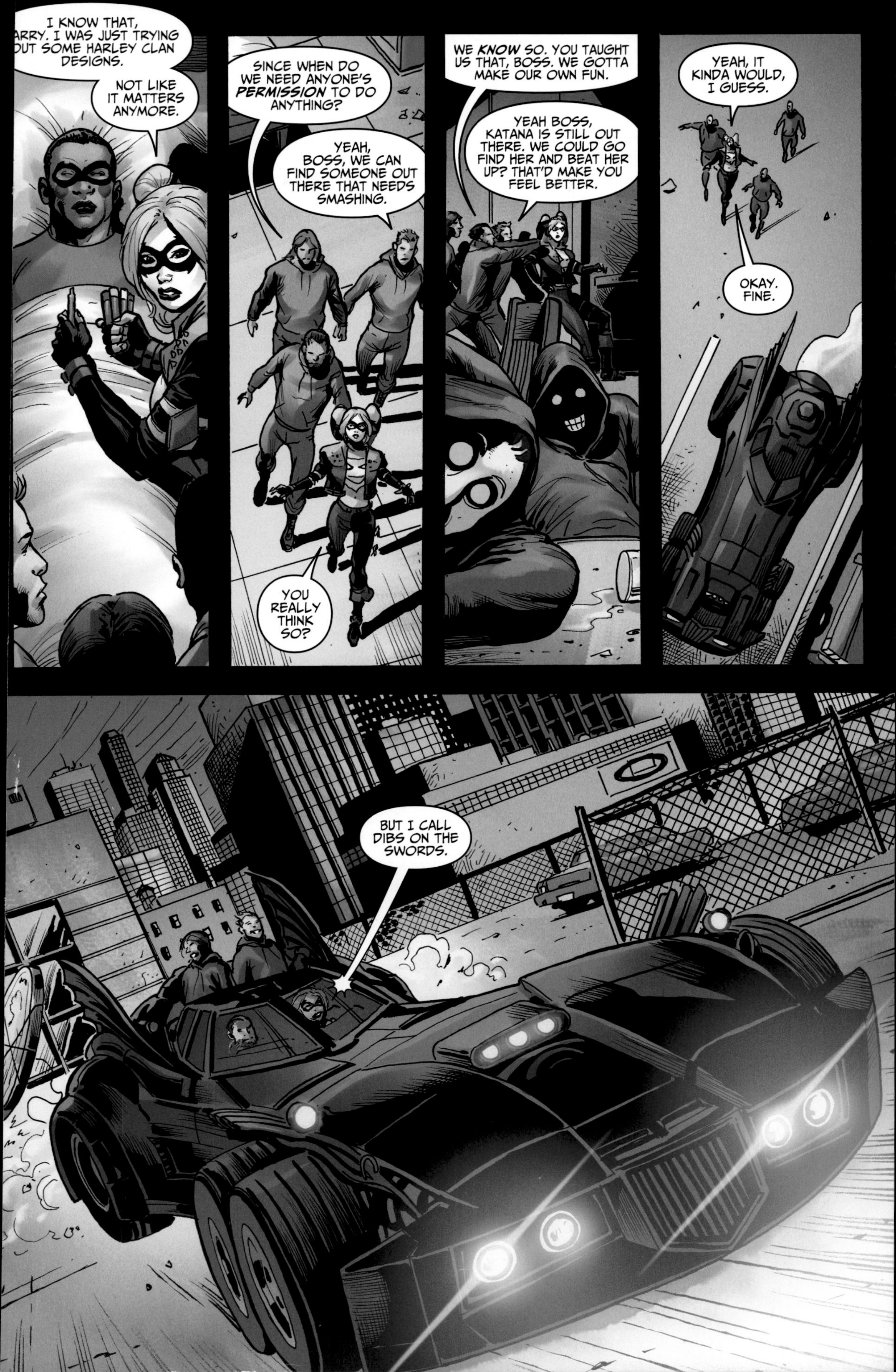
I KNOW THAT, ARRY. I WAS JUST TRYING OUT SOME HARLEY CLAN DESIGNS.
NOT LIKE IT MATTERS ANYMORE.
SINCE WHEN DO WE NEED ANYONE'S PERMISSION TO DO ANYTHING?
YEAH, BOSS, WE CAN FIND SOMEONE OUT THERE THAT NEEDS SMASHING.
YOU REALLY THINK SO?
WE KNOW SO. YOU TAUGHT US THAT, BOSS. WE GOTTA MAKE OUR OWN FUN.
YEAH BOSS, KATANA IS STILL OUT THERE. WE COULD GO FIND HER AND BEAT HER UP? THAT'D MAKE YOU FEEL BETTER.
YEAH, IT KINDA WOULD, I GUESS.
OKAY. FINE.
BUT I CALL DIBS ON THE SWORDS.

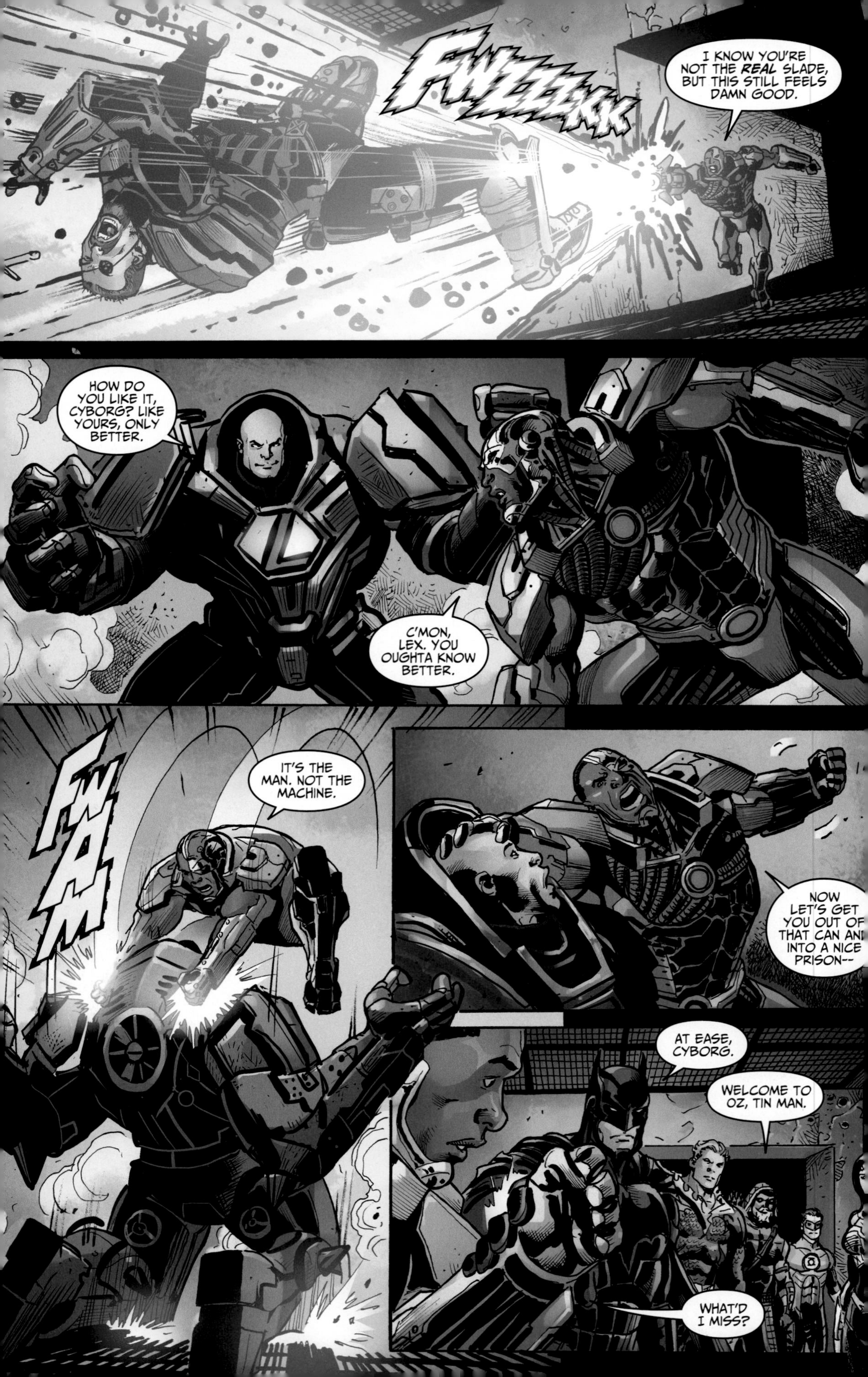

FWZZZKKK
I KNOW YOU'RE NOT THE REAL SLADE, BUT THIS STILL FEELS DAMN GOOD.
HOW DO YOU LIKE IT, CYBORG? LIKE YOURS, ONLY BETTER.
C'MON, LEX. YOU OUGHTA KNOW BETTER.
FWAM
IT'S THE MAN. NOT THE MACHINE.
NOW LET'S GET YOU OUT OF THAT CAN AN INTO A NICE PRISON--
AT EASE, CYBORG.
WELCOME TO OZ, TIN MAN.
WHAT'D I MISS?

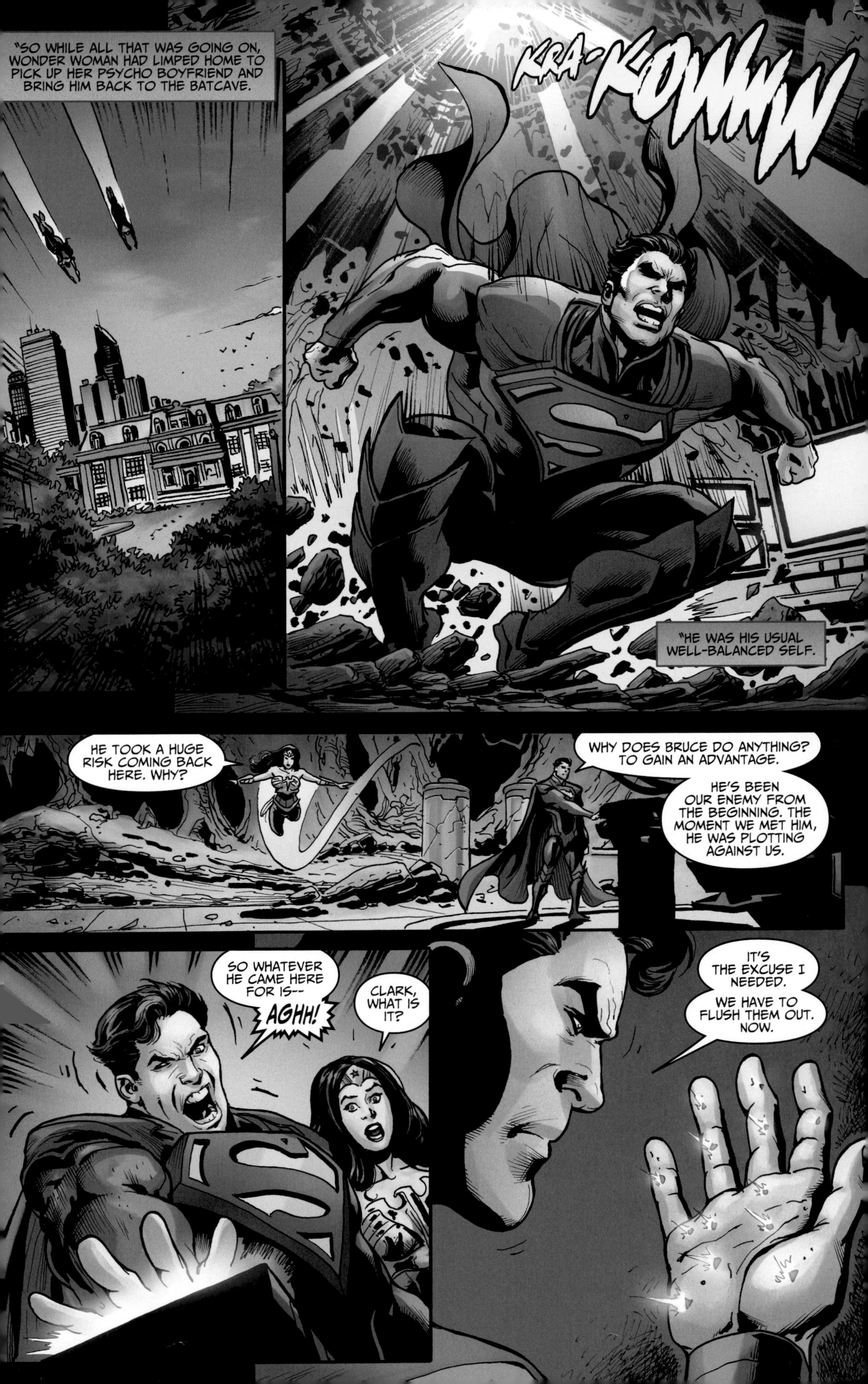
"SO WHILE ALL THAT WAS GOING ON, WONDER WOMAN HAD LIMPED HOME TO PICK UP HER PSYCHO BOYFRIEND AND BRING HIM BACK TO THE BATCAVE.
KRA-KOWWW
"HE WAS HIS USUAL WELL-BALANCED SELF.
HE TOOK A HUGE RISK COMING BACK HERE. WHY?
WHY DOES BRUCE DO ANYTHING? TO GAIN AN ADVANTAGE.
HE'S BEEN OUR ENEMY FROM THE BEGINNING. THE MOMENT WE MET HIM, HE WAS PLOTTING AGAINST US.
SO WHATEVER HE CAME HERE FOR IS--
AGHH!
CLARK, WHAT IS IT?
IT'S THE EXCUSE I NEEDED.
WE HAVE TO FLUSH THEM OUT. NOW.

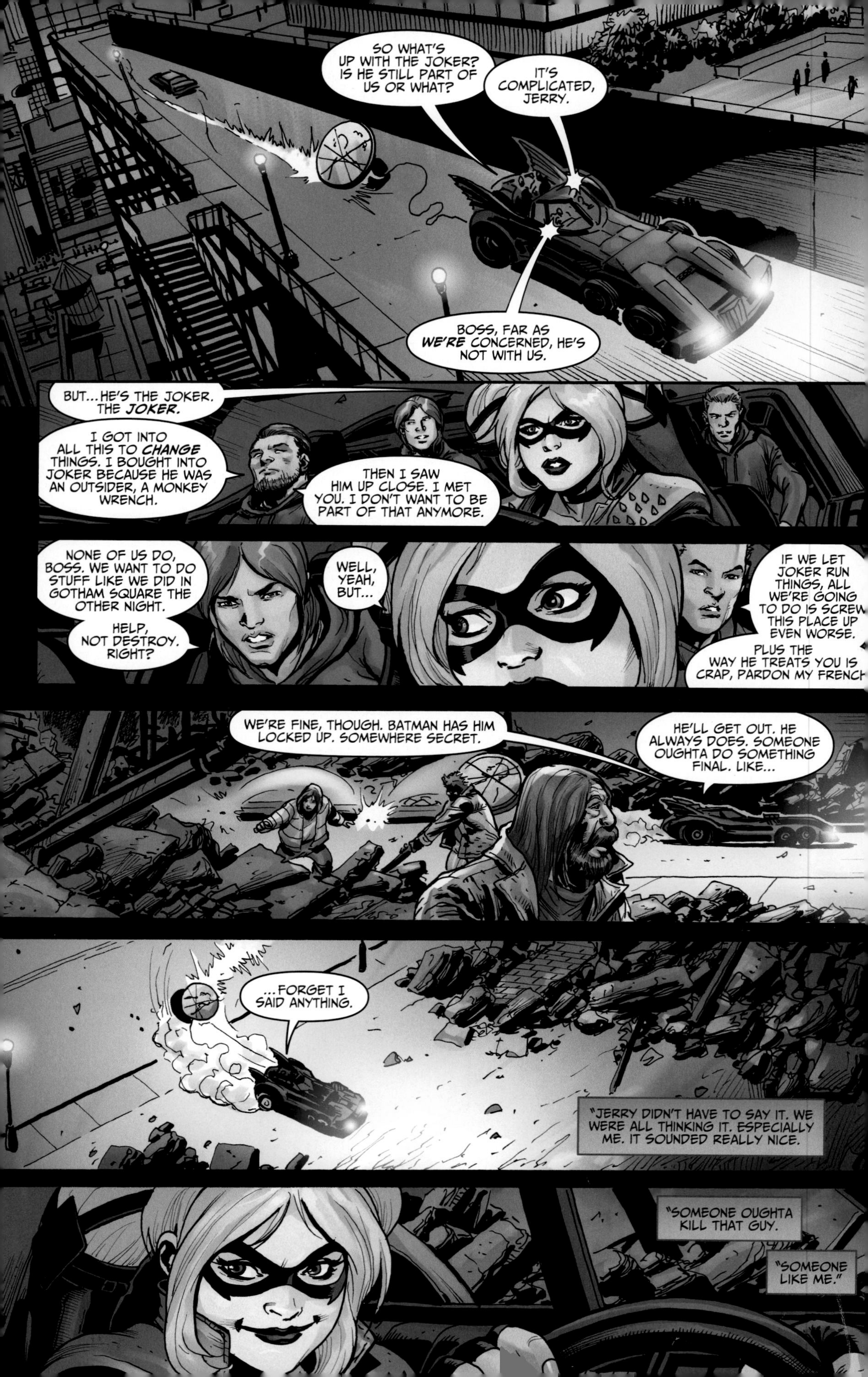
SO WHAT'S UP WITH THE JOKER? IS HE STILL PART OF US OR WHAT?
IT'S COMPLICATED, JERRY.
BOSS, FAR AS WE'RE CONCERNED, HE'S NOT WITH US.
BUT... HE'S THE JOKER. THE JOKER.
I GOT INTO ALL THIS TO CHANGE THINGS. I BOUGHT INTO JOKER BECAUSE HE WAS AN OUTSIDER, A MONKEY WRENCH.
THEN I SAW HIM UP CLOSE. I MET YOU. I DON'T WANT TO BE PART OF THAT ANYMORE.
NONE OF US DO, BOSS. WE WANT TO DO STUFF LIKE WE DID IN GOTHAM SQUARE THE OTHER NIGHT.
HELP, NOT DESTROY. RIGHT?
WELL, YEAH, BUT...
IF WE LET JOKER RUN THINGS, ALL WE'RE GOING TO DO IS SCREW THIS PLACE UP EVEN WORSE.
PLUS THE WAY HE TREATS YOU IS CRAP, PARDON MY FRENCH
WE'RE FINE, THOUGH. BATMAN HAS HIM LOCKED UP. SOMEWHERE SECRET.
HE'LL GET OUT. HE ALWAYS DOES. SOMEONE OUGHTA DO SOMETHING FINAL. LIKE...
...FORGET I SAID ANYTHING.
"JERRY DIDN'T HAVE TO SAY IT. WE WERE ALL THINKING IT. ESPECIALLY ME. IT SOUNDED REALLY NICE.
"SOMEONE OUGHTA KILL THAT GUY.
"SOMEONE LIKE ME."

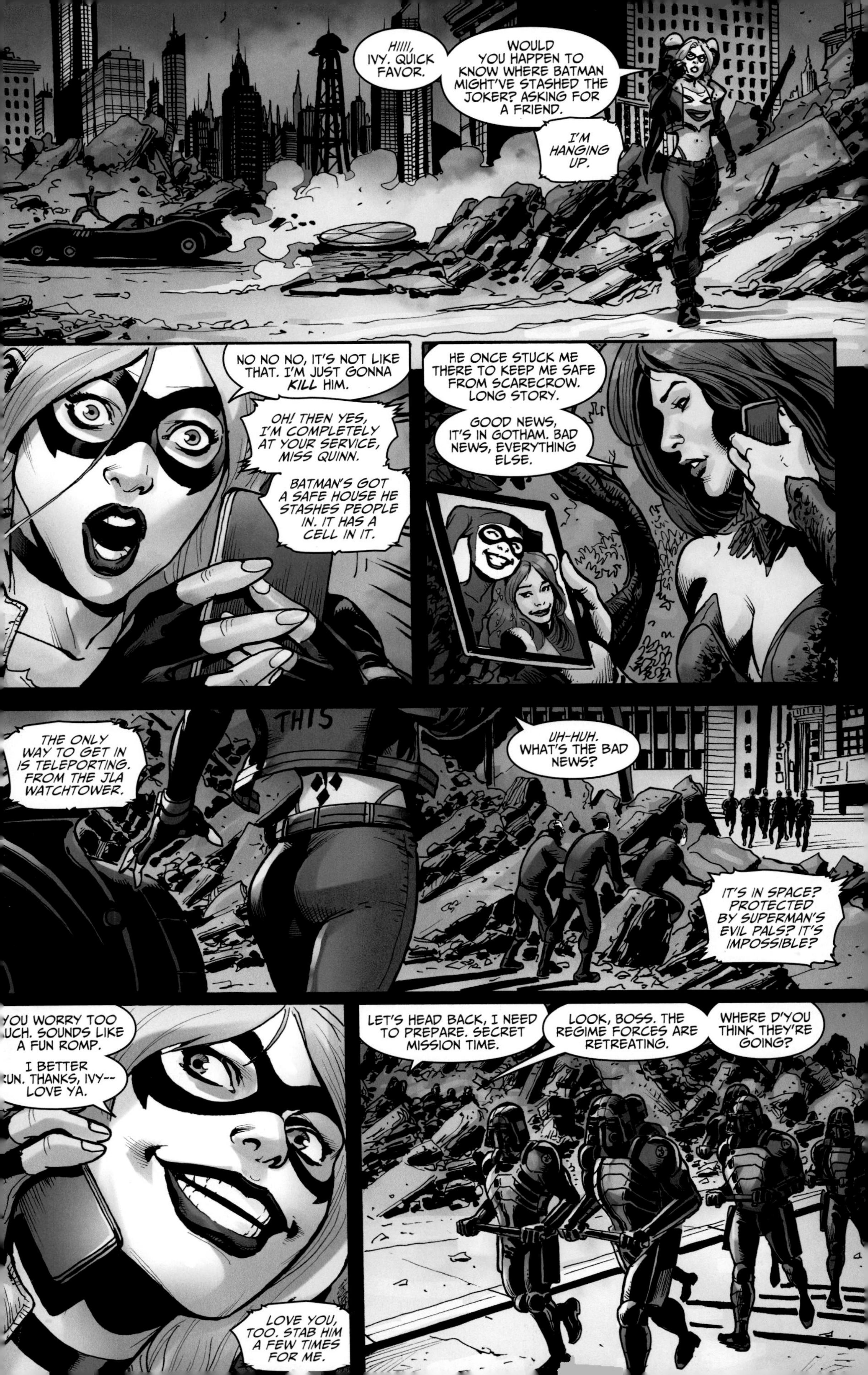
HIIII, IVY. QUICK FAVOR.
WOULD YOU HAPPEN TO KNOW WHERE BATMAN MIGHT'VE STASHED THE JOKER? ASKING FOR A FRIEND.
I'M HANGING UP.
NO NO NO, IT'S NOT LIKE THAT. I'M JUST GONNA KILL HIM.
OH! THEN YES, I'M COMPLETELY AT YOUR SERVICE, MISS QUINN.
BATMAN'S GOT A SAFE HOUSE HE STASHES PEOPLE IN. IT HAS A CELL IN IT.
HE ONCE STUCK ME THERE TO KEEP ME SAFE FROM SCARECROW. LONG STORY.
GOOD NEWS, IT'S IN GOTHAM. BAD NEWS, EVERYTHING ELSE.
THE ONLY WAY TO GET IN IS TELEPORTING. FROM THE JLA WATCHTOWER.
UH-HUH. WHAT'S THE BAD NEWS?
IT'S IN SPACE? PROTECTED BY SUPERMAN'S EVIL PALS? IT'S IMPOSSIBLE?
YOU WORRY TOO UCH. SOUNDS LIKE A FUN ROMP.
I BETTER UN. THANKS, IVY-- LOVE YA.
LOVE YOU, TOO. STAB HIM A FEW TIMES FOR ME.
LET'S HEAD BACK, I NEED TO PREPARE. SECRET MISSION TIME.
LOOK, BOSS. THE REGIME FORCES ARE RETREATING.
WHERE D'YOU THINK THEY'RE GOING?

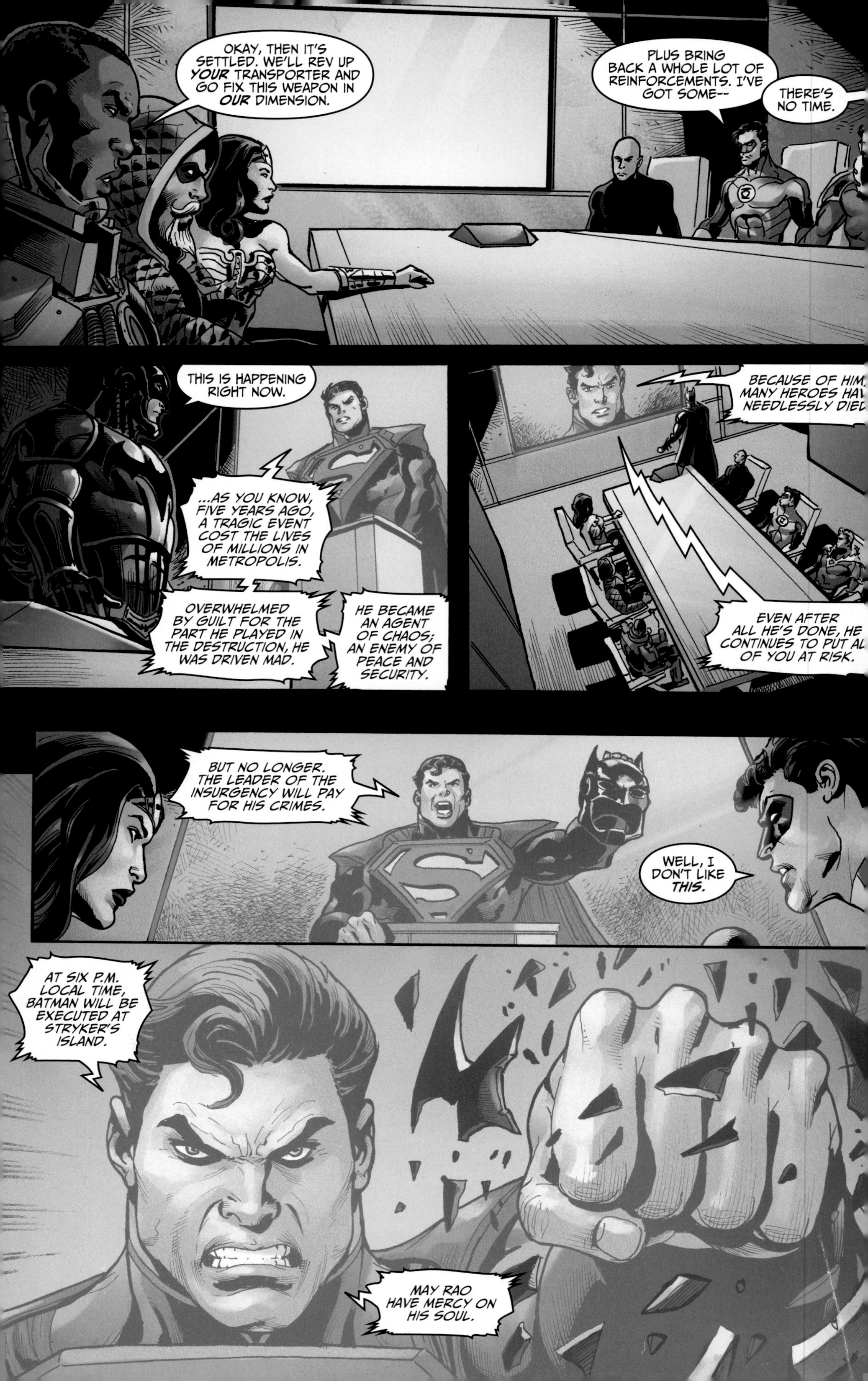
OKAY, THEN IT'S SETTLED. WE'LL REV UP YOUR TRANSPORTER AND GO FIX THIS WEAPON IN OUR DIMENSION.
PLUS BRING BACK A WHOLE LOT OF REINFORCEMENTS. I'VE GOT SOME--
THERE'S NO TIME.
THIS IS HAPPENING RIGHT NOW.
...AS YOU KNOW, FIVE YEARS AGO, A TRAGIC EVENT COST THE LIVES OF MILLIONS IN METROPOLIS.
OVERWHELMED BY GUILT FOR THE PART HE PLAYED IN THE DESTRUCTION, HE WAS DRIVEN MAD.
HE BECAME AN AGENT OF CHAOS; AN ENEMY OF PEACE AND SECURITY.
BECAUSE OF HIM, MANY HEROES HAV NEEDLESSLY DIED
EVEN AFTER ALL HE'S DONE, HE CONTINUES TO PUT AL OF YOU AT RISK.
BUT NO LONGER. THE LEADER OF THE INSURGENCY WILL PAY FOR HIS CRIMES.
WELL, I DON'T LIKE THIS.
AT SIX P.M. LOCAL TIME, BATMAN WILL BE EXECUTED AT STRYKER'S ISLAND.
MAY RAO HAVE MERCY ON HIS SOUL.

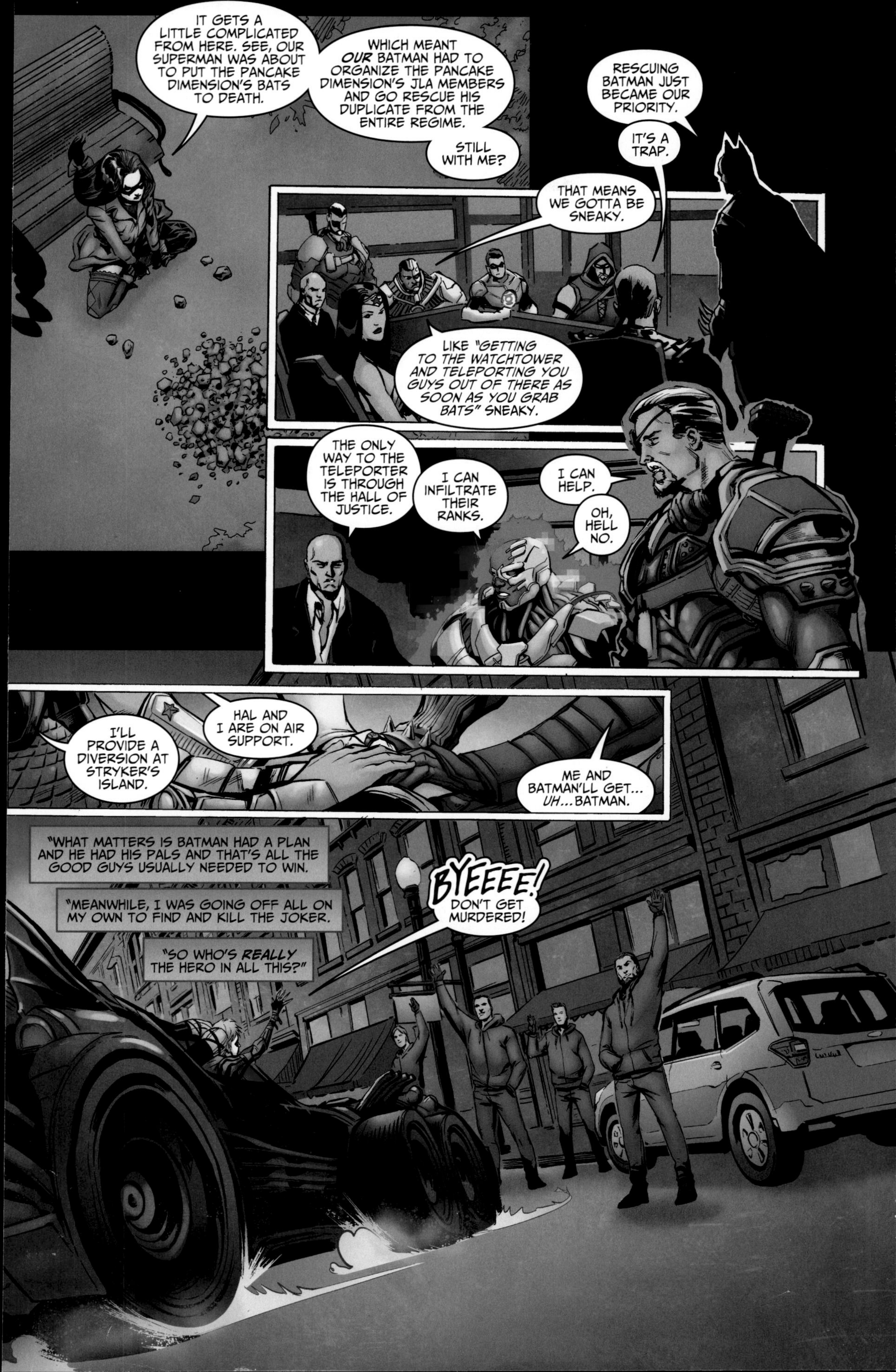
IT GETS A LITTLE COMPLICATED FROM HERE. SEE, OUR SUPERMAN WAS ABOUT TO PUT THE PANCAKE DIMENSION'S BATS TO DEATH.
WHICH MEANT *OUR* BATMAN HAD TO ORGANIZE THE PANCAKE DIMENSION'S JLA MEMBERS AND GO RESCUE HIS DUPLICATE FROM THE ENTIRE REGIME.
STILL WITH ME?
RESCUING BATMAN JUST BECAME OUR PRIORITY.
IT'S A TRAP.
THAT MEANS WE GOTTA BE SNEAKY.
LIKE *"GETTING TO THE WATCHTOWER AND TELEPORTING YOU GUYS OUT OF THERE AS SOON AS YOU GRAB BATS"* SNEAKY.
THE ONLY WAY TO THE TELEPORTER IS THROUGH THE HALL OF JUSTICE.
I CAN INFILTRATE THEIR RANKS.
I CAN HELP.
OH, HELL NO.
I'LL PROVIDE A DIVERSION AT STRYKER'S ISLAND.
HAL AND I ARE ON AIR SUPPORT.
ME AND BATMAN'LL GET... *UH*... BATMAN.
"WHAT MATTERS IS BATMAN HAD A PLAN AND HE HAD HIS PALS AND THAT'S ALL THE GOOD GUYS USUALLY NEEDED TO WIN.
"MEANWHILE, I WAS GOING OFF ALL ON MY OWN TO FIND AND KILL THE JOKER.
"SO WHO'S *REALLY* THE HERO IN ALL THIS?"
BYEEEE! DON'T GET MURDERED!

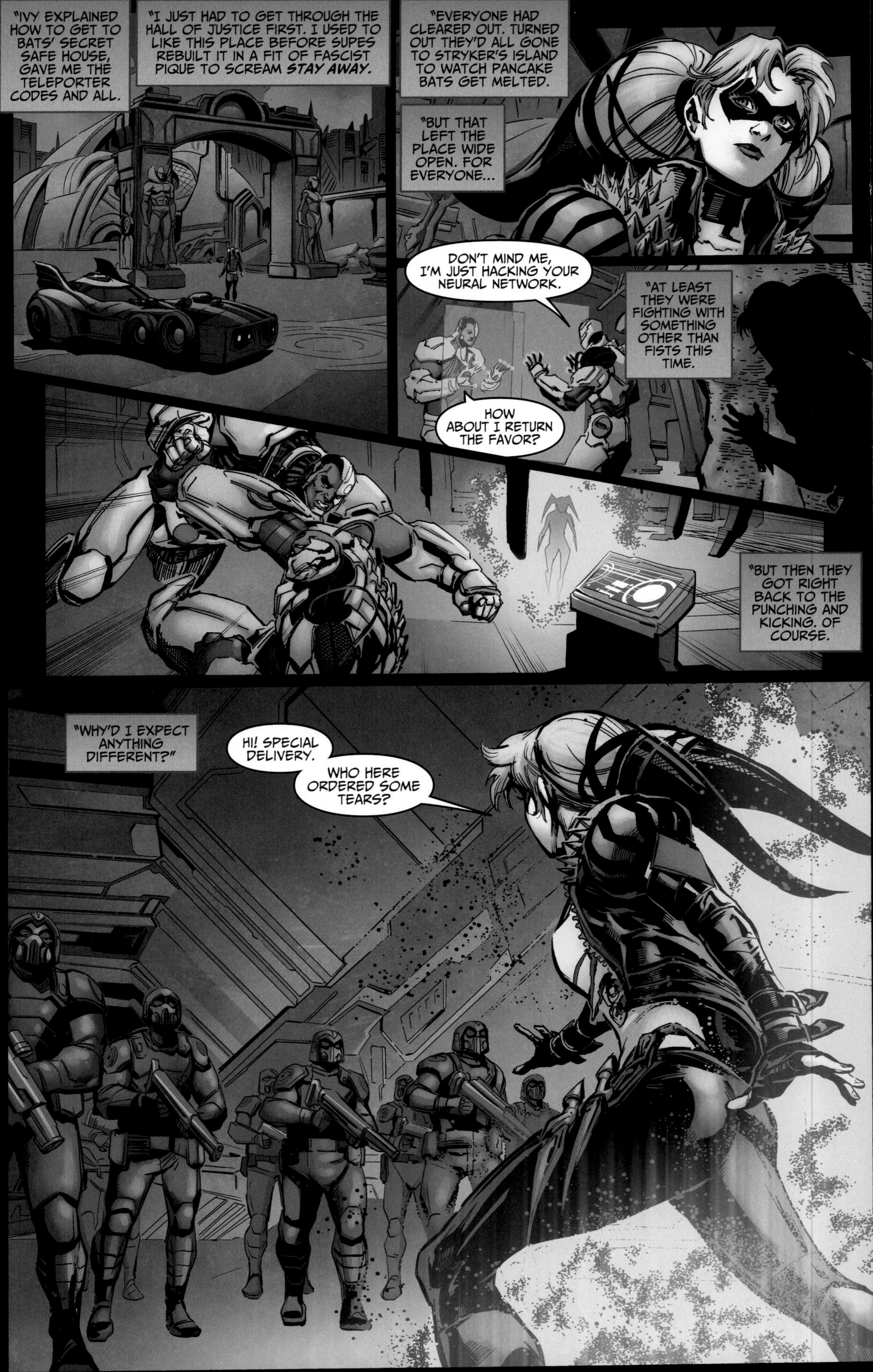
"IVY EXPLAINED HOW TO GET TO BATS' SECRET SAFE HOUSE, GAVE ME THE TELEPORTER CODES AND ALL.
"I JUST HAD TO GET THROUGH THE HALL OF JUSTICE FIRST. I USED TO LIKE THIS PLACE BEFORE SUPES REBUILT IT IN A FIT OF FASCIST PIQUE TO SCREAM STAY AWAY.
"EVERYONE HAD CLEARED OUT. TURNED OUT THEY'D ALL GONE TO STRYKER'S ISLAND TO WATCH PANCAKE BATS GET MELTED.
"BUT THAT LEFT THE PLACE WIDE OPEN. FOR EVERYONE...
DON'T MIND ME, I'M JUST HACKING YOUR NEURAL NETWORK.
"AT LEAST THEY WERE FIGHTING WITH SOMETHING OTHER THAN FISTS THIS TIME.
HOW ABOUT I RETURN THE FAVOR?
"BUT THEN THEY GOT RIGHT BACK TO THE PUNCHING AND KICKING. OF COURSE.
"WHY'D I EXPECT ANYTHING DIFFERENT?"
HI! SPECIAL DELIVERY.
WHO HERE ORDERED SOME TEARS?

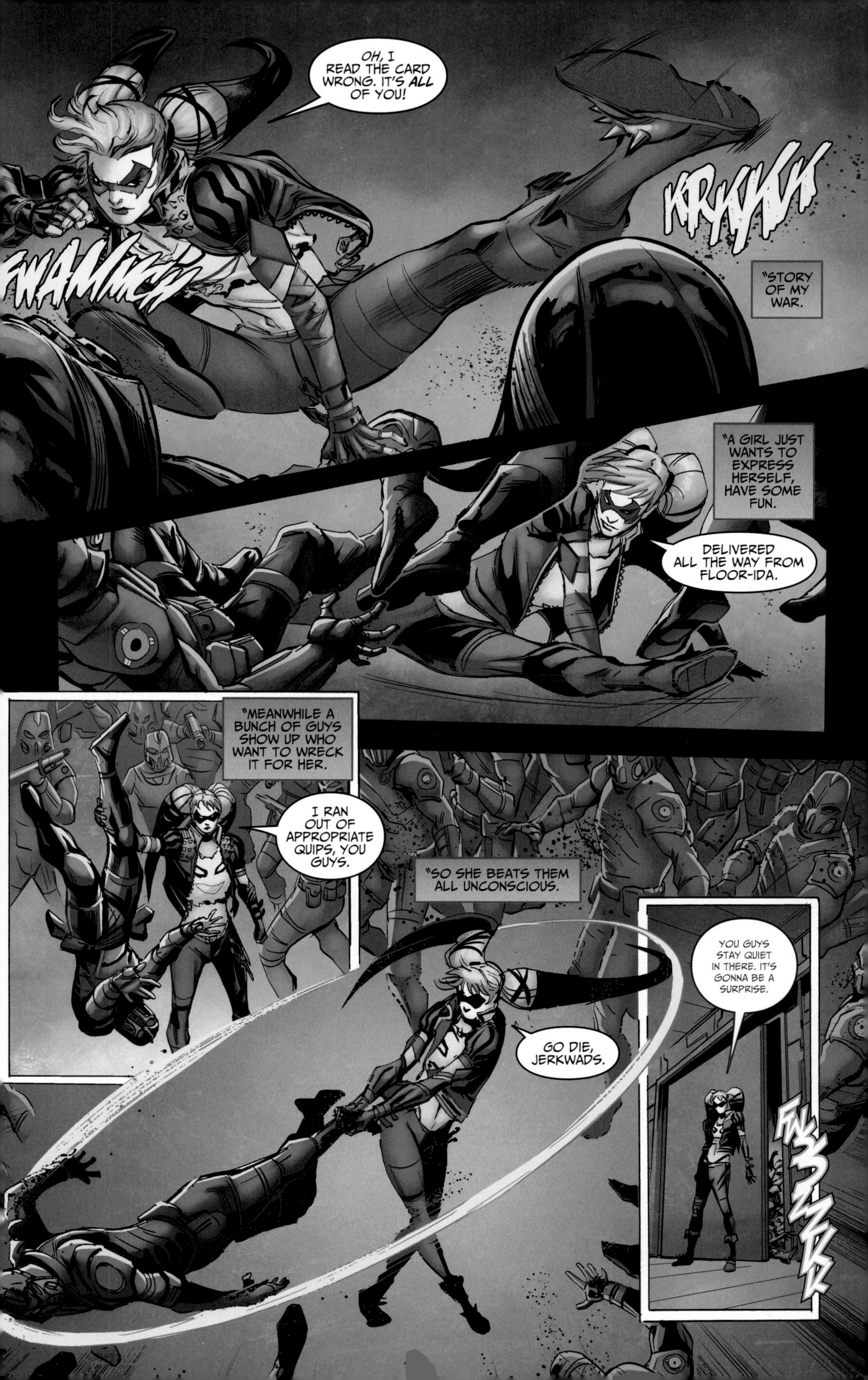
OH, I READ THE CARD WRONG. IT'S ALL OF YOU!
FWAMCH
"STORY OF MY WAR.
"A GIRL JUST WANTS TO EXPRESS HERSELF, HAVE SOME FUN.
DELIVERED ALL THE WAY FROM FLOOR-IDA.
"MEANWHILE A BUNCH OF GUYS SHOW UP WHO WANT TO WRECK IT FOR HER.
I RAN OUT OF APPROPRIATE QUIPS, YOU GUYS.
"SO SHE BEATS THEM ALL UNCONSCIOUS.
GO DIE, JERKWADS.
YOU GUYS STAY QUIET IN THERE. IT'S GONNA BE A SURPRISE.

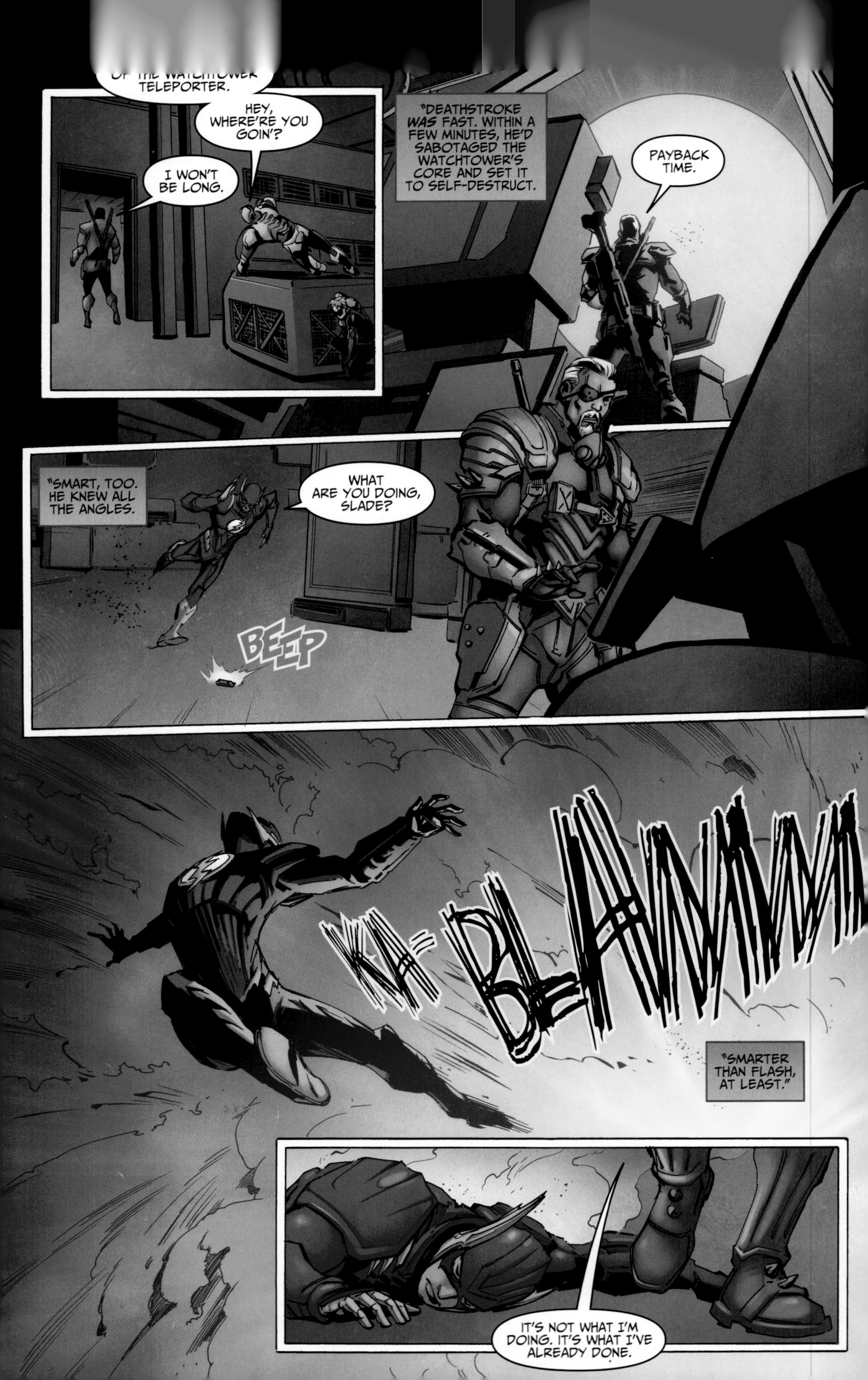

OF THE WATCHTOWER TELEPORTER.
HEY, WHERE'RE YOU GOIN'?
I WON'T BE LONG.
"DEATHSTROKE WAS FAST. WITHIN A FEW MINUTES, HE'D SABOTAGED THE WATCHTOWER'S CORE AND SET IT TO SELF-DESTRUCT.
PAYBACK TIME.
"SMART, TOO. HE KNEW ALL THE ANGLES.
WHAT ARE YOU DOING, SLADE?
BEEP
KA-BLAMM
"SMARTER THAN FLASH, AT LEAST."
IT'S NOT WHAT I'M DOING. IT'S WHAT I'VE ALREADY DONE.

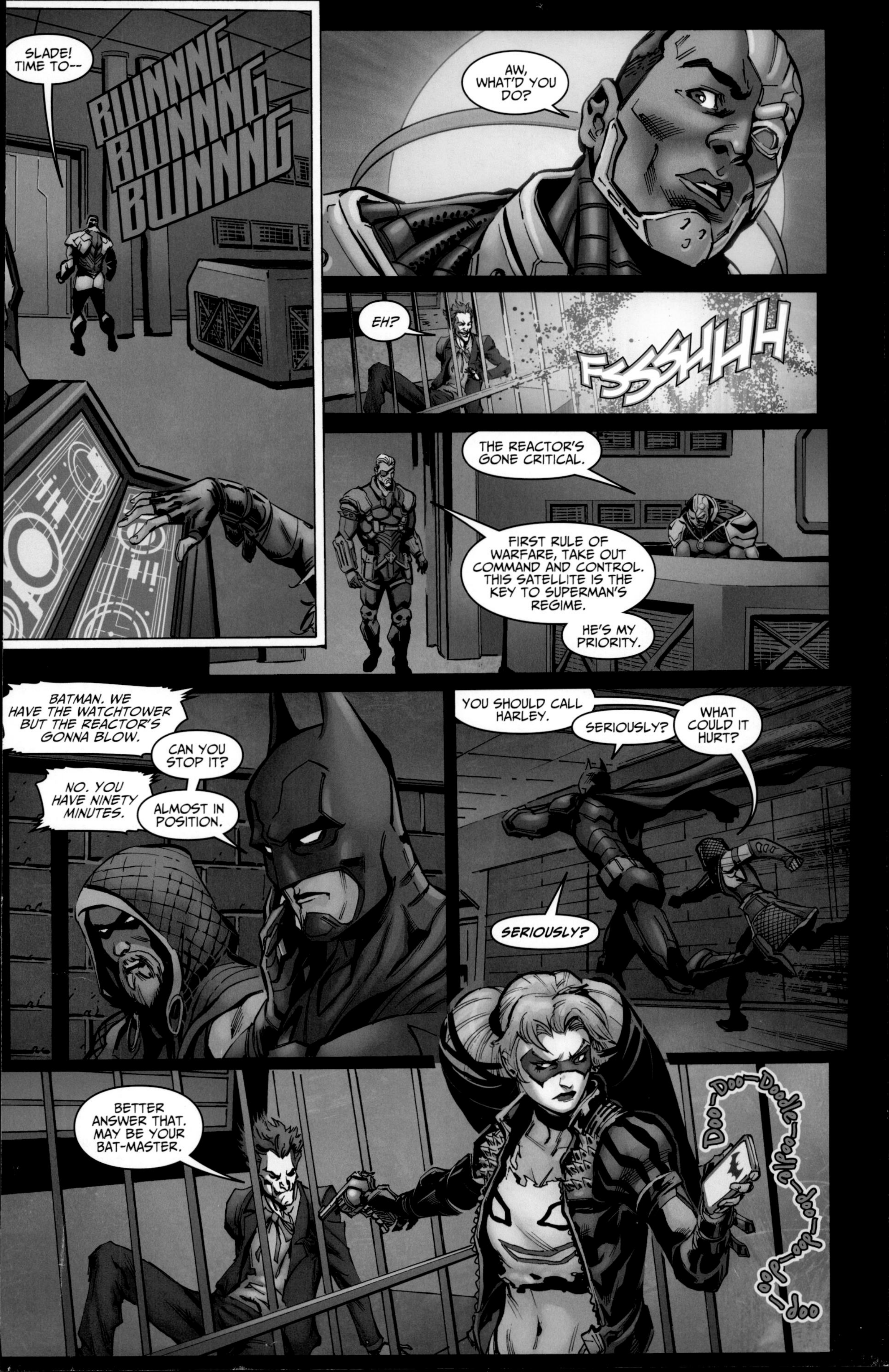
SLADE! TIME TO--
BWNNNG BWNNNG BWNNNG
AW, WHAT'D YOU DO?
EH?
FSSSHHH
THE REACTOR'S GONE CRITICAL.
FIRST RULE OF WARFARE, TAKE OUT COMMAND AND CONTROL. THIS SATELLITE IS THE KEY TO SUPERMAN'S REGIME.
HE'S MY PRIORITY.
BATMAN. WE HAVE THE WATCHTOWER BUT THE REACTOR'S GONNA BLOW.
CAN YOU STOP IT?
NO. YOU HAVE NINETY MINUTES.
ALMOST IN POSITION.
YOU SHOULD CALL HARLEY.
SERIOUSLY?
WHAT COULD IT HURT?
SERIOUSLY?
BETTER ANSWER THAT. MAY BE YOUR BAT-MASTER.
Doo-Doo-Doodle-oodle-doo-doo-doo-doo

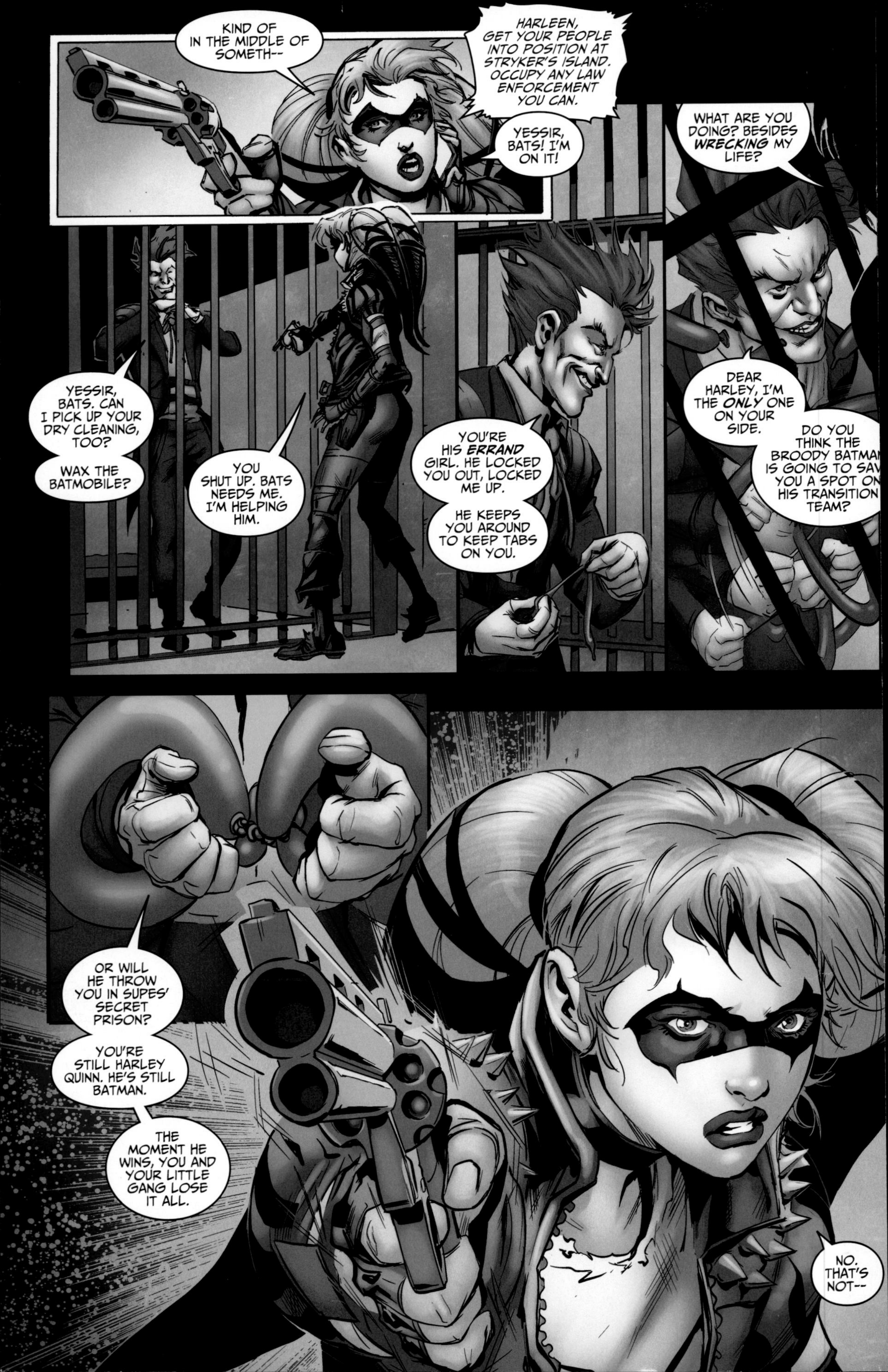

KIND OF IN THE MIDDLE OF SOMETH--
HARLEEN, GET YOUR PEOPLE INTO POSITION AT STRYKER'S ISLAND. OCCUPY ANY LAW ENFORCEMENT YOU CAN.
YESSIR, BATS! I'M ON IT!
YESSIR, BATS. CAN I PICK UP YOUR DRY CLEANING, TOO?
WAX THE BATMOBILE?
YOU SHUT UP. BATS NEEDS ME. I'M HELPING HIM.
YOU'RE HIS ERRAND GIRL. HE LOCKED YOU OUT, LOCKED ME UP.
HE KEEPS YOU AROUND TO KEEP TABS ON YOU.
WHAT ARE YOU DOING? BESIDES WRECKING MY LIFE?
DEAR HARLEY, I'M THE ONLY ONE ON YOUR SIDE.
DO YOU THINK THE BROODY BATMAN IS GOING TO SAVE YOU A SPOT ON HIS TRANSITION TEAM?
OR WILL HE THROW YOU IN SUPES' SECRET PRISON?
YOU'RE STILL HARLEY QUINN. HE'S STILL BATMAN.
THE MOMENT HE WINS, YOU AND YOUR LITTLE GANG LOSE IT ALL.
NO. THAT'S NOT--

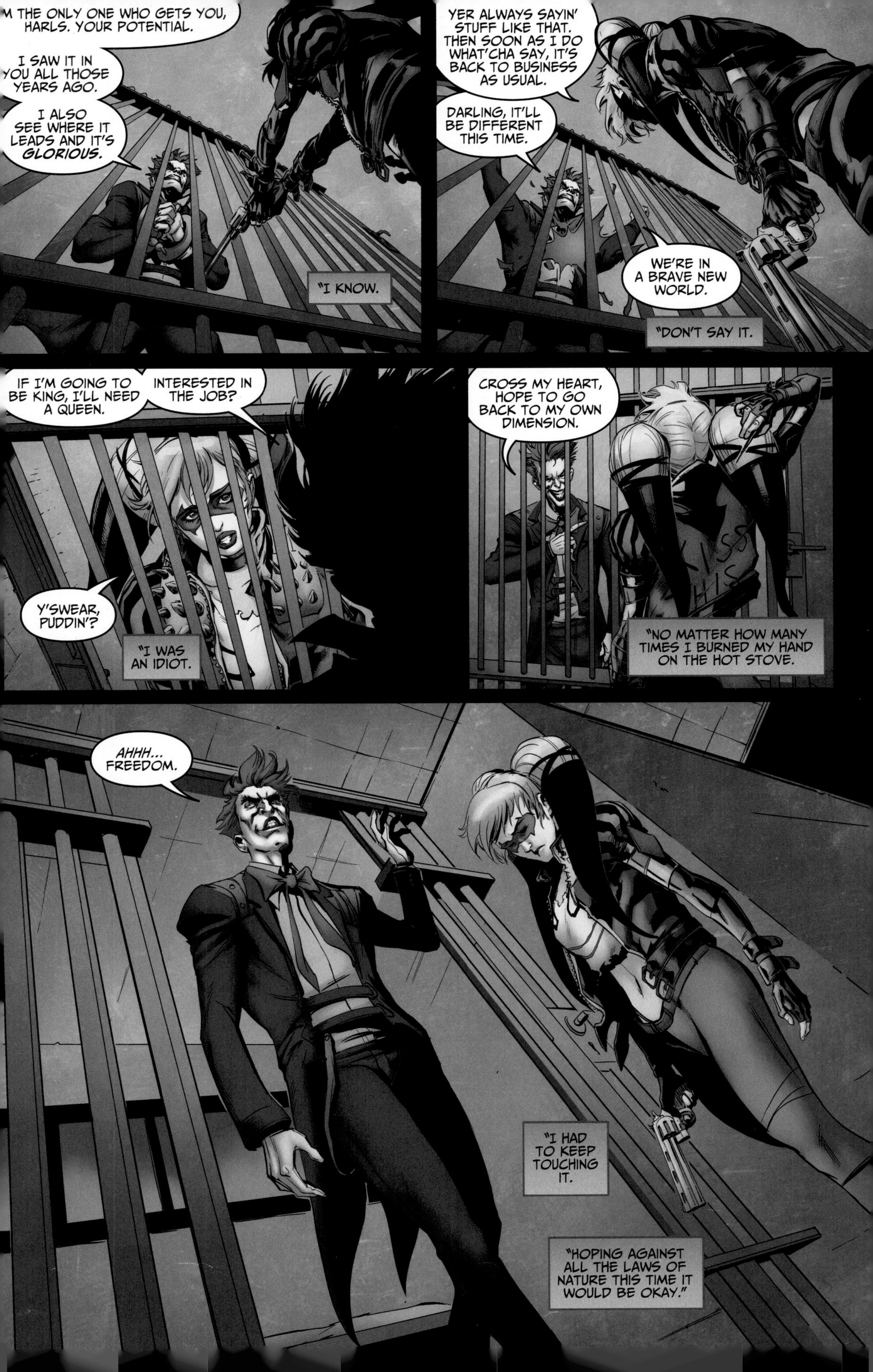
M THE ONLY ONE WHO GETS YOU, HARLS. YOUR POTENTIAL.
I SAW IT IN YOU ALL THOSE YEARS AGO.
I ALSO SEE WHERE IT LEADS AND IT'S *GLORIOUS.*
"I KNOW.
YER ALWAYS SAYIN' STUFF LIKE THAT. THEN SOON AS I DO WHAT'CHA SAY, IT'S BACK TO BUSINESS AS USUAL.
DARLING, IT'LL BE DIFFERENT THIS TIME.
WE'RE IN A BRAVE NEW WORLD.
"DON'T SAY IT.
IF I'M GOING TO BE KING, I'LL NEED A QUEEN.
INTERESTED IN THE JOB?
Y'SWEAR, PUDDIN'?
"I WAS AN IDIOT.
CROSS MY HEART, HOPE TO GO BACK TO MY OWN DIMENSION.
"NO MATTER HOW MANY TIMES I BURNED MY HAND ON THE HOT STOVE.
AHHH... FREEDOM.
"I HAD TO KEEP TOUCHING IT.
"HOPING AGAINST ALL THE LAWS OF NATURE THIS TIME IT WOULD BE OKAY."

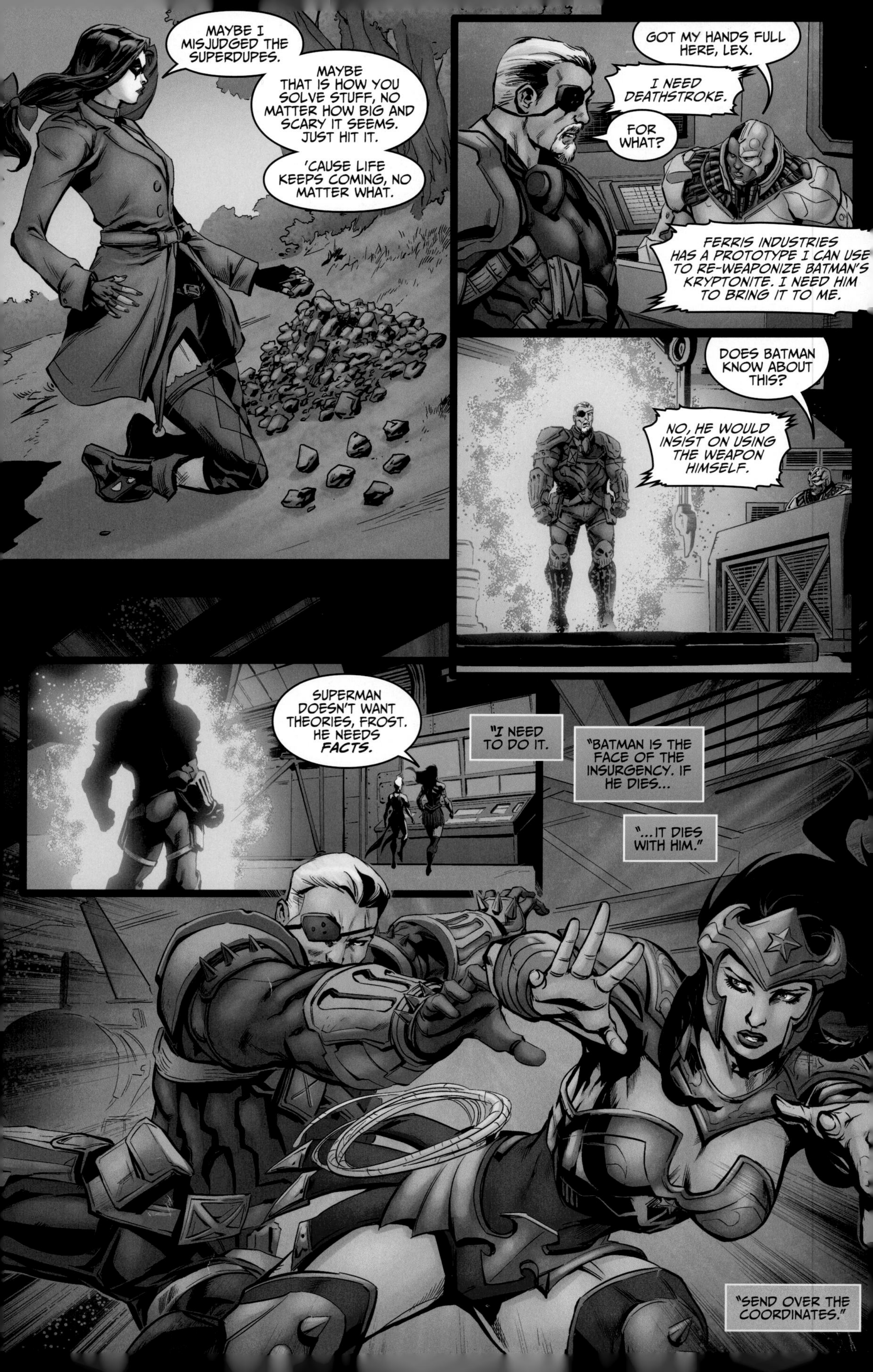
MAYBE I MISJUDGED THE SUPERDUPES.
MAYBE THAT IS HOW YOU SOLVE STUFF, NO MATTER HOW BIG AND SCARY IT SEEMS. JUST HIT IT.
'CAUSE LIFE KEEPS COMING, NO MATTER WHAT.
GOT MY HANDS FULL HERE, LEX.
I NEED DEATHSTROKE.
FOR WHAT?
FERRIS INDUSTRIES HAS A PROTOTYPE I CAN USE TO RE-WEAPONIZE BATMAN'S KRYPTONITE. I NEED HIM TO BRING IT TO ME.
DOES BATMAN KNOW ABOUT THIS?
NO, HE WOULD INSIST ON USING THE WEAPON HIMSELF.
SUPERMAN DOESN'T WANT THEORIES, FROST. HE NEEDS *FACTS.*
"I NEED TO DO IT.
"BATMAN IS THE FACE OF THE INSURGENCY. IF HE DIES...
"...IT DIES WITH HIM."
"SEND OVER THE COORDINATES."

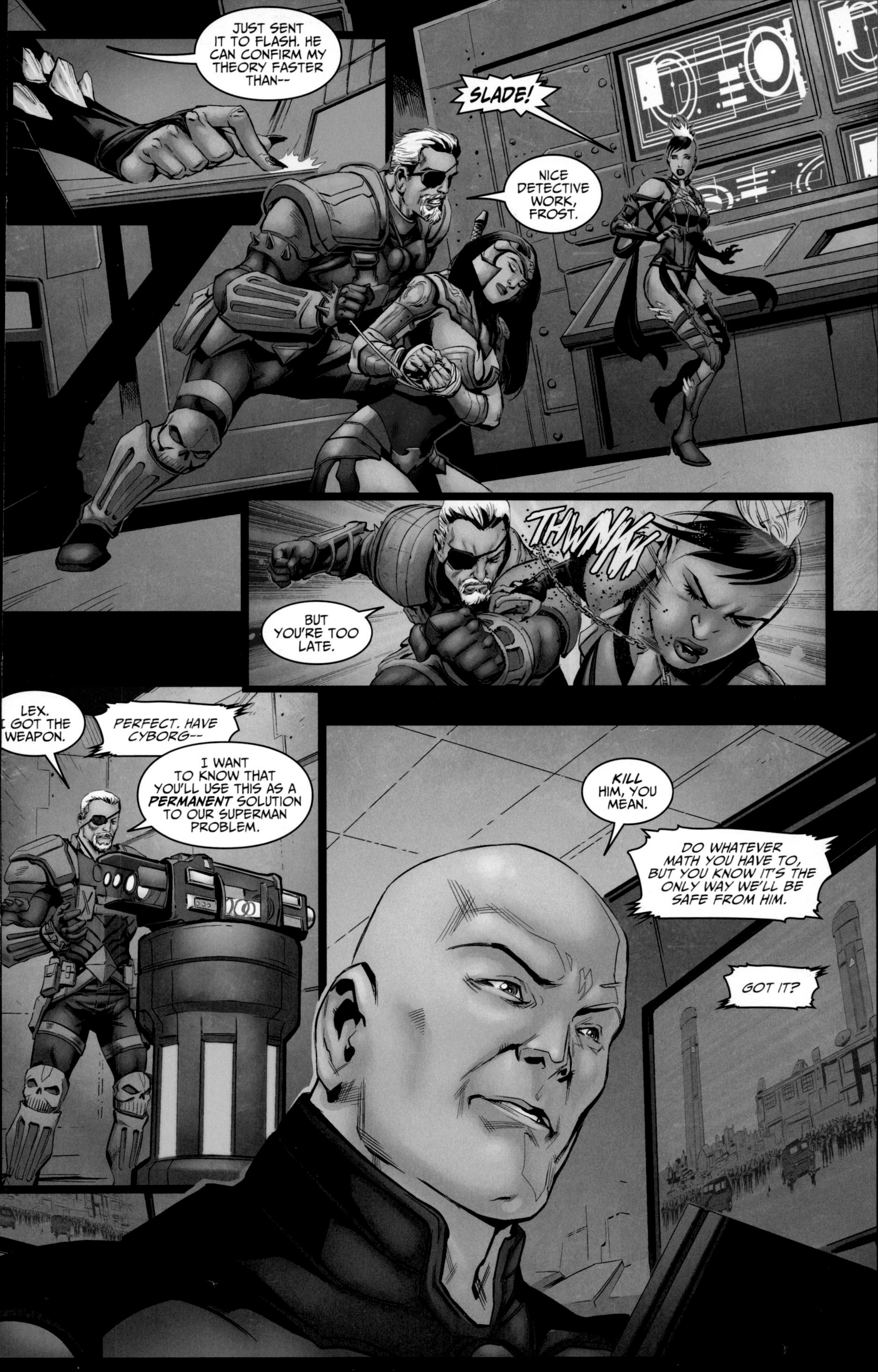
JUST SENT IT TO FLASH. HE CAN CONFIRM MY THEORY FASTER THAN--
SLADE!
NICE DETECTIVE WORK, FROST.
THWNK
BUT YOU'RE TOO LATE.
LEX. I GOT THE WEAPON.
PERFECT. HAVE CYBORG--
I WANT TO KNOW THAT YOU'LL USE THIS AS A PERMANENT SOLUTION TO OUR SUPERMAN PROBLEM.
KILL HIM, YOU MEAN.
DO WHATEVER MATH YOU HAVE TO, BUT YOU KNOW IT'S THE ONLY WAY WE'LL BE SAFE FROM HIM.
GOT IT?

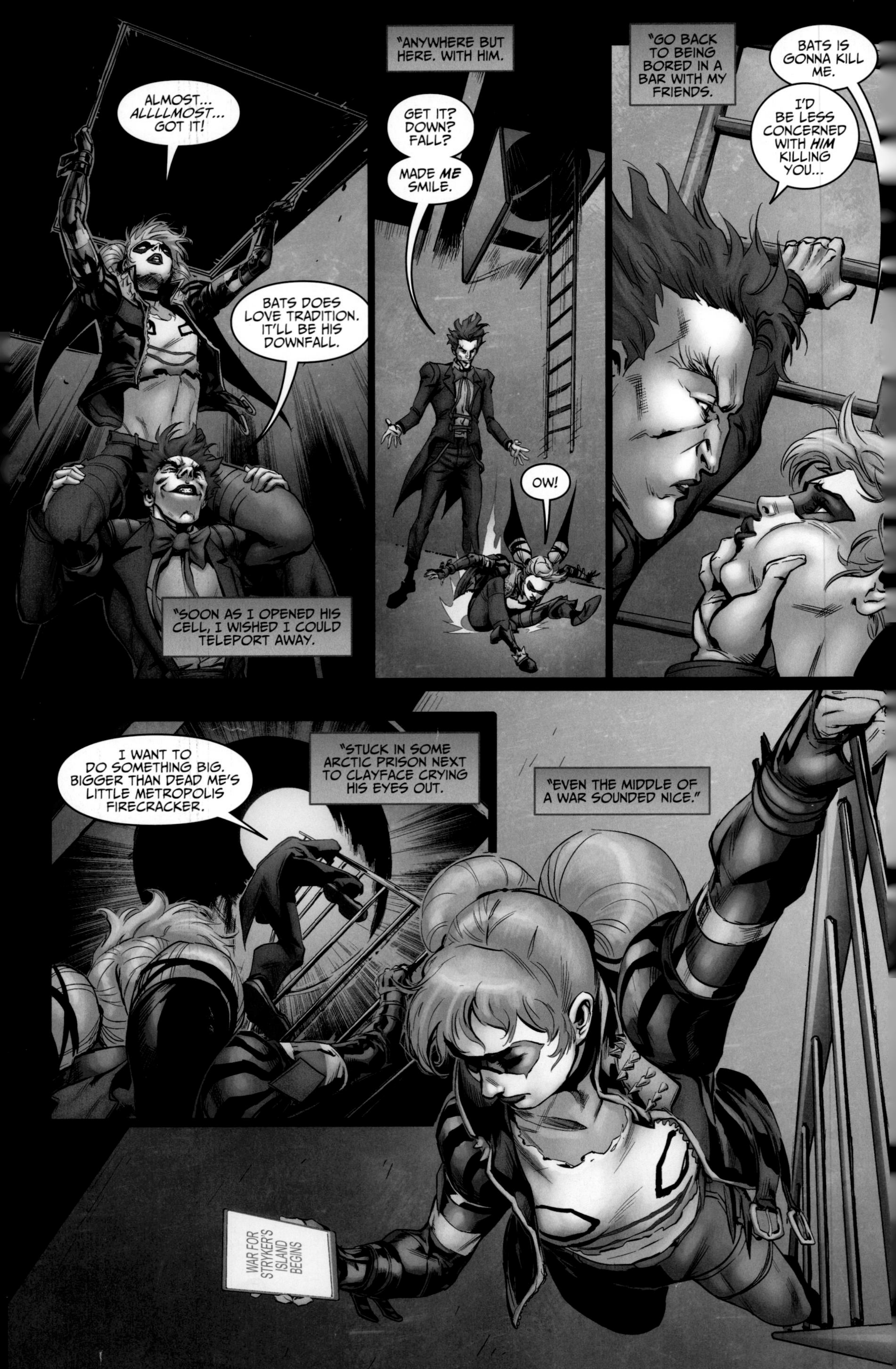
ALMOST... ALLLLMOST... GOT IT!
BATS DOES LOVE TRADITION. IT'LL BE HIS DOWNFALL.
"SOON AS I OPENED HIS CELL, I WISHED I COULD TELEPORT AWAY.
"ANYWHERE BUT HERE. WITH HIM.
GET IT? DOWN? FALL?
MADE ME SMILE.
OW!
"GO BACK TO BEING BORED IN A BAR WITH MY FRIENDS.
BATS IS GONNA KILL ME.
I'D BE LESS CONCERNED WITH HIM KILLING YOU...
I WANT TO DO SOMETHING BIG. BIGGER THAN DEAD ME'S LITTLE METROPOLIS FIRECRACKER.
"STUCK IN SOME ARCTIC PRISON NEXT TO CLAYFACE CRYING HIS EYES OUT.
"EVEN THE MIDDLE OF A WAR SOUNDED NICE."
WAR FOR STRYKER'S ISLAND BEGINS

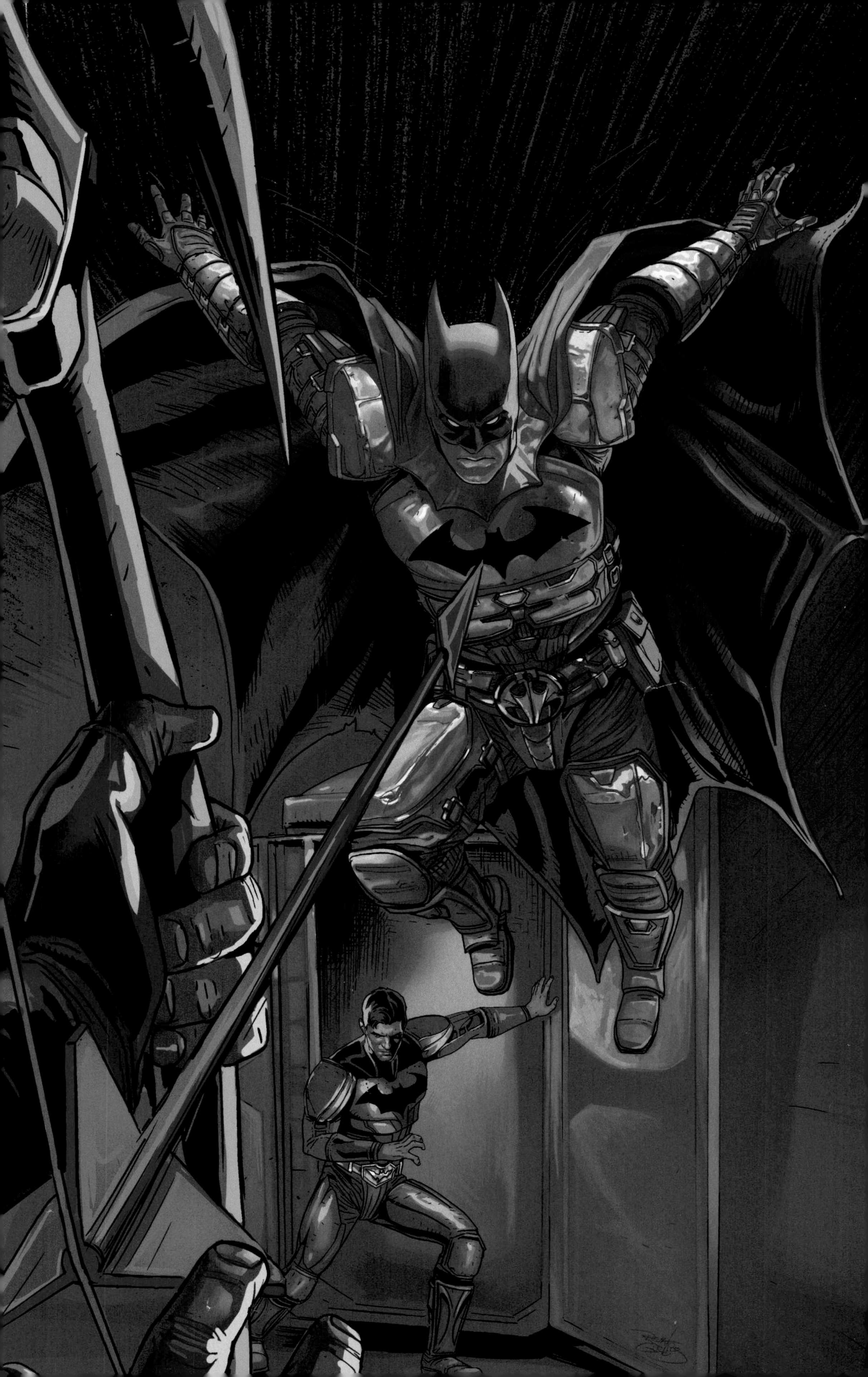

"Clowntime Is Over" **Derlis Santacruz** **Marco Santucci** Pencillers
Derlis Santacruz **Andy Owens** **Marco Santucci** Inkers **Rex Lokus** **J.Nanjan** Colorists Cover art by **Renato Guedes**

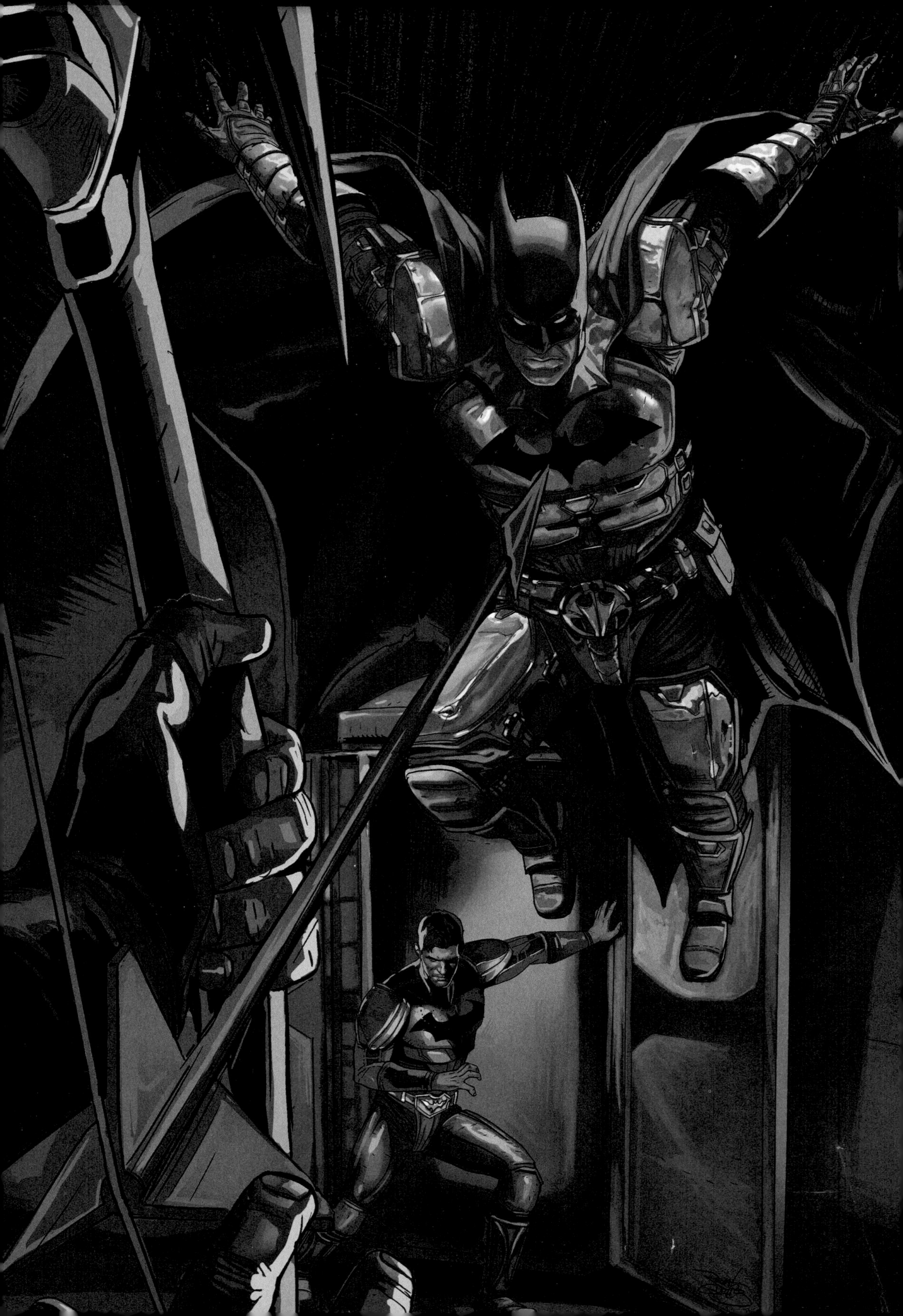

GOTHAM CITY.

THEY'D NEVER LET ME GET AWAY WITH THIS IN MY DIMENSION.

"MY BATS AND THE HEROES HE YANKED OVER FROM THE PANCAKE DIMENSION WERE STORMING STRYKER'S ISLAND.

THERE THEY ARE. RIGHT ON TIME.

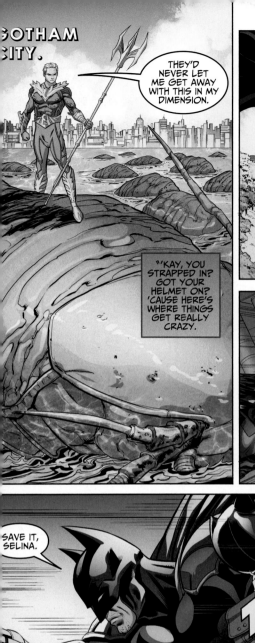

"'KAY, YOU STRAPPED IN? GOT YOUR HELMET ON? 'CAUSE HERE'S WHERE THINGS GET REALLY CRAZY.

"ALL TO RESCUE PANCAKE BATMAN, WHO NOT-SO-NEATO MUSSOLINI WAS ABOUT TO EXECUTE FOR GIGGLES.

HELLO, BRUCE. STILL AS HANDSOME AS EVER.

SAVE IT, SELINA.

"ABOUT THE ONLY CHUCKLES TO BE FOUND IN THE MIDDLE OF THIS BATTLEFIELD.

THNK

HEY, AREN'T WE SUPPOSED TO BE THERE?

LIVE: STRYKER'S ISLAND

"OH, RIGHT, I WASN'T AROUND EITHER.

"ABOUT THAT..."

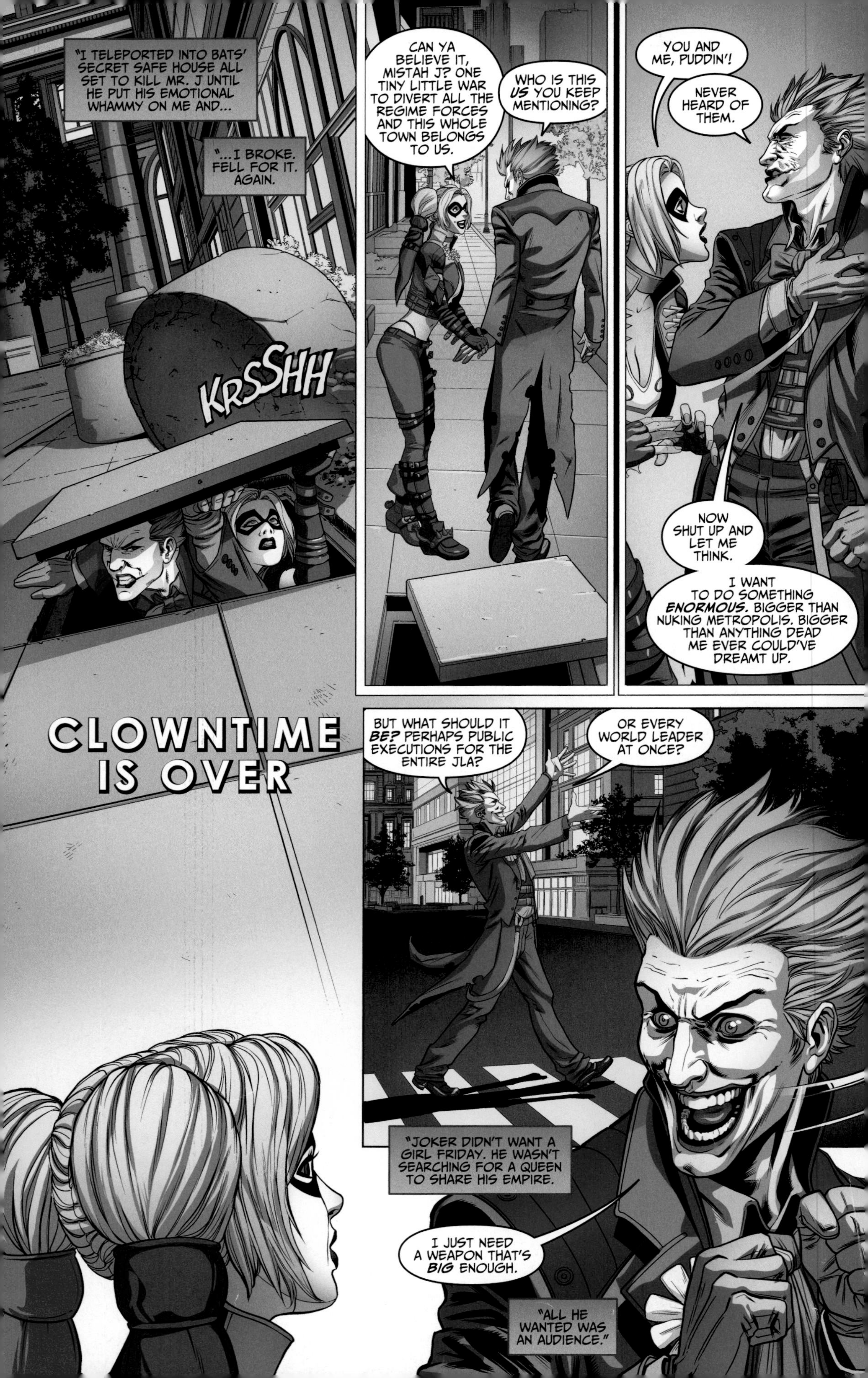
"I TELEPORTED INTO BATS' SECRET SAFE HOUSE ALL SET TO KILL MR. J UNTIL HE PUT HIS EMOTIONAL WHAMMY ON ME AND...
"...I BROKE. FELL FOR IT. AGAIN.
KRSSHH
CAN YA BELIEVE IT, MISTAH J? ONE TINY LITTLE WAR TO DIVERT ALL THE REGIME FORCES AND THIS WHOLE TOWN BELONGS TO US.
WHO IS THIS *US* YOU KEEP MENTIONING?
YOU AND ME, PUDDIN'!
NEVER HEARD OF THEM.
NOW SHUT UP AND LET ME THINK.
I WANT TO DO SOMETHING *ENORMOUS.* BIGGER THAN NUKING METROPOLIS. BIGGER THAN ANYTHING DEAD ME EVER COULD'VE DREAMT UP.
CLOWNTIME IS OVER
BUT WHAT SHOULD IT *BE?* PERHAPS PUBLIC EXECUTIONS FOR THE ENTIRE JLA?
OR EVERY WORLD LEADER AT ONCE?
"JOKER DIDN'T WANT A GIRL FRIDAY. HE WASN'T SEARCHING FOR A QUEEN TO SHARE HIS EMPIRE.
I JUST NEED A WEAPON THAT'S *BIG* ENOUGH.
"ALL HE WANTED WAS AN AUDIENCE."

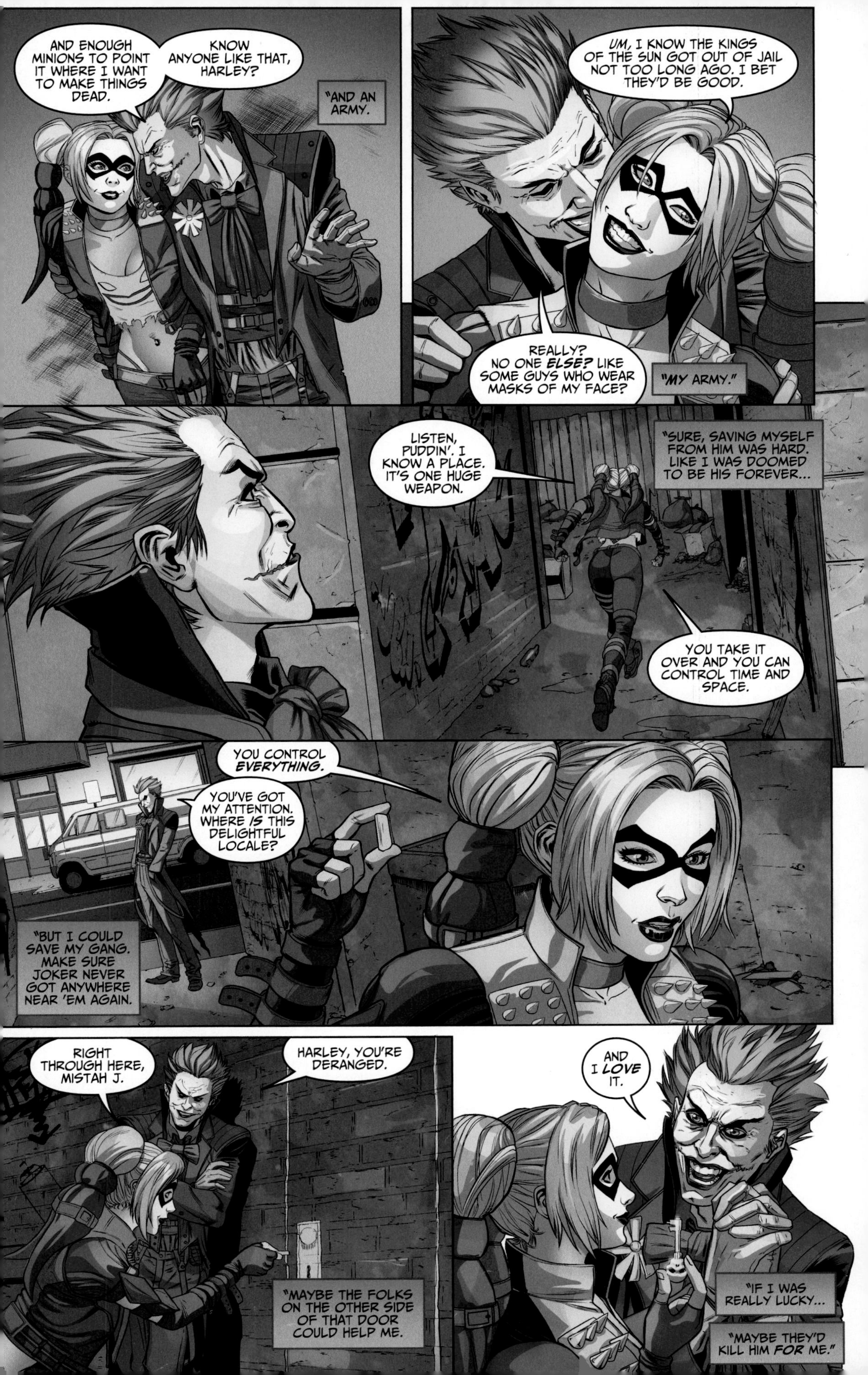
AND ENOUGH MINIONS TO POINT IT WHERE I WANT TO MAKE THINGS DEAD.
KNOW ANYONE LIKE THAT, HARLEY?
"AND AN ARMY.
UM, I KNOW THE KINGS OF THE SUN GOT OUT OF JAIL NOT TOO LONG AGO. I BET THEY'D BE GOOD.
REALLY? NO ONE ELSE? LIKE SOME GUYS WHO WEAR MASKS OF MY FACE?
"MY ARMY."
LISTEN, PUDDIN'. I KNOW A PLACE. IT'S ONE HUGE WEAPON.
"SURE, SAVING MYSELF FROM HIM WAS HARD. LIKE I WAS DOOMED TO BE HIS FOREVER...
YOU TAKE IT OVER AND YOU CAN CONTROL TIME AND SPACE.
YOU CONTROL EVERYTHING.
YOU'VE GOT MY ATTENTION. WHERE IS THIS DELIGHTFUL LOCALE?
"BUT I COULD SAVE MY GANG. MAKE SURE JOKER NEVER GOT ANYWHERE NEAR 'EM AGAIN.
RIGHT THROUGH HERE, MISTAH J.
HARLEY, YOU'RE DERANGED.
"MAYBE THE FOLKS ON THE OTHER SIDE OF THAT DOOR COULD HELP ME.
AND I LOVE IT.
"IF I WAS REALLY LUCKY...
"MAYBE THEY'D KILL HIM FOR ME."

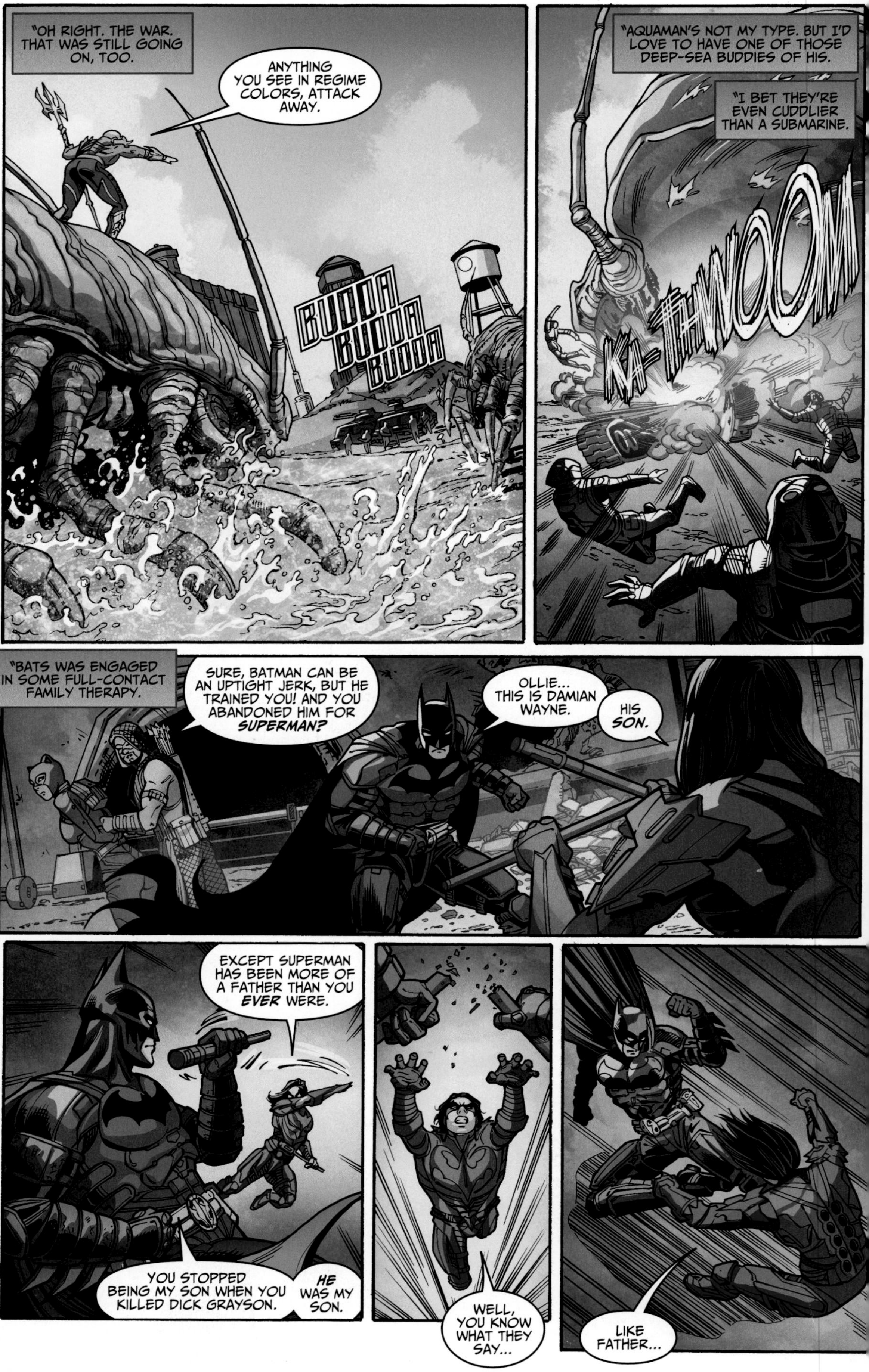
"OH RIGHT. THE WAR. THAT WAS STILL GOING ON, TOO.
ANYTHING YOU SEE IN REGIME COLORS, ATTACK AWAY.
BUDDA BUDDA BUDDA
"AQUAMAN'S NOT MY TYPE. BUT I'D LOVE TO HAVE ONE OF THOSE DEEP-SEA BUDDIES OF HIS.
"I BET THEY'RE EVEN CUDDLIER THAN A SUBMARINE.
KA-THWOOM
"BATS WAS ENGAGED IN SOME FULL-CONTACT FAMILY THERAPY.
SURE, BATMAN CAN BE AN UPTIGHT JERK, BUT HE TRAINED YOU! AND YOU ABANDONED HIM FOR SUPERMAN?
OLLIE... THIS IS DAMIAN WAYNE.
HIS SON.
EXCEPT SUPERMAN HAS BEEN MORE OF A FATHER THAN YOU EVER WERE.
YOU STOPPED BEING MY SON WHEN YOU KILLED DICK GRAYSON.
HE WAS MY SON.
WELL, YOU KNOW WHAT THEY SAY...
LIKE FATHER...

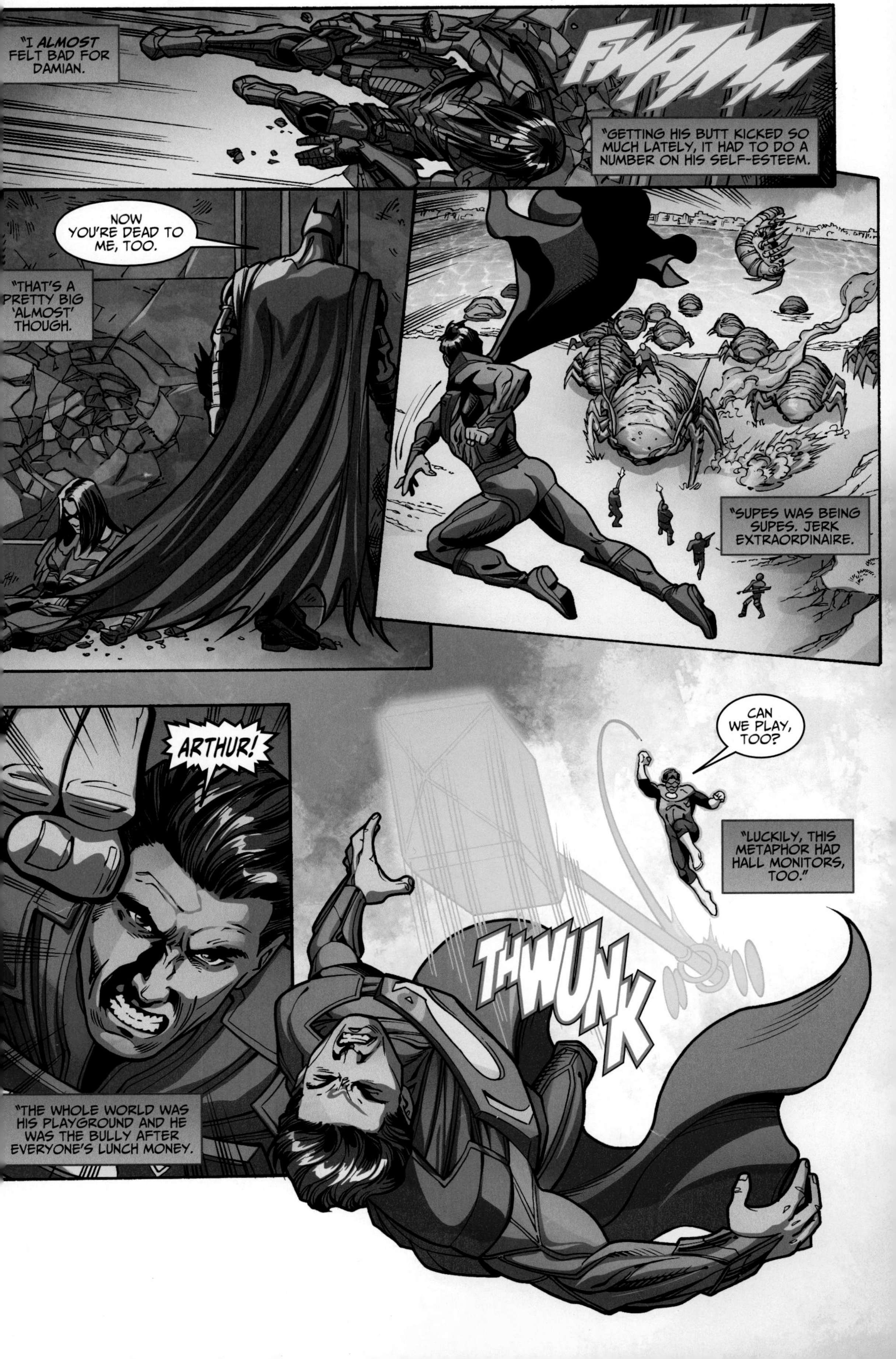
"I ALMOST FELT BAD FOR DAMIAN.
FWAMM
"GETTING HIS BUTT KICKED SO MUCH LATELY, IT HAD TO DO A NUMBER ON HIS SELF-ESTEEM.
NOW YOU'RE DEAD TO ME, TOO.
"THAT'S A PRETTY BIG 'ALMOST' THOUGH.
"SUPES WAS BEING SUPES. JERK EXTRAORDINAIRE.
ARTHUR!
CAN WE PLAY, TOO?
"LUCKILY, THIS METAPHOR HAD HALL MONITORS, TOO."
THWUNK
"THE WHOLE WORLD WAS HIS PLAYGROUND AND HE WAS THE BULLY AFTER EVERYONE'S LUNCH MONEY.

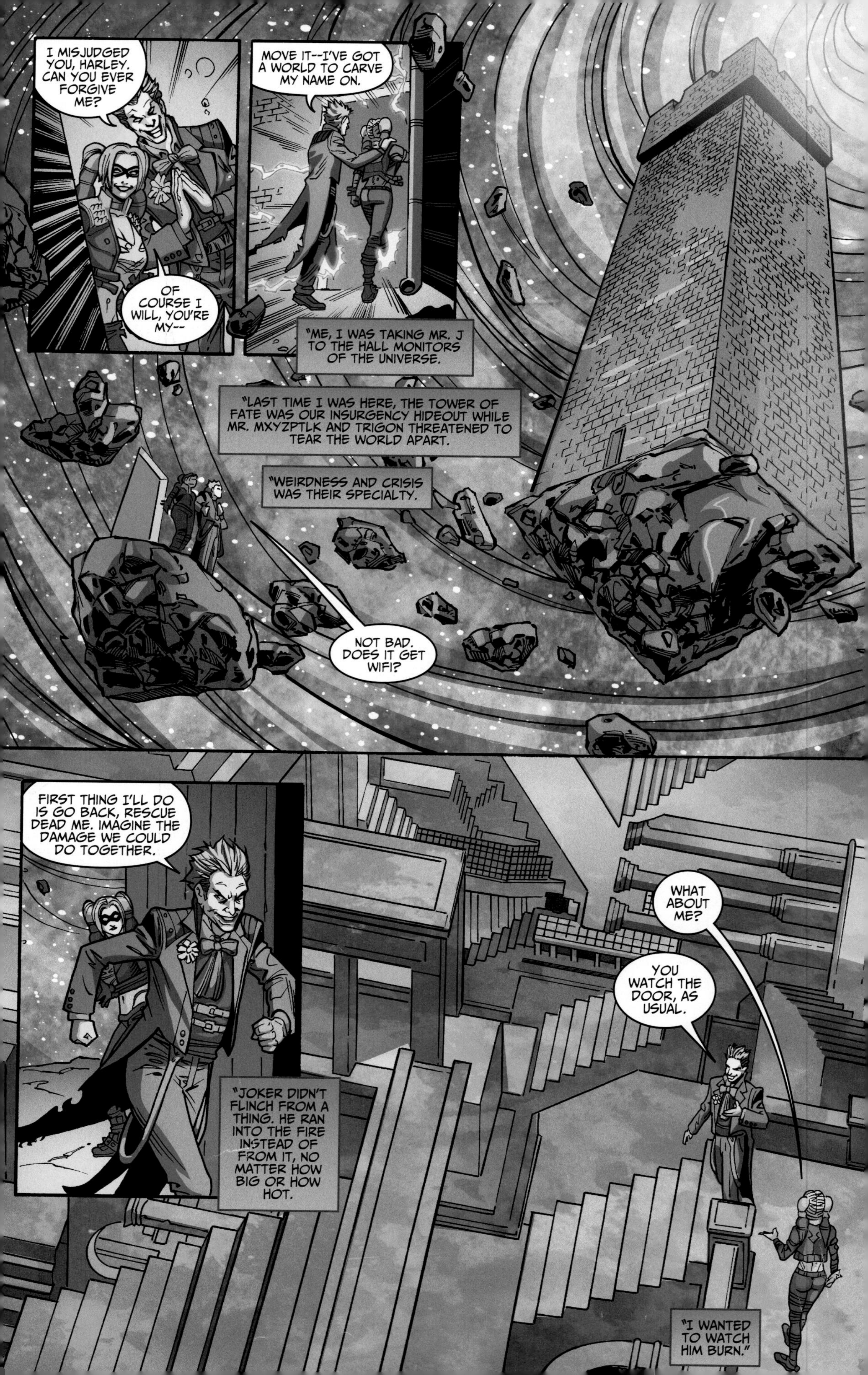
I MISJUDGED YOU, HARLEY. CAN YOU EVER FORGIVE ME?
OF COURSE I WILL, YOU'RE MY--
MOVE IT--I'VE GOT A WORLD TO CARVE MY NAME ON.
"ME, I WAS TAKING MR. J TO THE HALL MONITORS OF THE UNIVERSE.
"LAST TIME I WAS HERE, THE TOWER OF FATE WAS OUR INSURGENCY HIDEOUT WHILE MR. MXYZPTLK AND TRIGON THREATENED TO TEAR THE WORLD APART.
"WEIRDNESS AND CRISIS WAS THEIR SPECIALTY.
NOT BAD. DOES IT GET WIFI?
FIRST THING I'LL DO IS GO BACK, RESCUE DEAD ME. IMAGINE THE DAMAGE WE COULD DO TOGETHER.
WHAT ABOUT ME?
YOU WATCH THE DOOR, AS USUAL.
"JOKER DIDN'T FLINCH FROM A THING. HE RAN INTO THE FIRE INSTEAD OF FROM IT, NO MATTER HOW BIG OR HOW HOT.
"I WANTED TO WATCH HIM BURN."

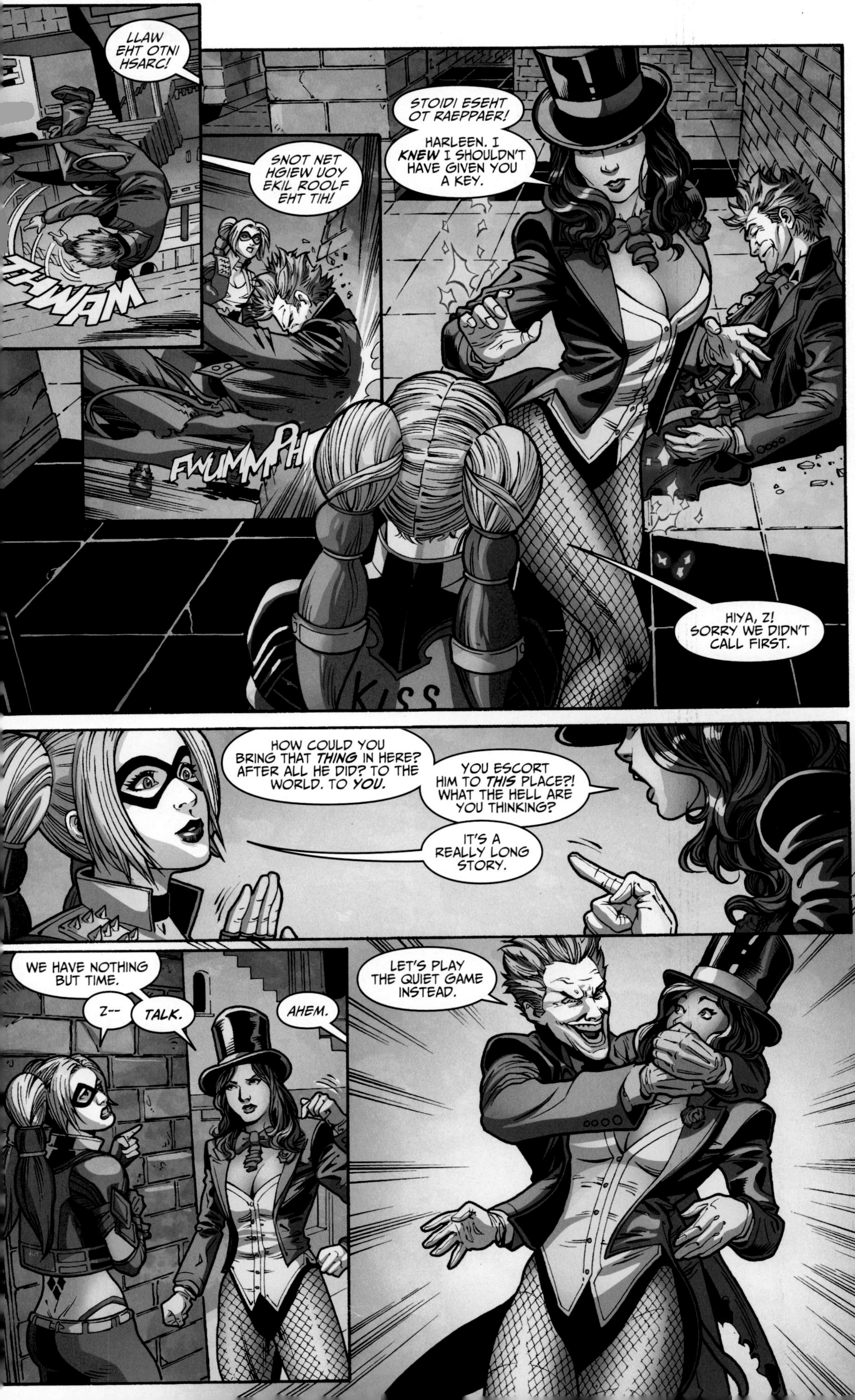

LLAW EHT OTNI HSARC!
THWAM
SNOT NET HGIEW UOY EKIL ROOLF EHT TIH!
FWUMMPH
STOIDI ESEHT OT RAEPPAER!
HARLEEN. I KNEW I SHOULDN'T HAVE GIVEN YOU A KEY.
HIYA, Z! SORRY WE DIDN'T CALL FIRST.
KISS
HOW COULD YOU BRING THAT THING IN HERE? AFTER ALL HE DID? TO THE WORLD. TO YOU.
YOU ESCORT HIM TO THIS PLACE?! WHAT THE HELL ARE YOU THINKING?
IT'S A REALLY LONG STORY.
WE HAVE NOTHING BUT TIME.
Z--
TALK.
AHEM.
LET'S PLAY THE QUIET GAME INSTEAD.

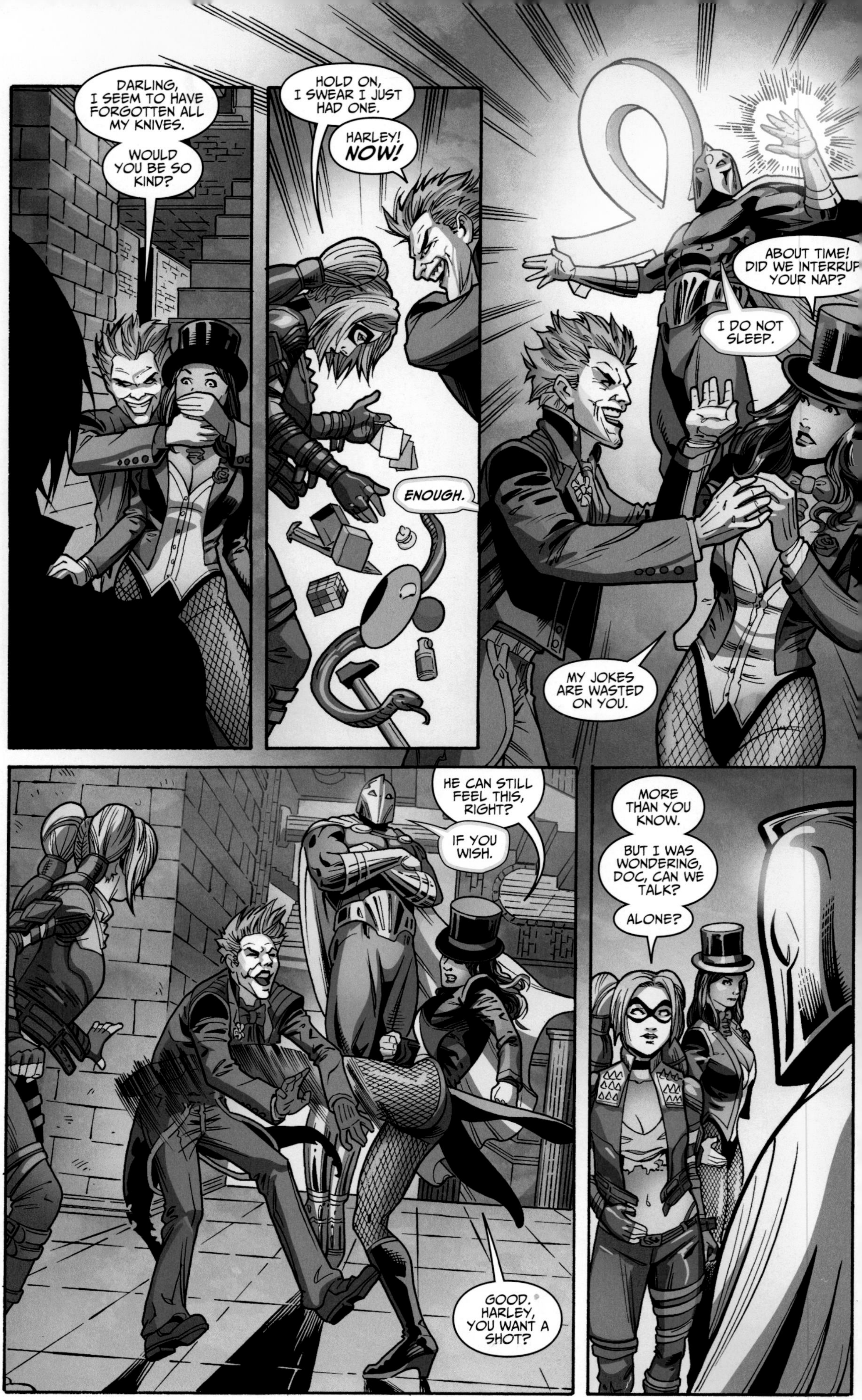
DARLING, I SEEM TO HAVE FORGOTTEN ALL MY KNIVES.
WOULD YOU BE SO KIND?
HOLD ON, I SWEAR I JUST HAD ONE.
HARLEY! NOW!
ENOUGH.
ABOUT TIME! DID WE INTERRUP YOUR NAP?
I DO NOT SLEEP.
MY JOKES ARE WASTED ON YOU.
HE CAN STILL FEEL THIS, RIGHT?
IF YOU WISH.
GOOD. HARLEY, YOU WANT A SHOT?
MORE THAN YOU KNOW.
BUT I WAS WONDERING, DOC, CAN WE TALK?
ALONE?

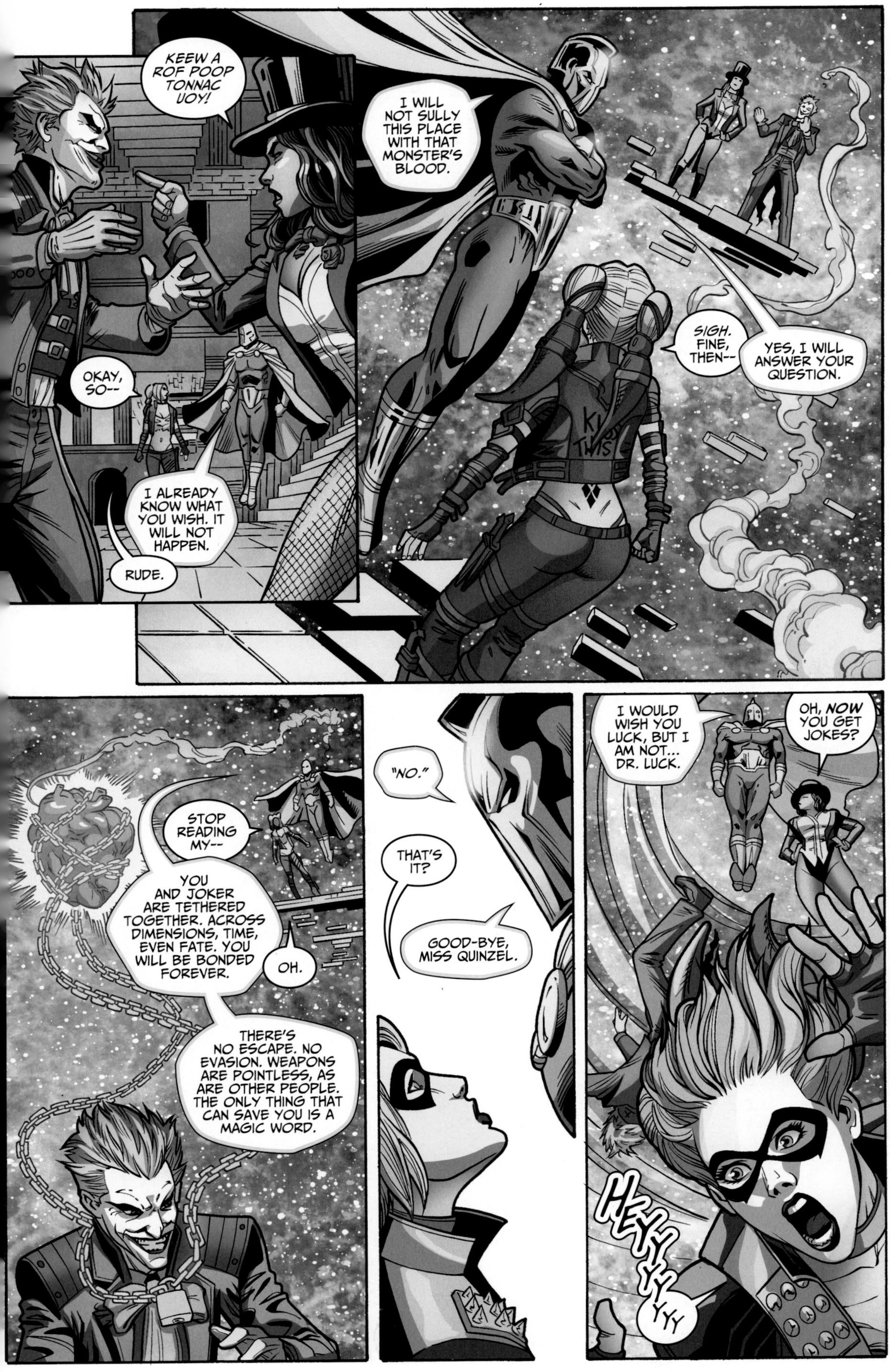
KEEW A ROF POOP TONNAC UOY!
OKAY, SO--
I ALREADY KNOW WHAT YOU WISH. IT WILL NOT HAPPEN.
RUDE.
I WILL NOT SULLY THIS PLACE WITH THAT MONSTER'S BLOOD.
SIGH. FINE, THEN--
YES, I WILL ANSWER YOUR QUESTION.
STOP READING MY--
YOU AND JOKER ARE TETHERED TOGETHER. ACROSS DIMENSIONS, TIME, EVEN FATE. YOU WILL BE BONDED FOREVER.
OH.
THERE'S NO ESCAPE. NO EVASION. WEAPONS ARE POINTLESS, AS ARE OTHER PEOPLE. THE ONLY THING THAT CAN SAVE YOU IS A MAGIC WORD.
"NO."
THAT'S IT?
GOOD-BYE, MISS QUINZEL.
I WOULD WISH YOU LUCK, BUT I AM NOT... DR. LUCK.
OH, *NOW* YOU GET JOKES?
HEYYYYYY

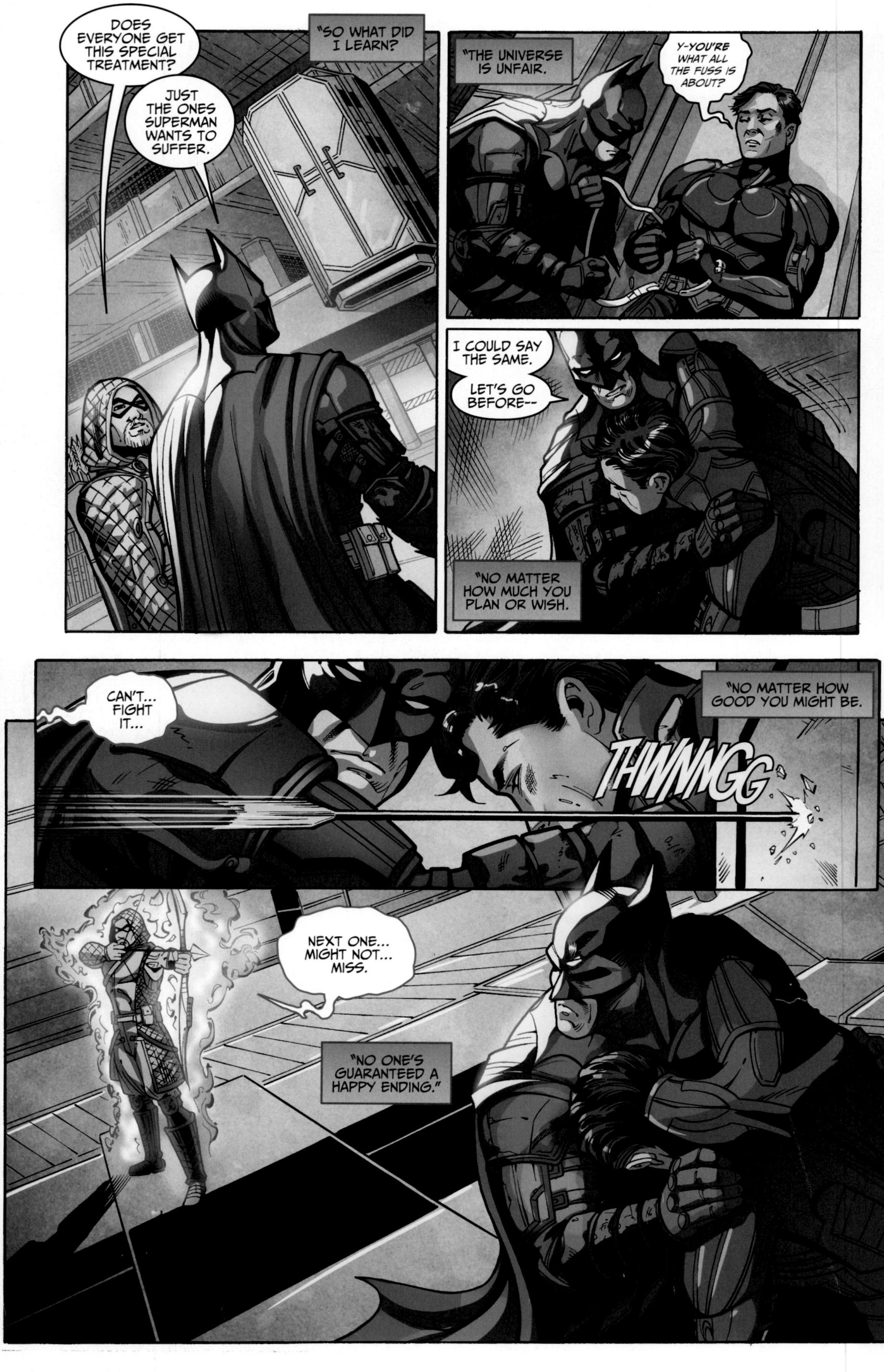
DOES EVERYONE GET THIS SPECIAL TREATMENT?
JUST THE ONES SUPERMAN WANTS TO SUFFER.
"SO WHAT DID I LEARN?
"THE UNIVERSE IS UNFAIR.
Y-YOU'RE WHAT ALL THE FUSS IS ABOUT?
I COULD SAY THE SAME.
LET'S GO BEFORE--
"NO MATTER HOW MUCH YOU PLAN OR WISH.
CAN'T... FIGHT IT...
"NO MATTER HOW GOOD YOU MIGHT BE.
THWNNGG
NEXT ONE... MIGHT NOT... MISS.
"NO ONE'S GUARANTEED A HAPPY ENDING."

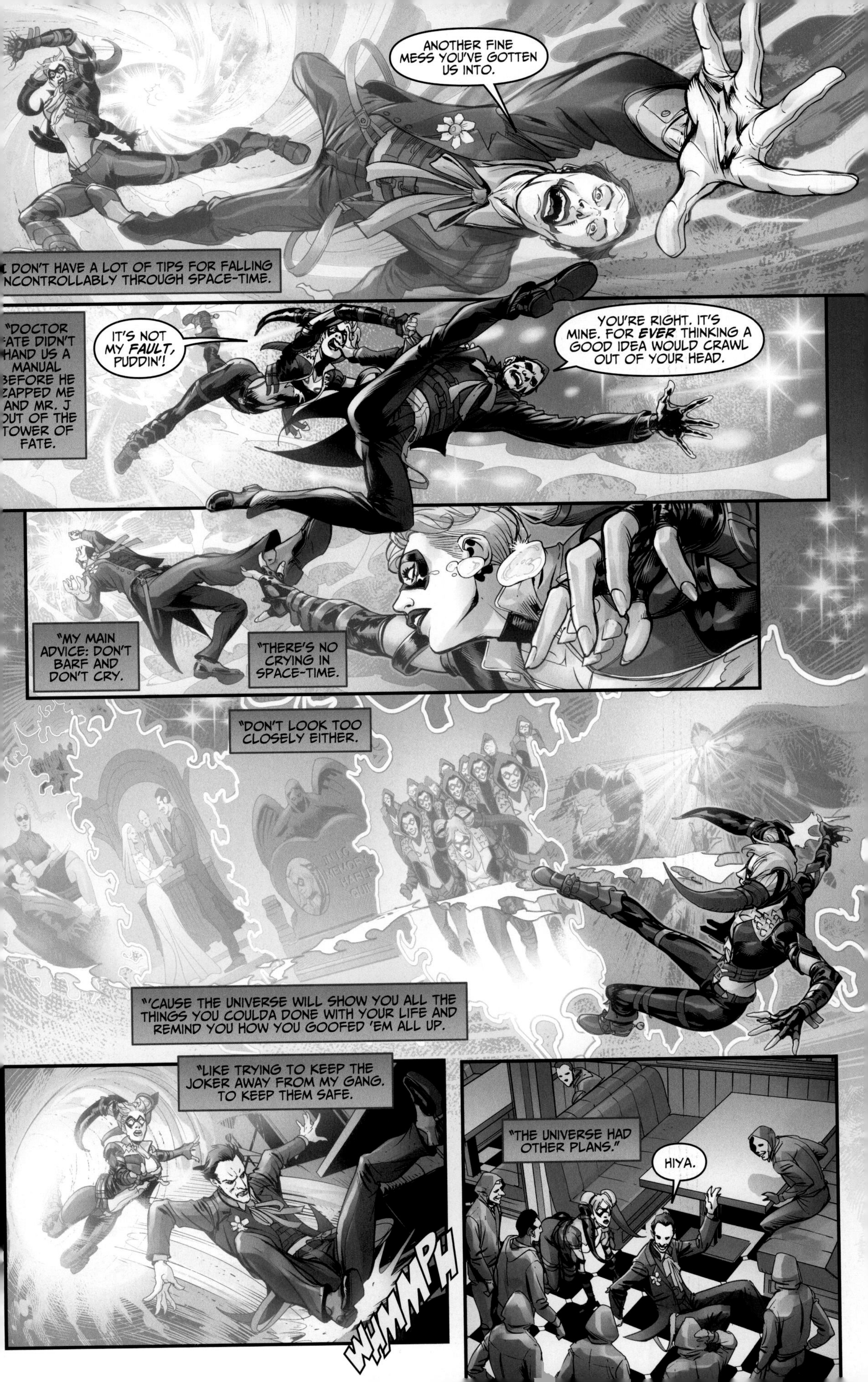
ANOTHER FINE MESS YOU'VE GOTTEN US INTO.
I DON'T HAVE A LOT OF TIPS FOR FALLING
NCONTROLLABLY THROUGH SPACE-TIME.
"DOCTOR FATE DIDN'T HAND US A MANUAL BEFORE HE ZAPPED ME AND MR. J OUT OF THE TOWER OF FATE.
IT'S NOT MY FAULT, PUDDIN'!
YOU'RE RIGHT. IT'S MINE. FOR EVER THINKING A GOOD IDEA WOULD CRAWL OUT OF YOUR HEAD.
"MY MAIN ADVICE: DON'T BARF AND DON'T CRY.
"THERE'S NO CRYING IN SPACE-TIME.
"DON'T LOOK TOO CLOSELY EITHER.
"'CAUSE THE UNIVERSE WILL SHOW YOU ALL THE THINGS YOU COULDA DONE WITH YOUR LIFE AND REMIND YOU HOW YOU GOOFED 'EM ALL UP.
"LIKE TRYING TO KEEP THE JOKER AWAY FROM MY GANG. TO KEEP THEM SAFE.
WHMMPH
"THE UNIVERSE HAD OTHER PLANS."
HIYA.

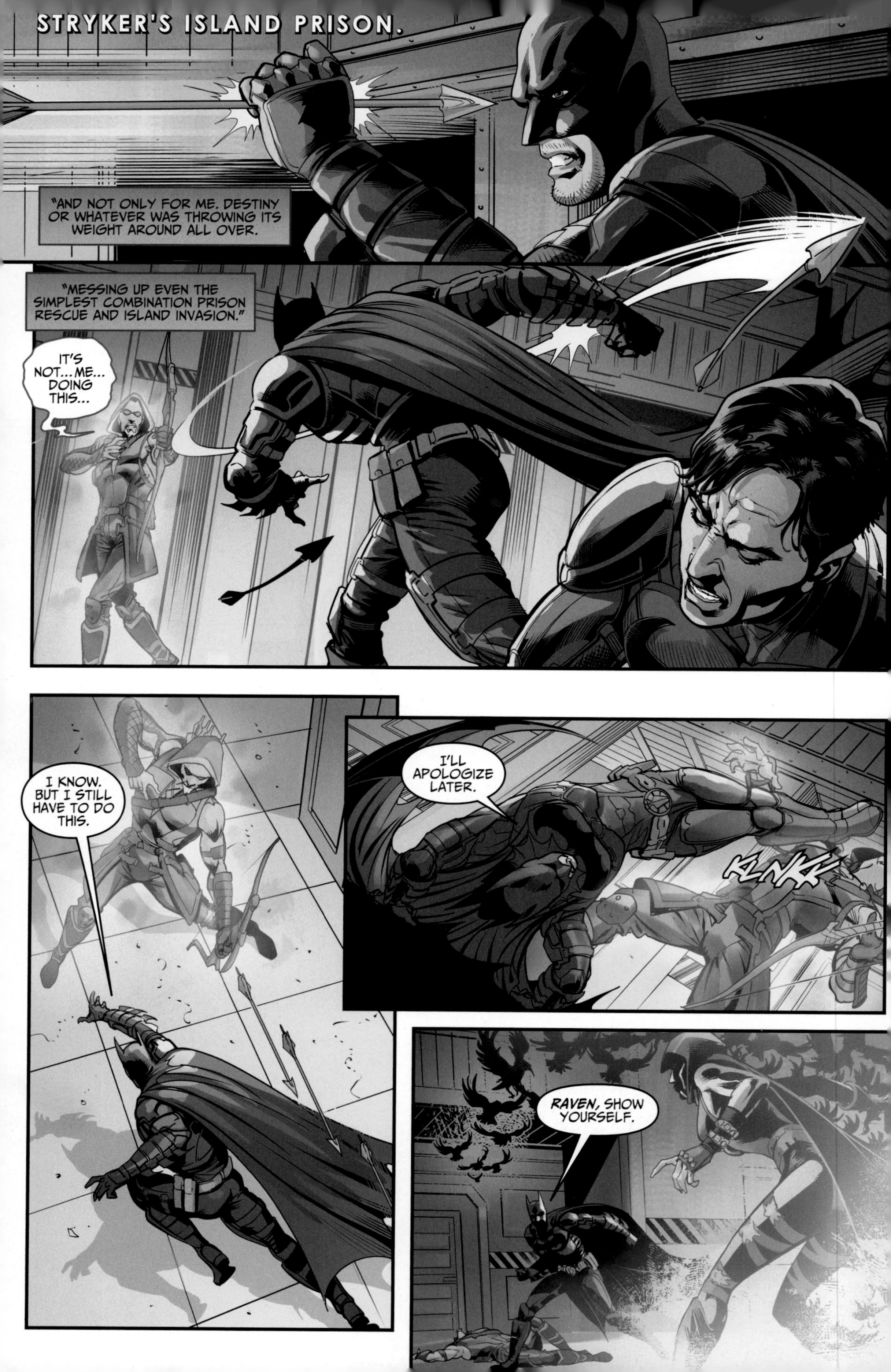
STRYKER'S ISLAND PRISON.
"AND NOT ONLY FOR ME. DESTINY OR WHATEVER WAS THROWING ITS WEIGHT AROUND ALL OVER.
"MESSING UP EVEN THE SIMPLEST COMBINATION PRISON RESCUE AND ISLAND INVASION."
IT'S NOT... ME... DOING THIS...
I KNOW. BUT I STILL HAVE TO DO THIS.
I'LL APOLOGIZE LATER.
KLNKK
RAVEN, SHOW YOURSELF.

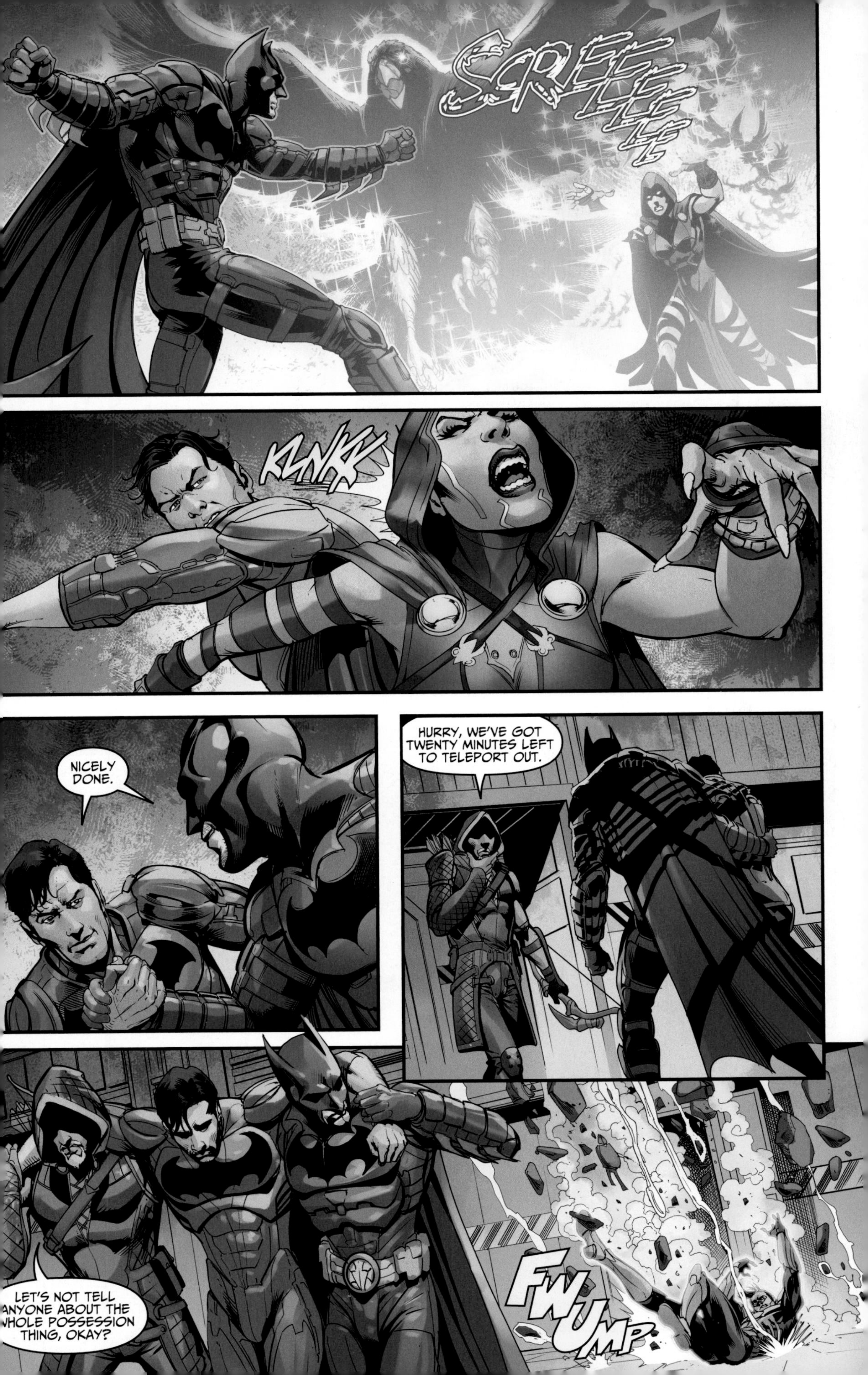
SCREEEEEE
KLNKK
NICELY DONE.
HURRY, WE'VE GOT TWENTY MINUTES LEFT TO TELEPORT OUT.
LET'S NOT TELL ANYONE ABOUT THE WHOLE POSSESSION THING, OKAY?
FWUMP

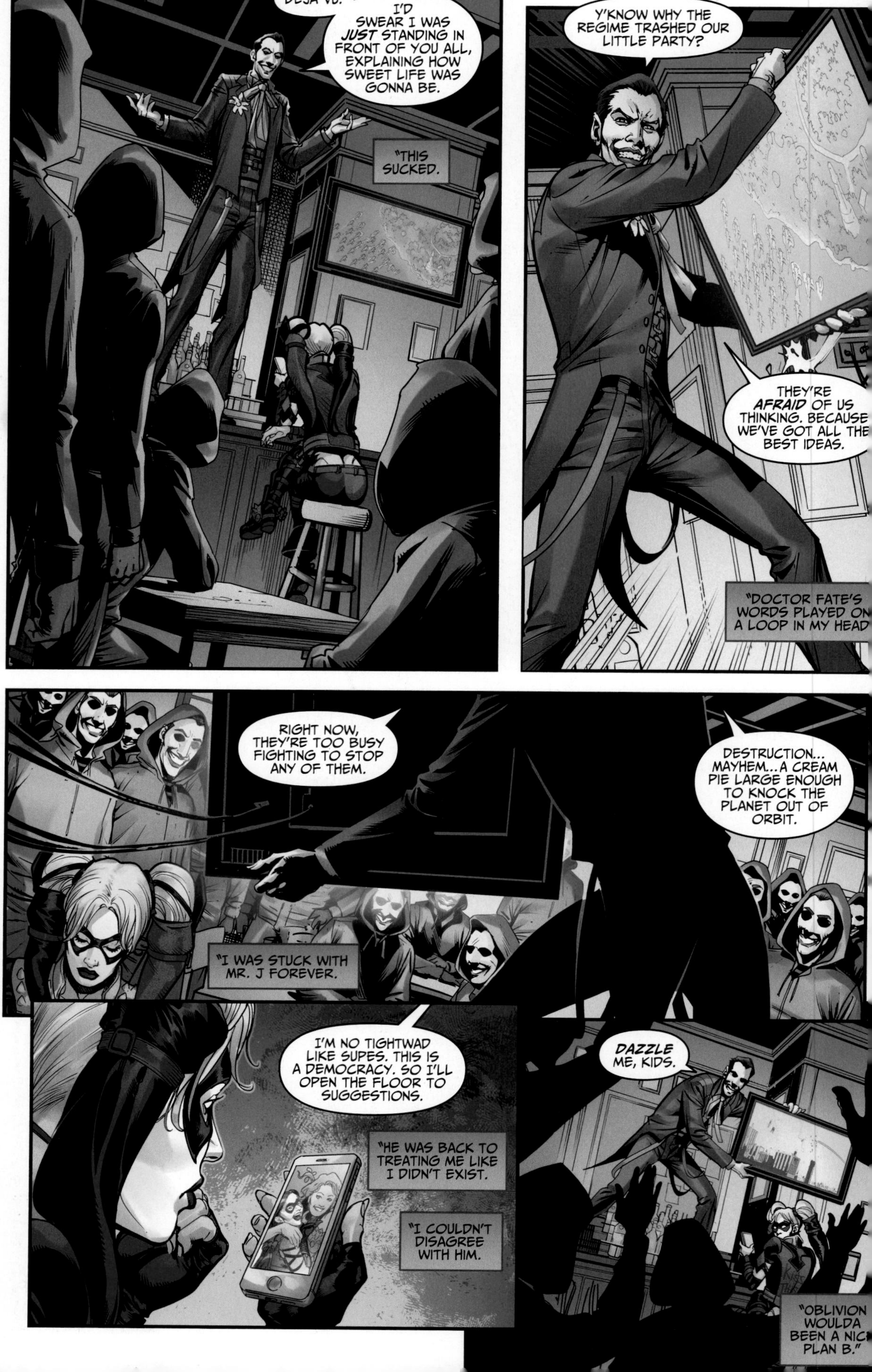
DÉJÀ VU.
I'D SWEAR I WAS JUST STANDING IN FRONT OF YOU ALL, EXPLAINING HOW SWEET LIFE WAS GONNA BE.
"THIS SUCKED.
Y'KNOW WHY THE REGIME TRASHED OUR LITTLE PARTY?
THEY'RE AFRAID OF US THINKING. BECAUSE WE'VE GOT ALL THE BEST IDEAS.
"DOCTOR FATE'S WORDS PLAYED ON A LOOP IN MY HEAD
RIGHT NOW, THEY'RE TOO BUSY FIGHTING TO STOP ANY OF THEM.
"I WAS STUCK WITH MR. J FOREVER.
DESTRUCTION... MAYHEM...A CREAM PIE LARGE ENOUGH TO KNOCK THE PLANET OUT OF ORBIT.
I'M NO TIGHTWAD LIKE SUPES. THIS IS A DEMOCRACY. SO I'LL OPEN THE FLOOR TO SUGGESTIONS.
"HE WAS BACK TO TREATING ME LIKE I DIDN'T EXIST.
"I COULDN'T DISAGREE WITH HIM.
DAZZLE ME, KIDS.
"OBLIVION WOULDA BEEN A NIC PLAN B."

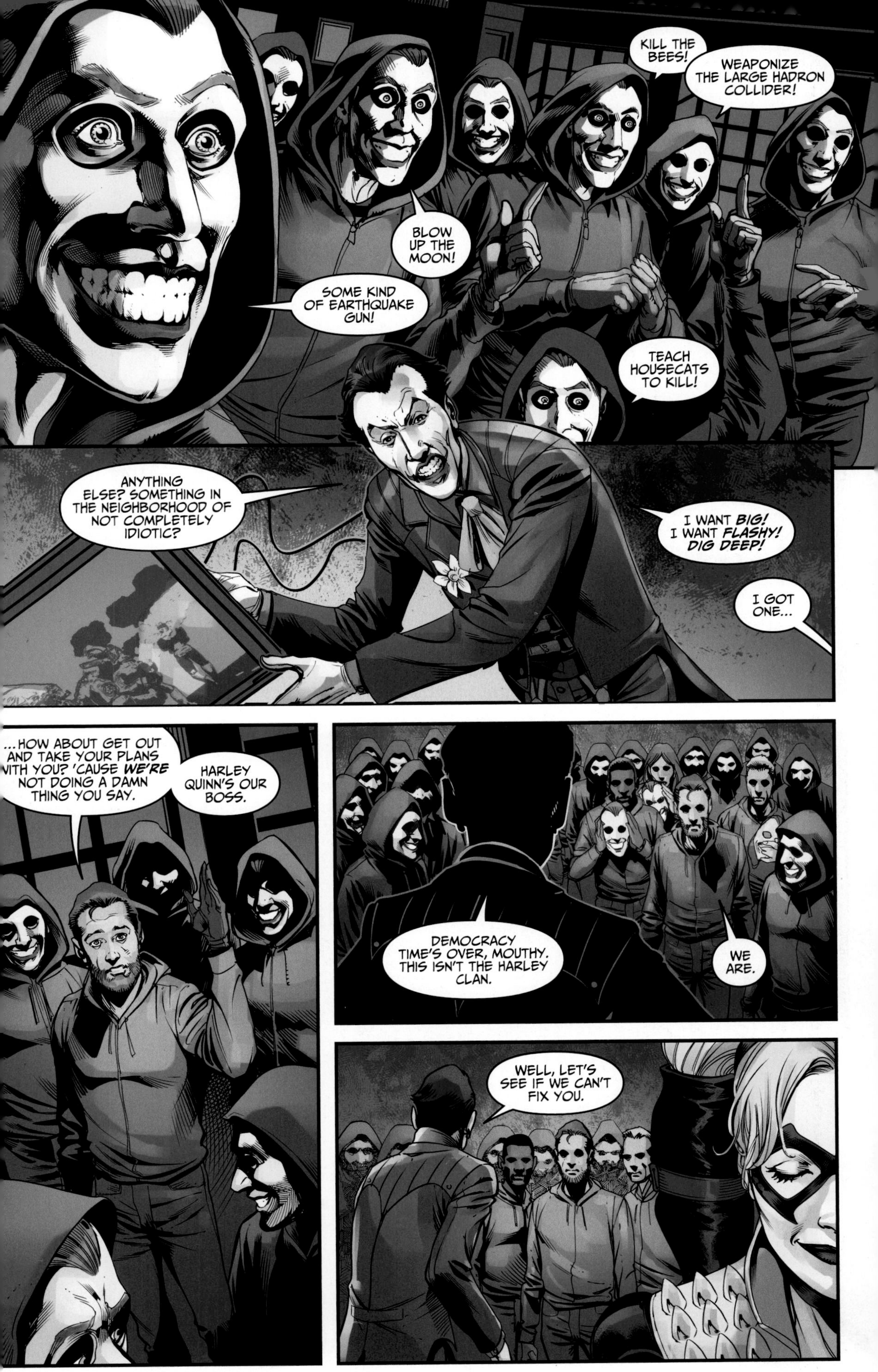
KILL THE BEES!
WEAPONIZE THE LARGE HADRON COLLIDER!
BLOW UP THE MOON!
SOME KIND OF EARTHQUAKE GUN!
TEACH HOUSECATS TO KILL!
ANYTHING ELSE? SOMETHING IN THE NEIGHBORHOOD OF NOT COMPLETELY IDIOTIC?
I WANT BIG! I WANT FLASHY! DIG DEEP!
I GOT ONE...
...HOW ABOUT GET OUT AND TAKE YOUR PLANS WITH YOU? 'CAUSE WE'RE NOT DOING A DAMN THING YOU SAY.
HARLEY QUINN'S OUR BOSS.
DEMOCRACY TIME'S OVER, MOUTHY. THIS ISN'T THE HARLEY CLAN.
WE ARE.
WELL, LET'S SEE IF WE CAN'T FIX YOU.

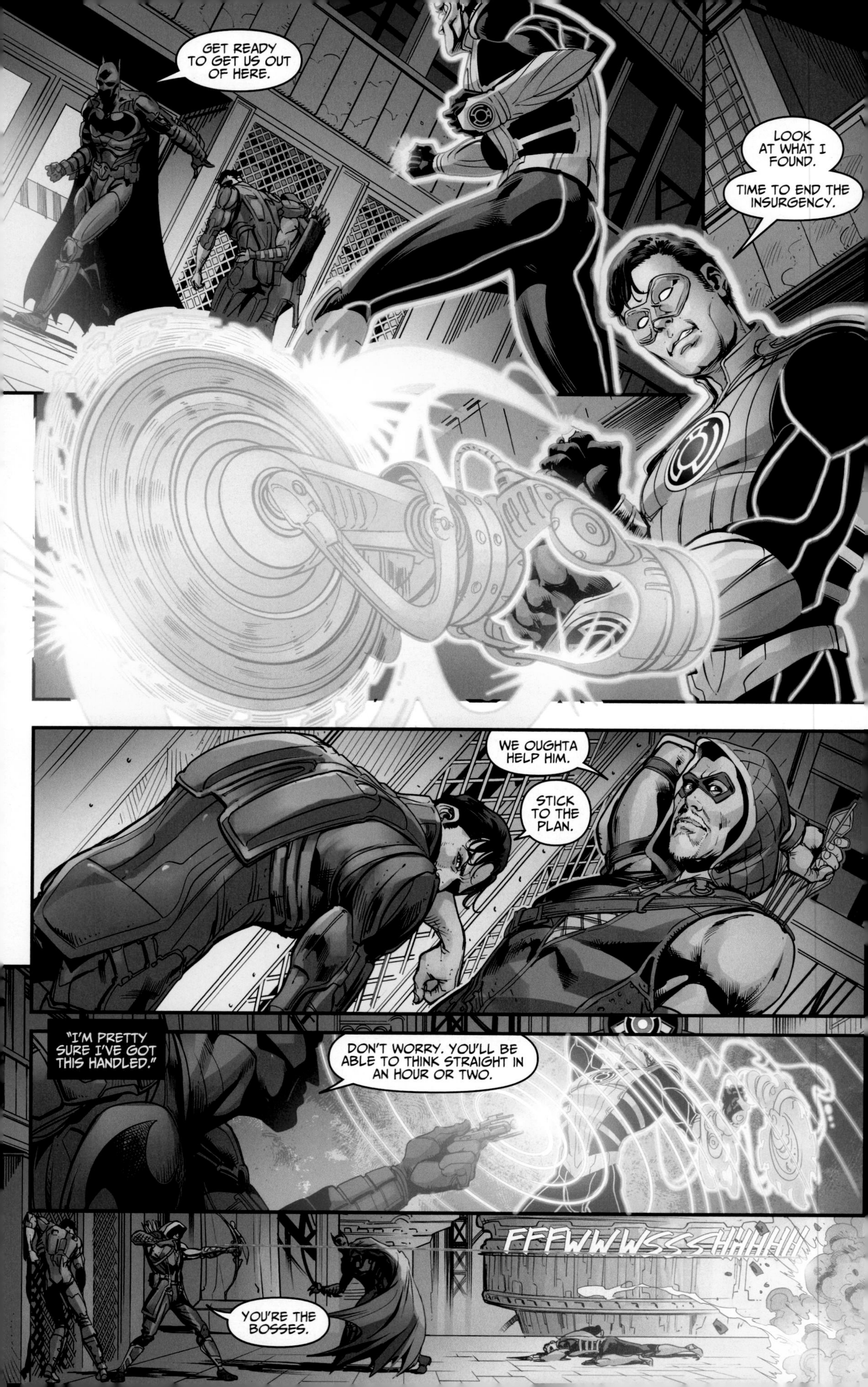
GET READY TO GET US OUT OF HERE.
LOOK AT WHAT I FOUND.
TIME TO END THE INSURGENCY.
WE OUGHTA HELP HIM.
STICK TO THE PLAN.
"I'M PRETTY SURE I'VE GOT THIS HANDLED."
DON'T WORRY. YOU'LL BE ABLE TO THINK STRAIGHT IN AN HOUR OR TWO.
FFFWWWSSSSHHHHH
YOU'RE THE BOSSES.

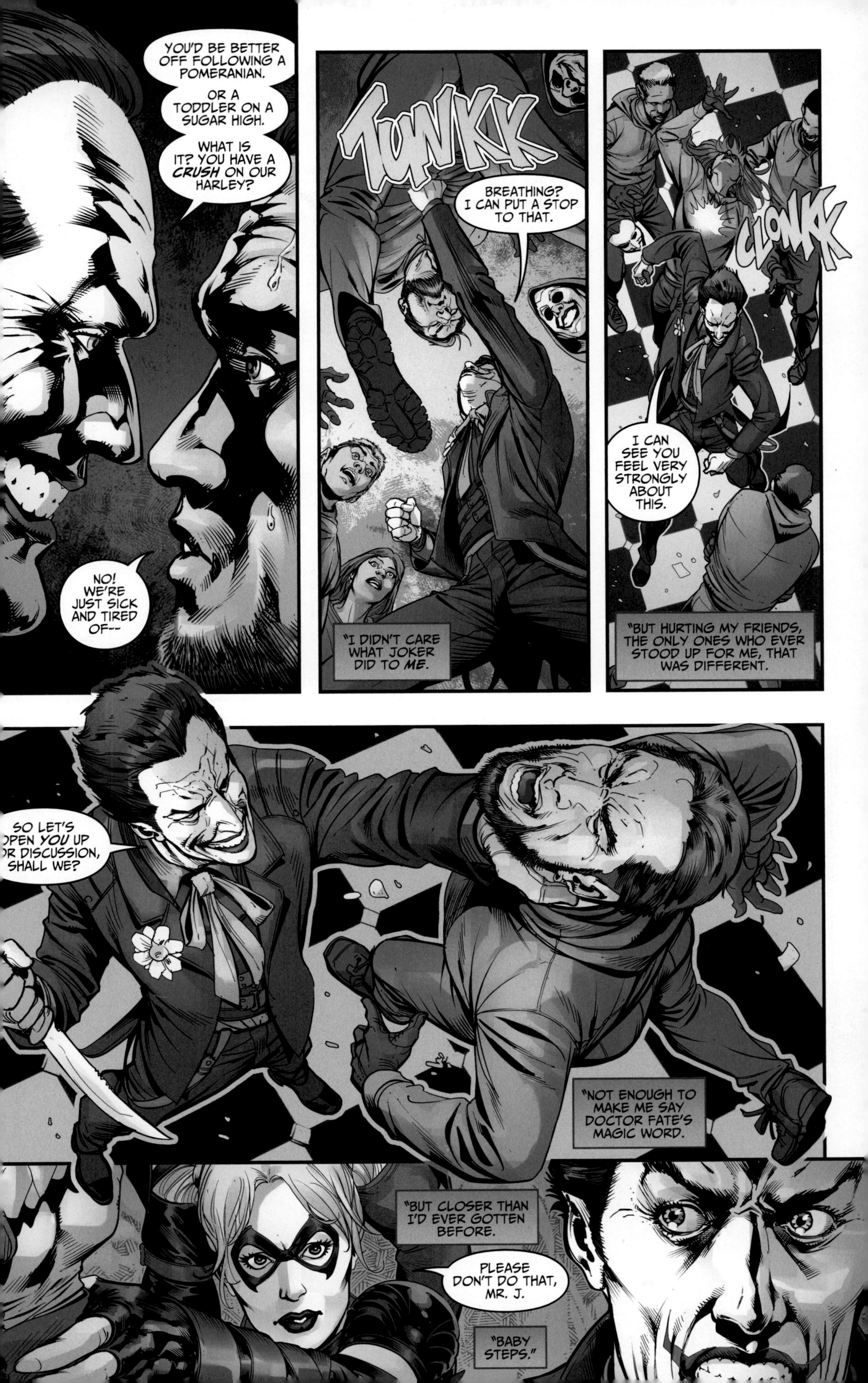

YOU'D BE BETTER OFF FOLLOWING A POMERANIAN.
OR A TODDLER ON A SUGAR HIGH.
WHAT IS IT? YOU HAVE A CRUSH ON OUR HARLEY?
NO! WE'RE JUST SICK AND TIRED OF--
TUNKK
BREATHING? I CAN PUT A STOP TO THAT.
"I DIDN'T CARE WHAT JOKER DID TO ME.
CLONKK
I CAN SEE YOU FEEL VERY STRONGLY ABOUT THIS.
"BUT HURTING MY FRIENDS, THE ONLY ONES WHO EVER STOOD UP FOR ME, THAT WAS DIFFERENT.
SO LET'S OPEN YOU UP FOR DISCUSSION, SHALL WE?
"NOT ENOUGH TO MAKE ME SAY DOCTOR FATE'S MAGIC WORD.
"BUT CLOSER THAN I'D EVER GOTTEN BEFORE.
PLEASE DON'T DO THAT, MR. J.
"BABY STEPS."

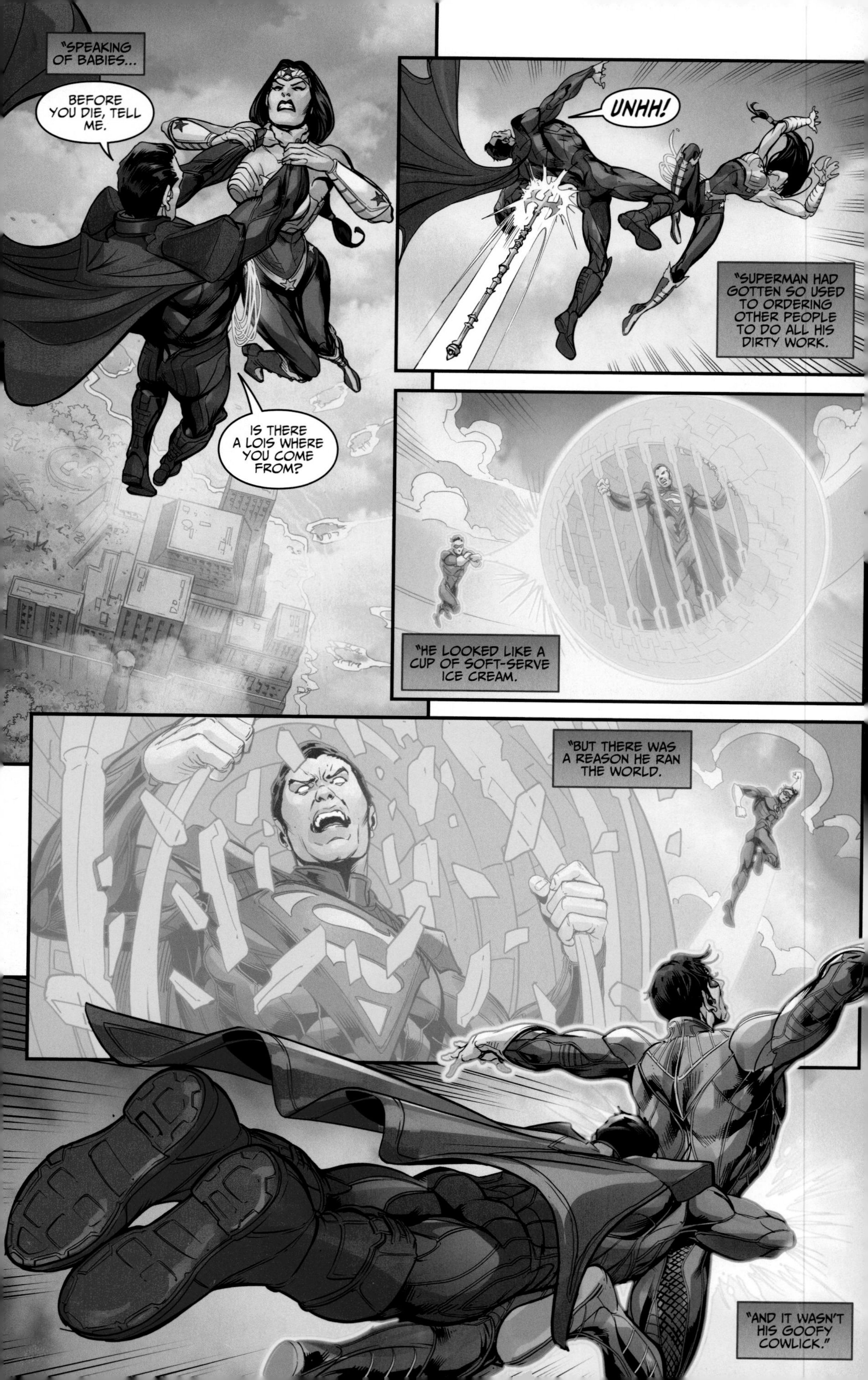
"SPEAKING OF BABIES...
BEFORE YOU DIE, TELL ME.
IS THERE A LOIS WHERE YOU COME FROM?
UNHH!
"SUPERMAN HAD GOTTEN SO USED TO ORDERING OTHER PEOPLE TO DO ALL HIS DIRTY WORK.
"HE LOOKED LIKE A CUP OF SOFT-SERVE ICE CREAM.
"BUT THERE WAS A REASON HE RAN THE WORLD.
"AND IT WASN'T HIS GOOFY COWLICK."

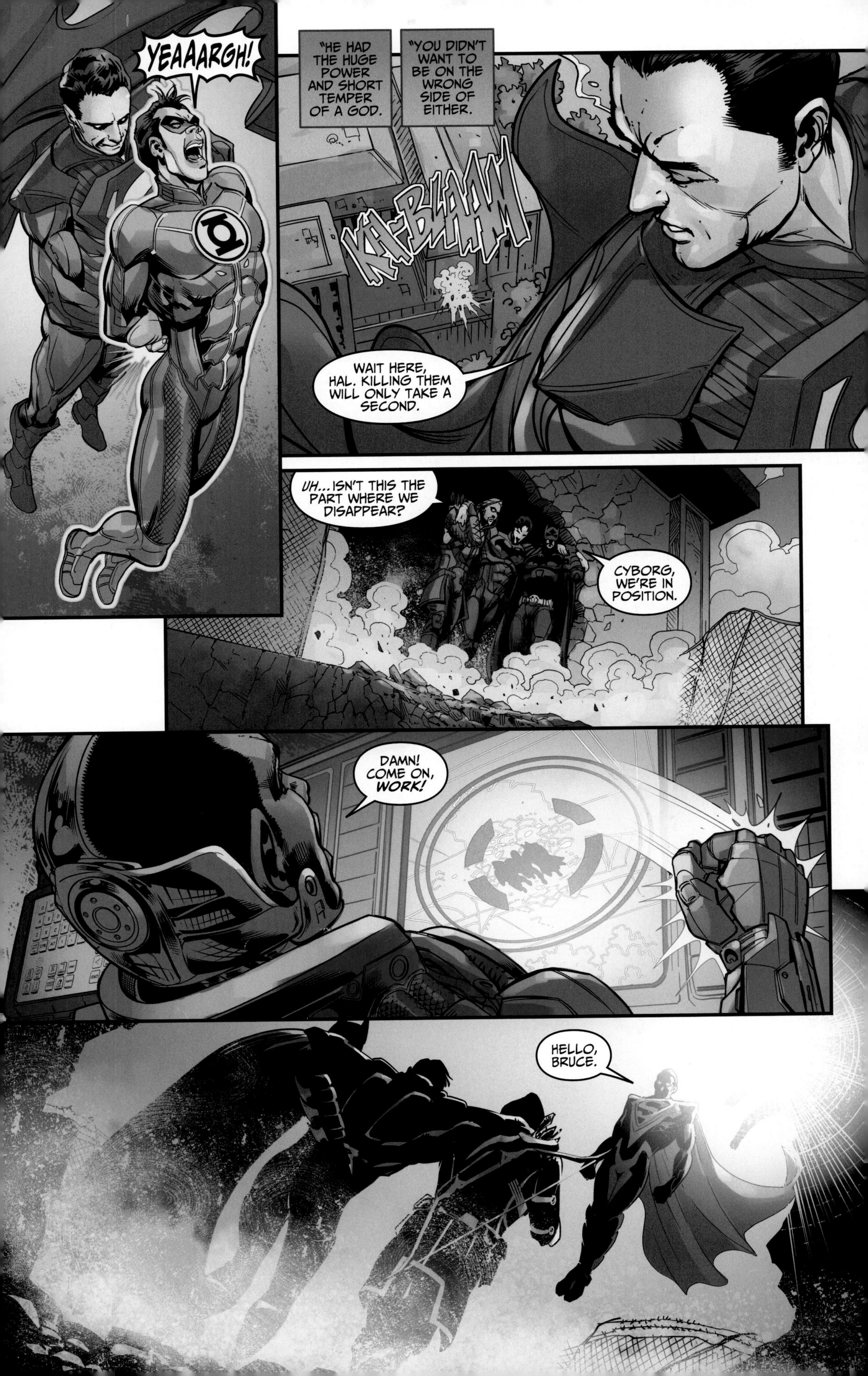
YEAAARGH!
"HE HAD THE HUGE POWER AND SHORT TEMPER OF A GOD.
"YOU DIDN'T WANT TO BE ON THE WRONG SIDE OF EITHER.
KA-BLAAM
WAIT HERE, HAL. KILLING THEM WILL ONLY TAKE A SECOND.
UH...ISN'T THIS THE PART WHERE WE DISAPPEAR?
CYBORG, WE'RE IN POSITION.
DAMN! COME ON, WORK!
HELLO, BRUCE.

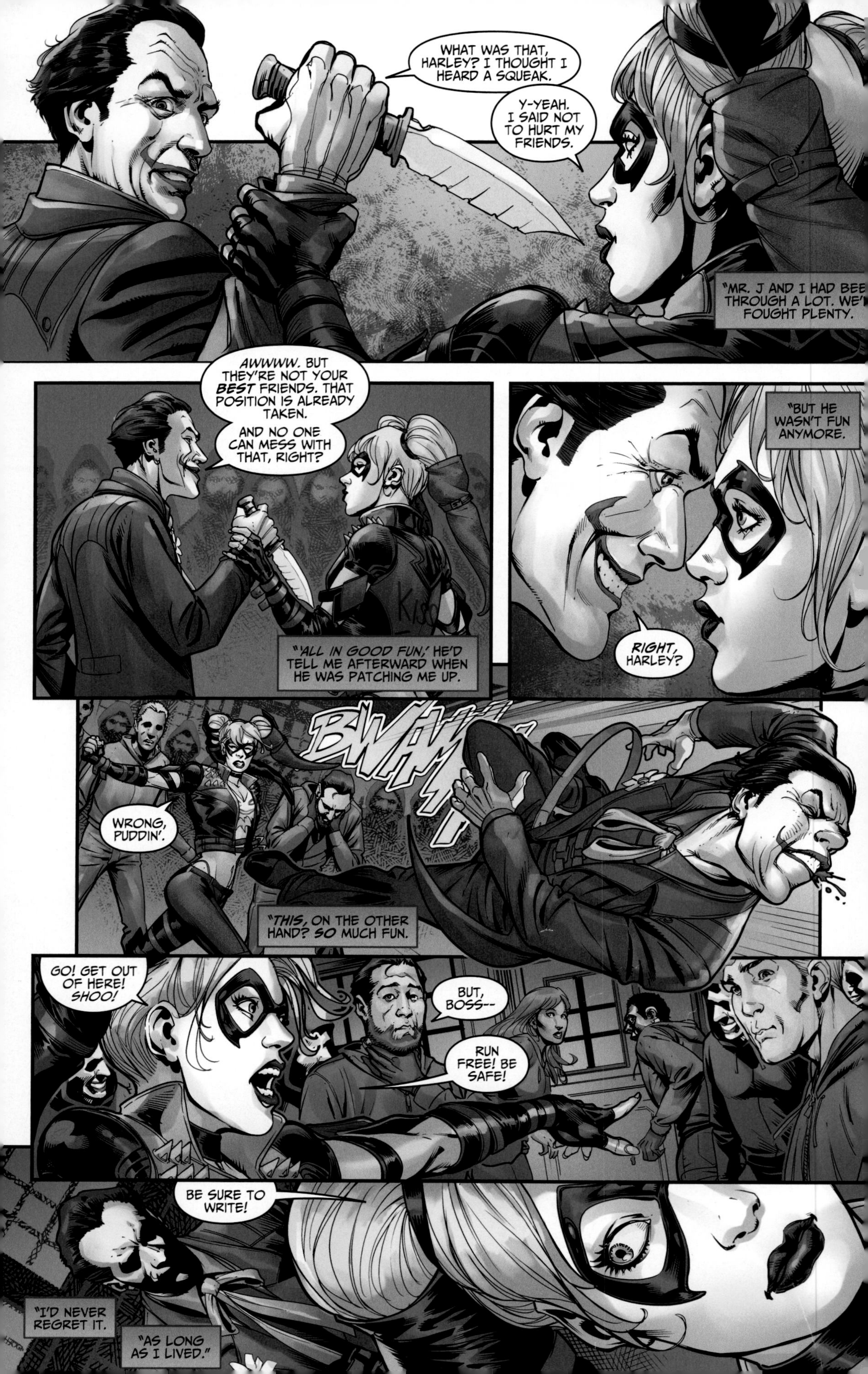
WHAT WAS THAT, HARLEY? I THOUGHT I HEARD A SQUEAK.
Y-YEAH. I SAID NOT TO HURT MY FRIENDS.
"MR. J AND I HAD BEE THROUGH A LOT. WE' FOUGHT PLENTY.
AWWWW. BUT THEY'RE NOT YOUR BEST FRIENDS. THAT POSITION IS ALREADY TAKEN.
AND NO ONE CAN MESS WITH THAT, RIGHT?
"'ALL IN GOOD FUN,' HE'D TELL ME AFTERWARD WHEN HE WAS PATCHING ME UP.
"BUT HE WASN'T FUN ANYMORE.
RIGHT, HARLEY?
WRONG, PUDDIN'.
"THIS, ON THE OTHER HAND? SO MUCH FUN.
GO! GET OUT OF HERE! SHOO!
BUT, BOSS--
RUN FREE! BE SAFE!
BE SURE TO WRITE!
"I'D NEVER REGRET IT.
"AS LONG AS I LIVED."

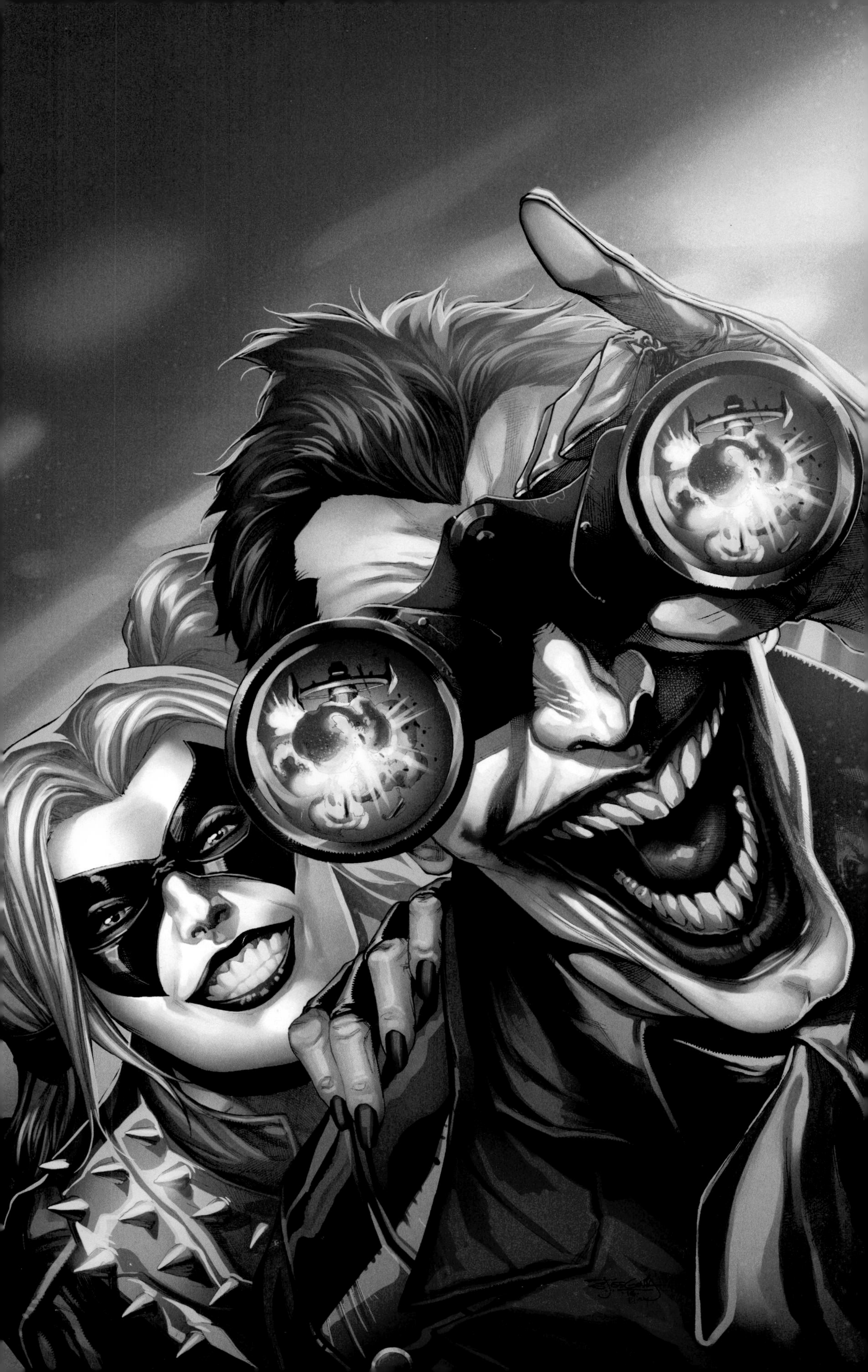

"Fall Down, Go Boom" **Daniel Sampere** **Tom Derenick** Pencillers
Juan Albarran **Tom Derenick** Inkers **J.Nanjan** Colorist
Cover art by **Stephen Segovia** and **Elmer Santos**

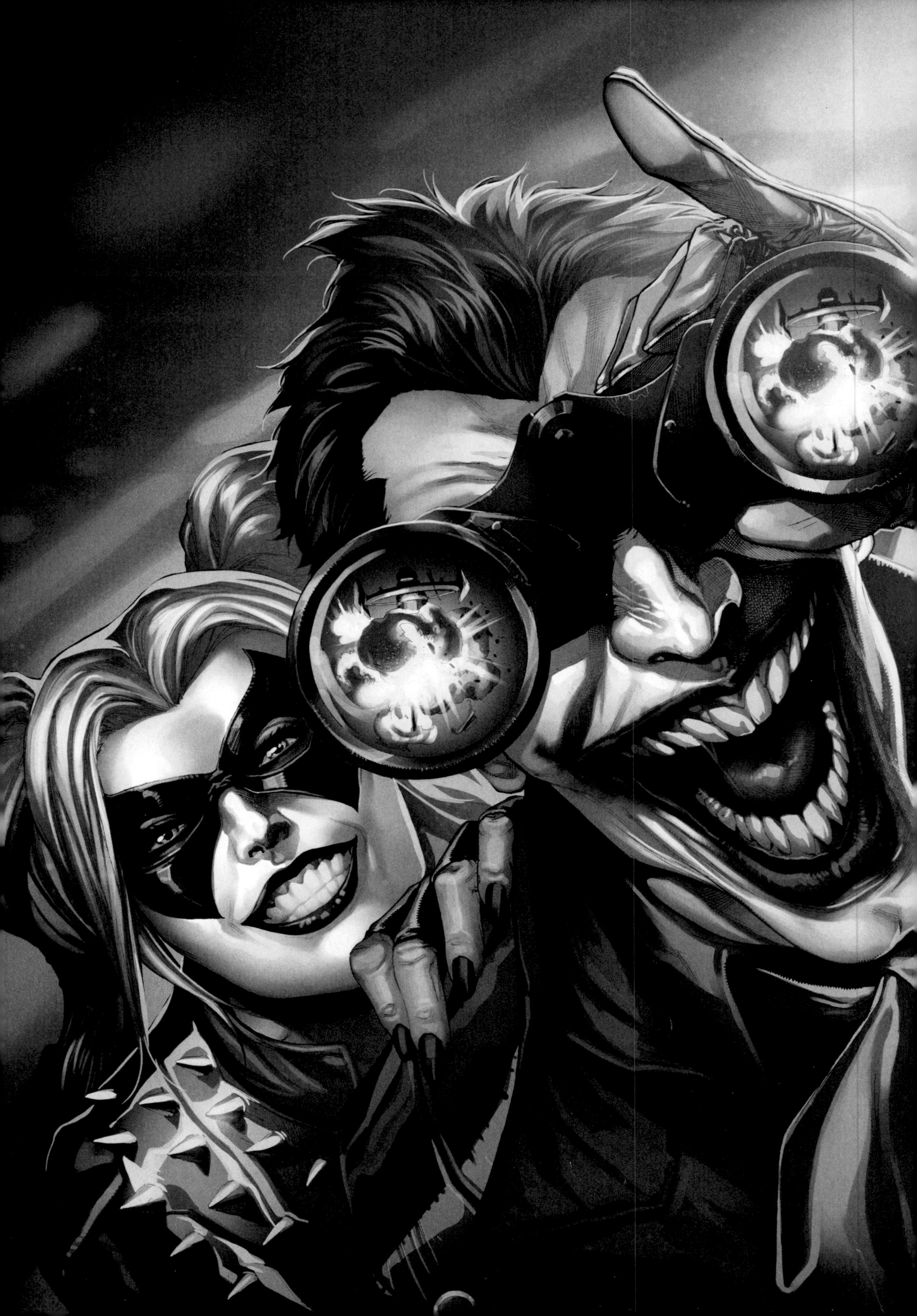

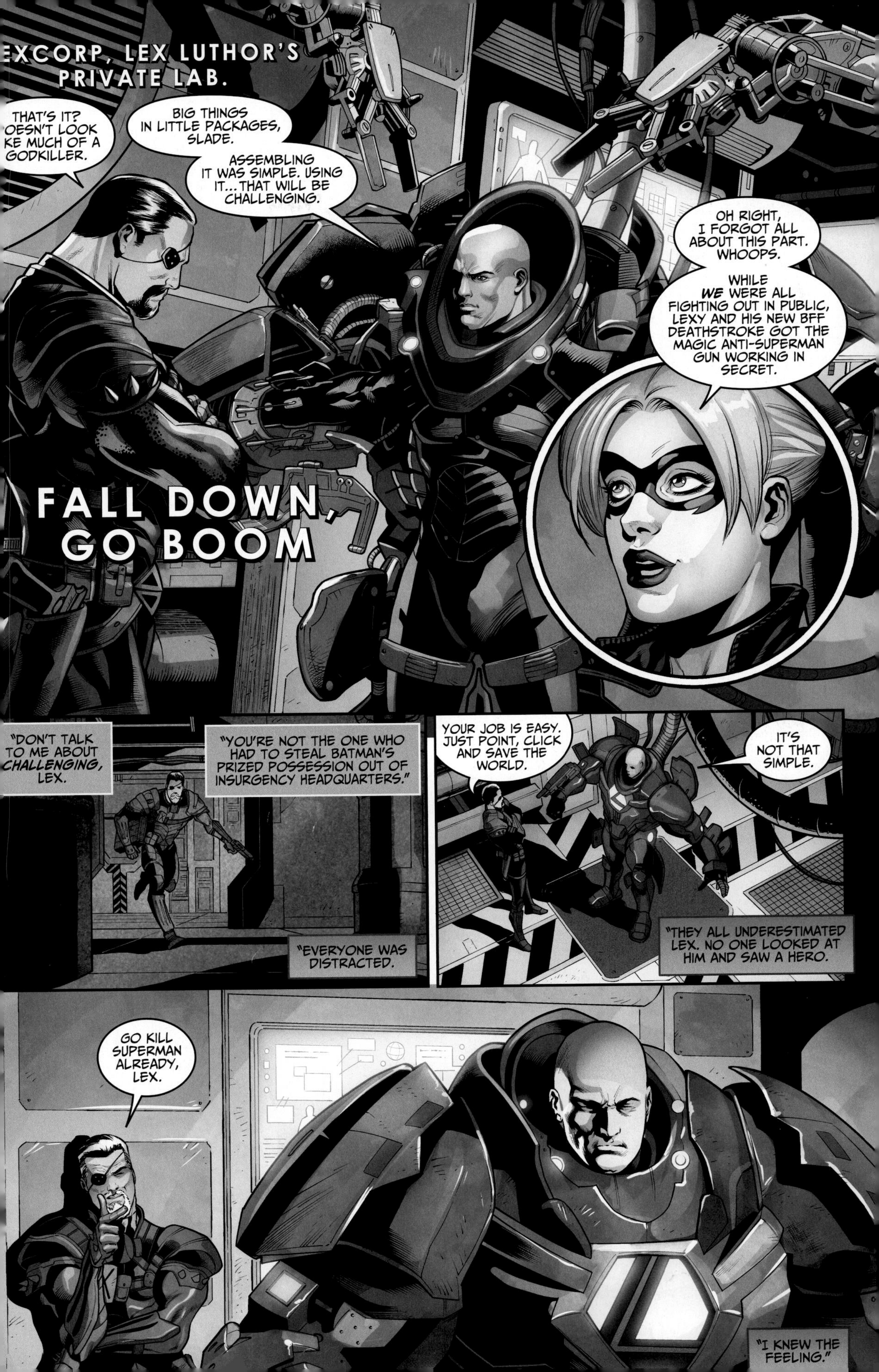

EXCORP, LEX LUTHOR'S PRIVATE LAB.
THAT'S IT? OESN'T LOOK KE MUCH OF A GODKILLER.
BIG THINGS IN LITTLE PACKAGES, SLADE.
ASSEMBLING IT WAS SIMPLE. USING IT... THAT WILL BE CHALLENGING.
OH RIGHT, I FORGOT ALL ABOUT THIS PART. WHOOPS.
WHILE WE WERE ALL FIGHTING OUT IN PUBLIC, LEXY AND HIS NEW BFF DEATHSTROKE GOT THE MAGIC ANTI-SUPERMAN GUN WORKING IN SECRET.
FALL DOWN, GO BOOM
"DON'T TALK TO ME ABOUT CHALLENGING, LEX.
"YOU'RE NOT THE ONE WHO HAD TO STEAL BATMAN'S PRIZED POSSESSION OUT OF INSURGENCY HEADQUARTERS."
"EVERYONE WAS DISTRACTED.
YOUR JOB IS EASY. JUST POINT, CLICK AND SAVE THE WORLD.
IT'S NOT THAT SIMPLE.
"THEY ALL UNDERESTIMATED LEX. NO ONE LOOKED AT HIM AND SAW A HERO.
GO KILL SUPERMAN ALREADY, LEX.
"I KNEW THE FEELING."

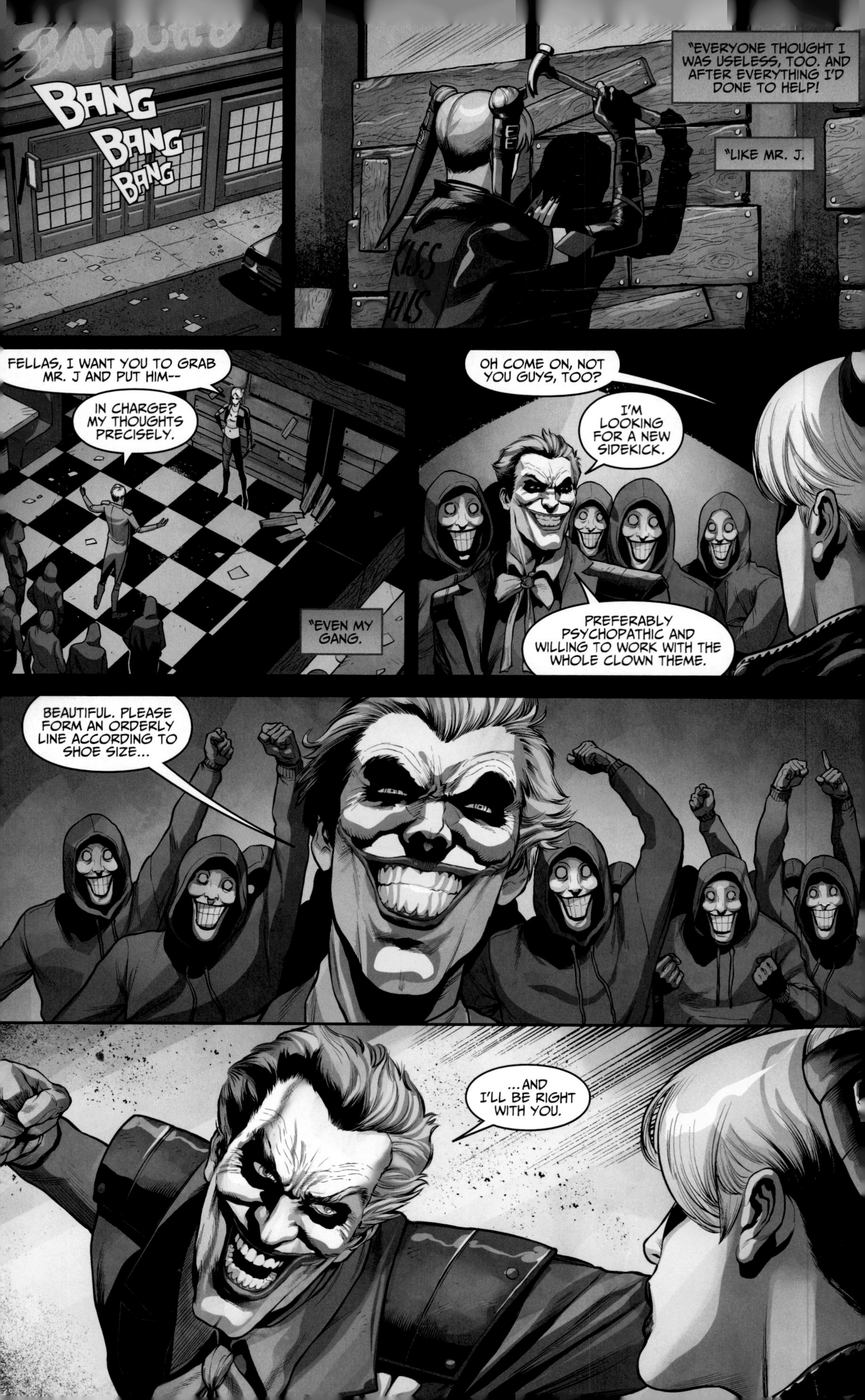
BANG
BANG
BANG
"EVERYONE THOUGHT I WAS USELESS, TOO. AND AFTER EVERYTHING I'D DONE TO HELP!
"LIKE MR. J.
FELLAS, I WANT YOU TO GRAB MR. J AND PUT HIM--
IN CHARGE? MY THOUGHTS PRECISELY.
"EVEN MY GANG.
OH COME ON, NOT YOU GUYS, TOO?
I'M LOOKING FOR A NEW SIDEKICK.
PREFERABLY PSYCHOPATHIC AND WILLING TO WORK WITH THE WHOLE CLOWN THEME.
BEAUTIFUL. PLEASE FORM AN ORDERLY LINE ACCORDING TO SHOE SIZE...
...AND I'LL BE RIGHT WITH YOU.

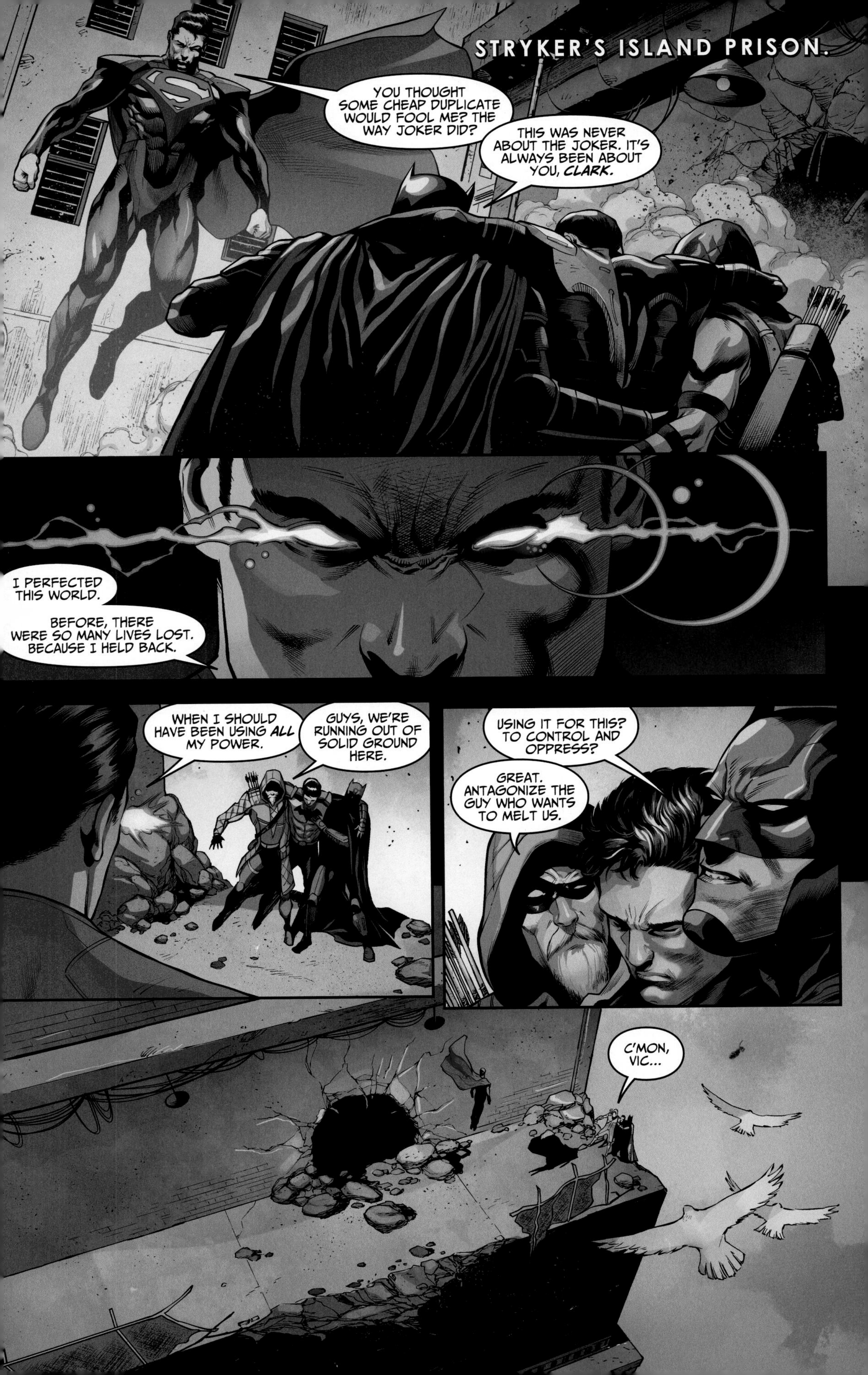
STRYKER'S ISLAND PRISON.
YOU THOUGHT SOME CHEAP DUPLICATE WOULD FOOL ME? THE WAY JOKER DID?
THIS WAS NEVER ABOUT THE JOKER. IT'S ALWAYS BEEN ABOUT YOU, CLARK.
I PERFECTED THIS WORLD.
BEFORE, THERE WERE SO MANY LIVES LOST. BECAUSE I HELD BACK.
WHEN I SHOULD HAVE BEEN USING ALL MY POWER.
GUYS, WE'RE RUNNING OUT OF SOLID GROUND HERE.
USING IT FOR THIS? TO CONTROL AND OPPRESS?
GREAT. ANTAGONIZE THE GUY WHO WANTS TO MELT US.
C'MON, VIC...

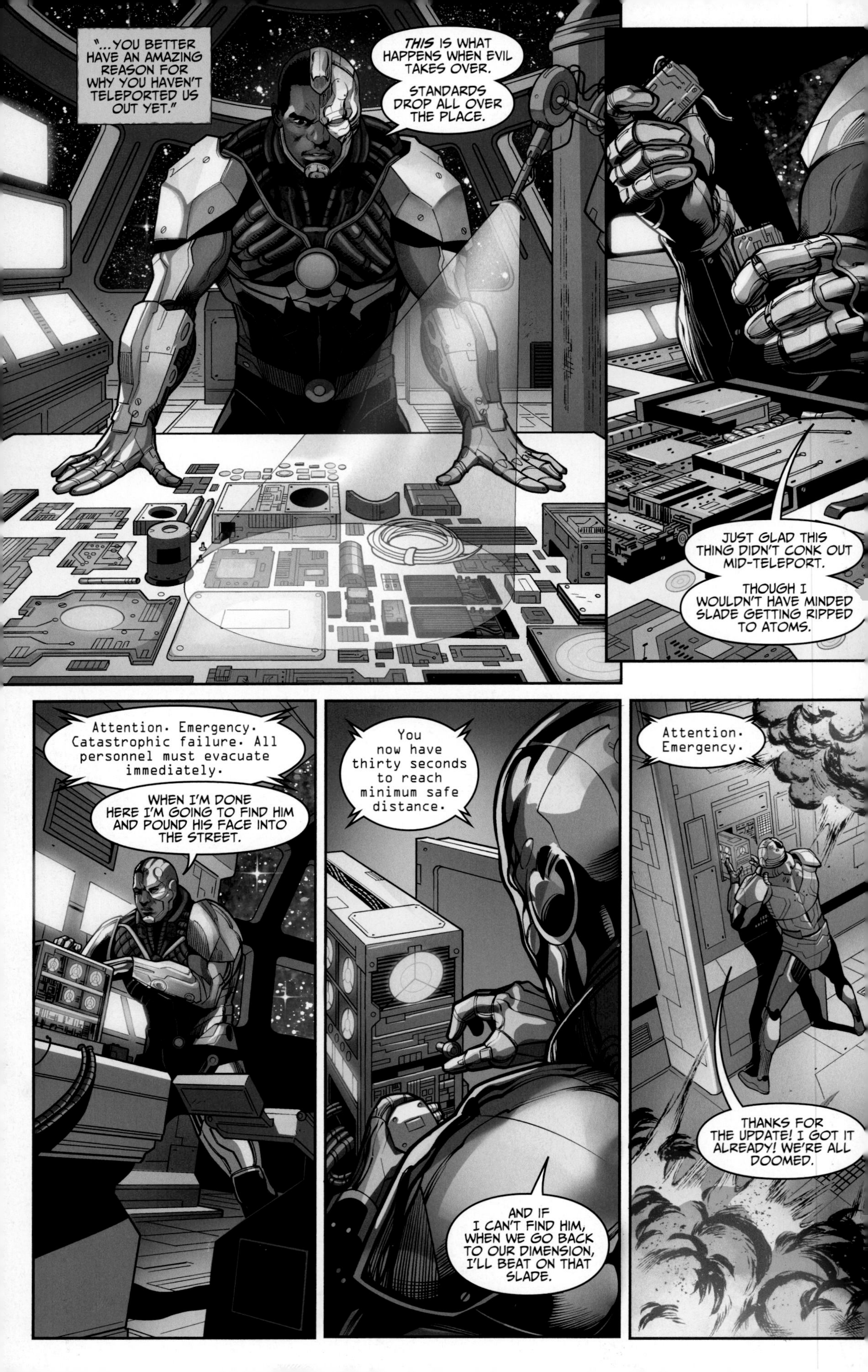
"...YOU BETTER HAVE AN AMAZING REASON FOR WHY YOU HAVEN'T TELEPORTED US OUT YET."
THIS IS WHAT HAPPENS WHEN EVIL TAKES OVER.
STANDARDS DROP ALL OVER THE PLACE.
JUST GLAD THIS THING DIDN'T CONK OUT MID-TELEPORT.
THOUGH I WOULDN'T HAVE MINDED SLADE GETTING RIPPED TO ATOMS.
Attention. Emergency. Catastrophic failure. All personnel must evacuate immediately.
WHEN I'M DONE HERE I'M GOING TO FIND HIM AND POUND HIS FACE INTO THE STREET.
You now have thirty seconds to reach minimum safe distance.
AND IF I CAN'T FIND HIM, WHEN WE GO BACK TO OUR DIMENSION, I'LL BEAT ON THAT SLADE.
Attention. Emergency.
THANKS FOR THE UPDATE! I GOT IT ALREADY! WE'RE ALL DOOMED.

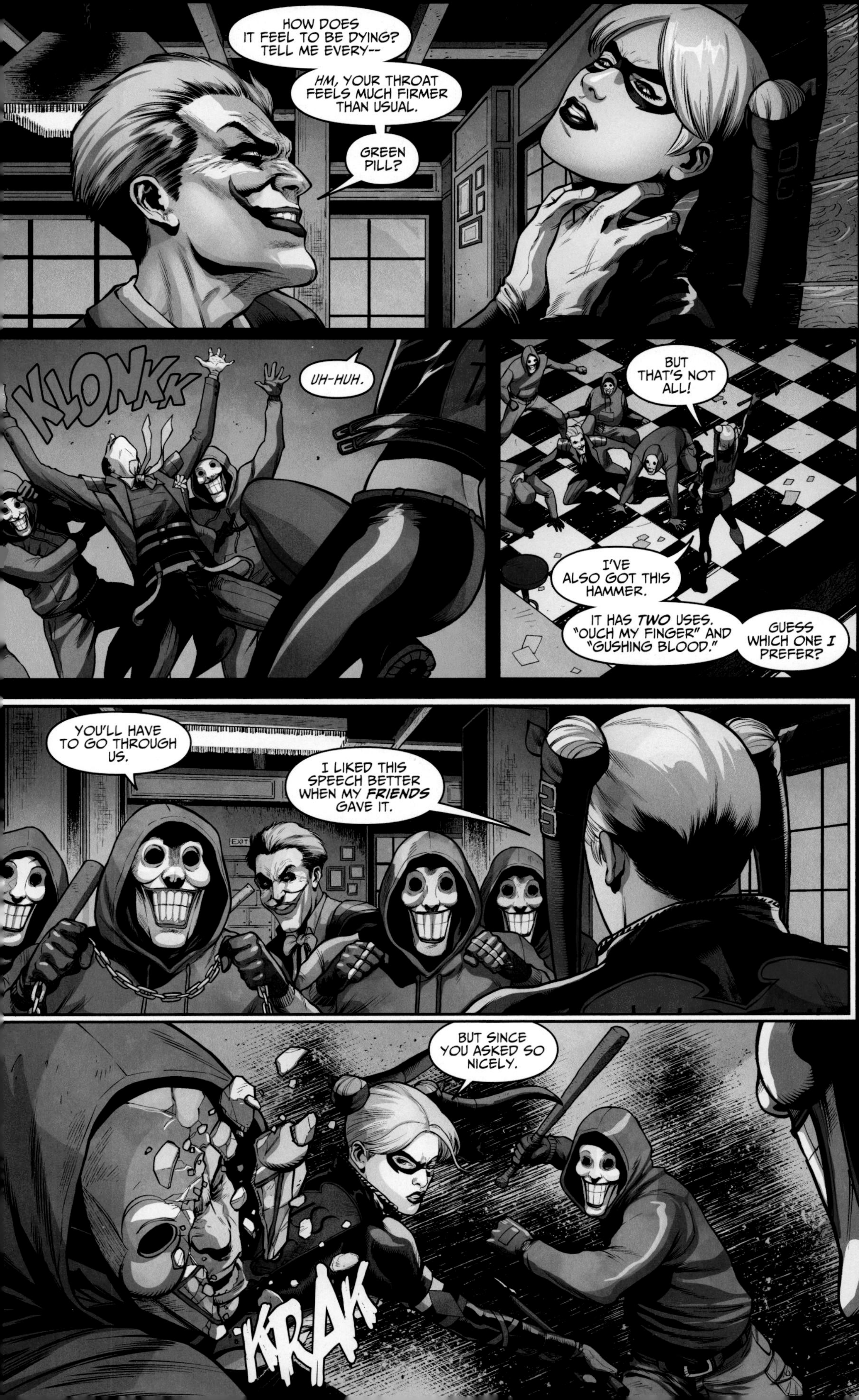
HOW DOES IT FEEL TO BE DYING? TELL ME EVERY--
HM, YOUR THROAT FEELS MUCH FIRMER THAN USUAL.
GREEN PILL?
KLONKK
UH-HUH.
BUT THAT'S NOT ALL!
I'VE ALSO GOT THIS HAMMER.
IT HAS TWO USES. "OUCH MY FINGER" AND "GUSHING BLOOD."
GUESS WHICH ONE I PREFER?
YOU'LL HAVE TO GO THROUGH US.
I LIKED THIS SPEECH BETTER WHEN MY FRIENDS GAVE IT.
EXIT
BUT SINCE YOU ASKED SO NICELY.
KRAK

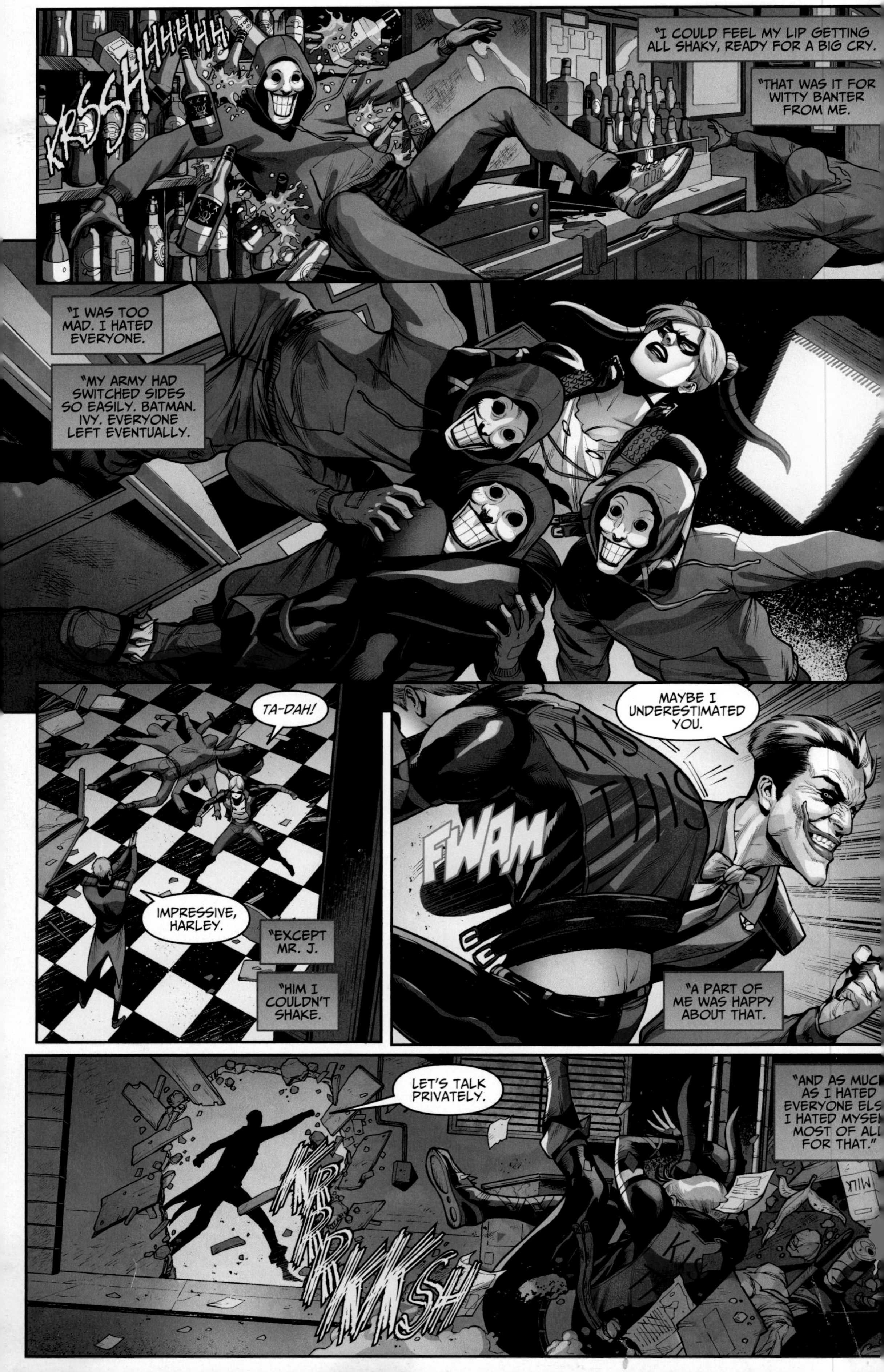
KRSSHHHHH
"I COULD FEEL MY LIP GETTING ALL SHAKY, READY FOR A BIG CRY.
"THAT WAS IT FOR WITTY BANTER FROM ME.
"I WAS TOO MAD. I HATED EVERYONE.
"MY ARMY HAD SWITCHED SIDES SO EASILY. BATMAN. IVY. EVERYONE LEFT EVENTUALLY.
TA-DAH!
IMPRESSIVE, HARLEY.
"EXCEPT MR. J.
"HIM I COULDN'T SHAKE.
MAYBE I UNDERESTIMATED YOU.
FWAM
"A PART OF ME WAS HAPPY ABOUT THAT.
LET'S TALK PRIVATELY.
KRRRKKSH
"AND AS MUC AS I HATED EVERYONE ELS I HATED MYSE MOST OF AL FOR THAT."

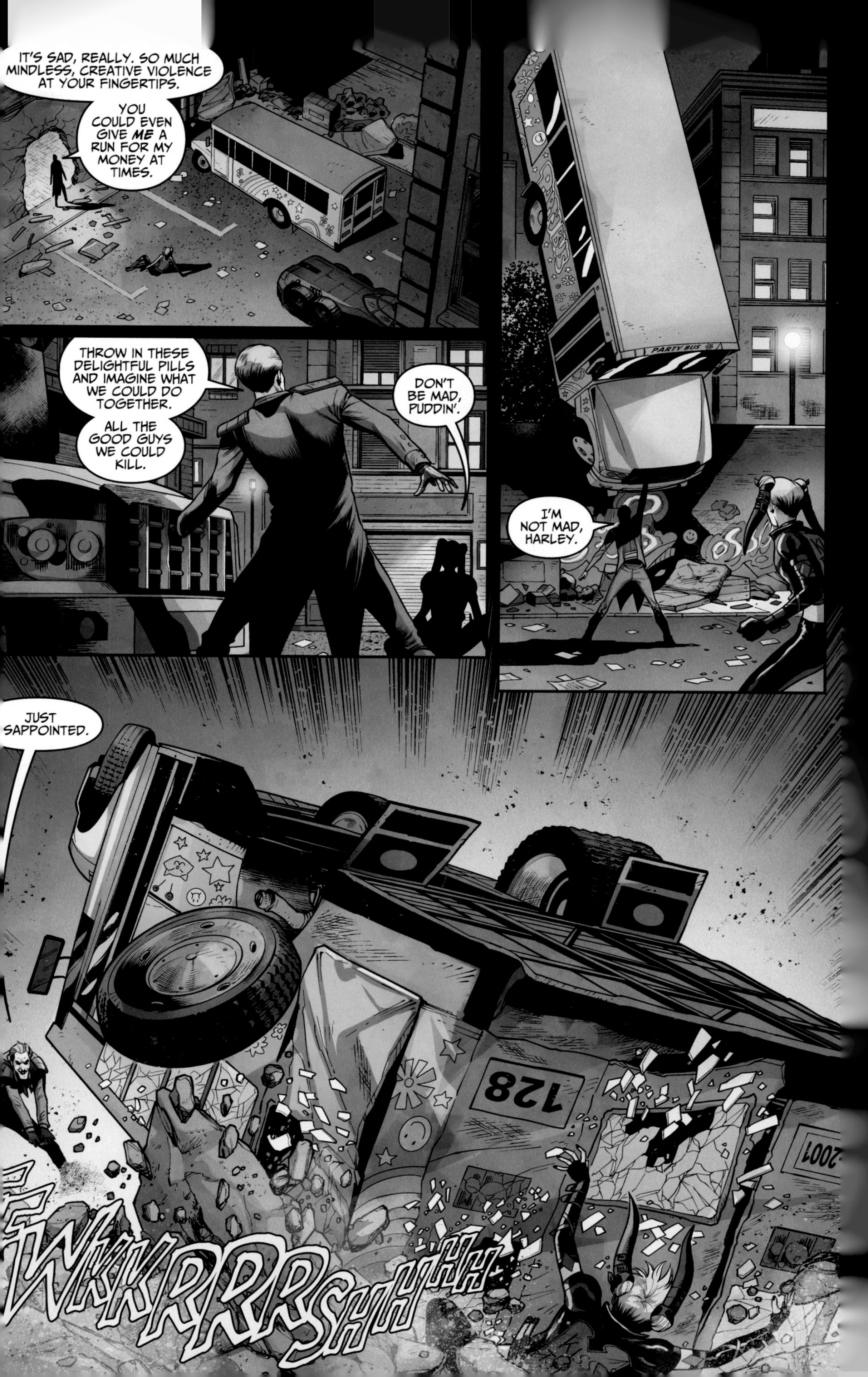
IT'S SAD, REALLY. SO MUCH MINDLESS, CREATIVE VIOLENCE AT YOUR FINGERTIPS.
YOU COULD EVEN GIVE ME A RUN FOR MY MONEY AT TIMES.
THROW IN THESE DELIGHTFUL PILLS AND IMAGINE WHAT WE COULD DO TOGETHER.
ALL THE GOOD GUYS WE COULD KILL.
DON'T BE MAD, PUDDIN'.
PARTY BUS
I'M NOT MAD, HARLEY.
JUST SAPPOINTED.
128
2001
WKKRRRSHHHH

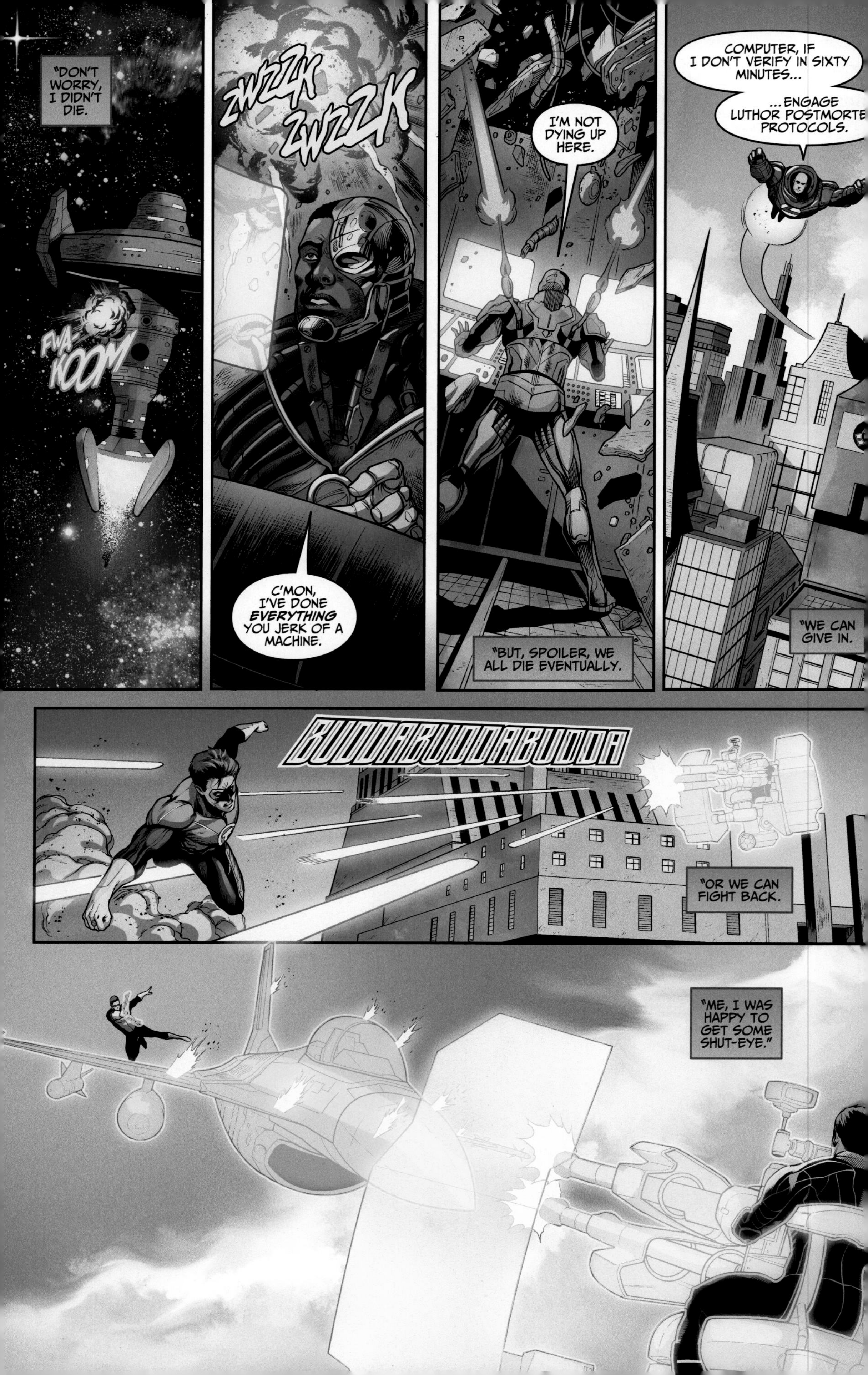
"DON'T WORRY, I DIDN'T DIE.
FWA-KOOM
ZWZZK ZWZZK
C'MON, I'VE DONE EVERYTHING YOU JERK OF A MACHINE.
I'M NOT DYING UP HERE.
"BUT, SPOILER, WE ALL DIE EVENTUALLY.
COMPUTER, IF I DON'T VERIFY IN SIXTY MINUTES...
...ENGAGE LUTHOR POSTMORTE PROTOCOLS.
"WE CAN GIVE IN.
BUDDABUDDABUDDA
"OR WE CAN FIGHT BACK.
"ME, I WAS HAPPY TO GET SOME SHUT-EYE."

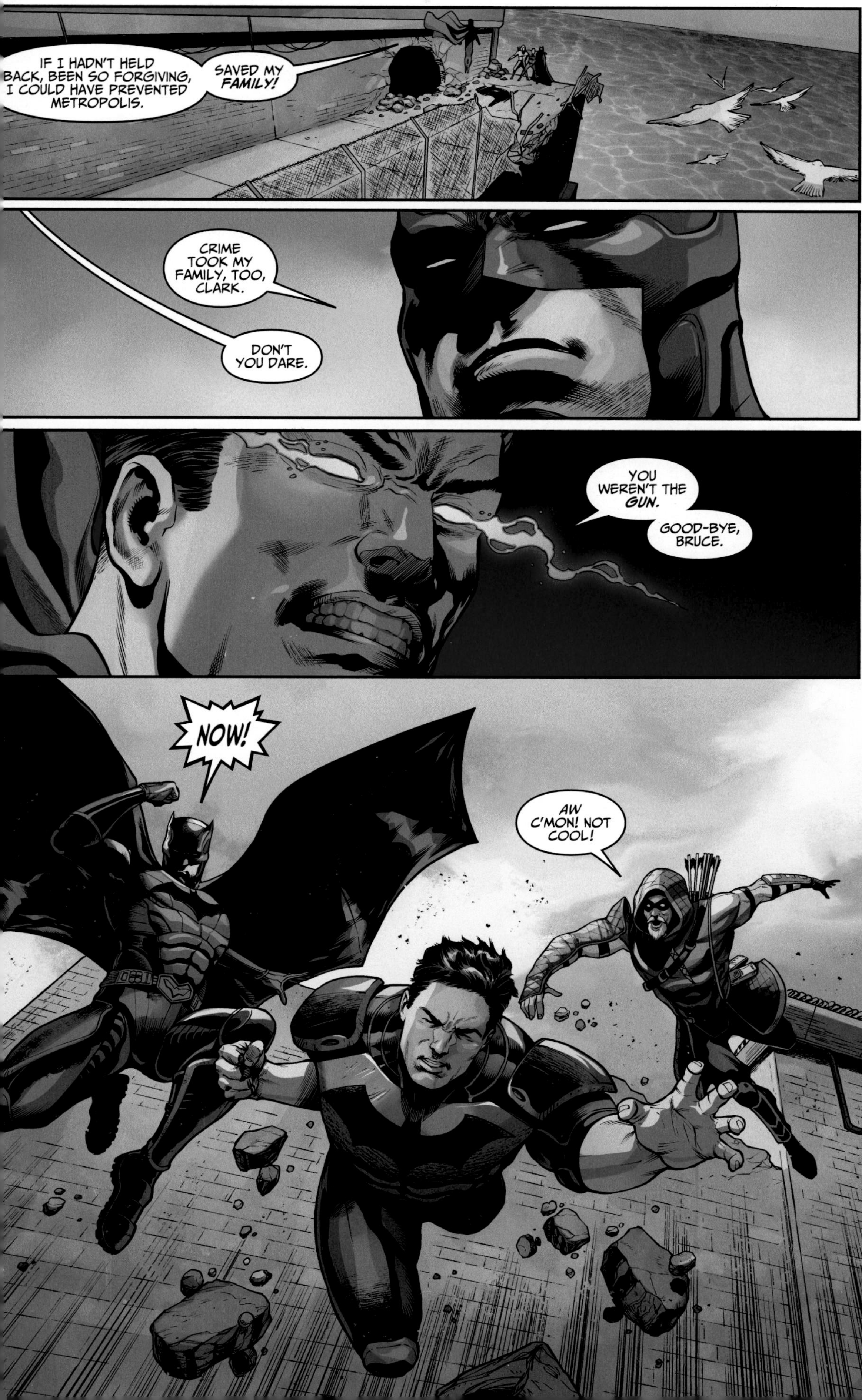
IF I HADN'T HELD BACK, BEEN SO FORGIVING, I COULD HAVE PREVENTED METROPOLIS.
SAVED MY FAMILY!
CRIME TOOK MY FAMILY, TOO, CLARK.
DON'T YOU DARE.
YOU WEREN'T THE GUN.
GOOD-BYE, BRUCE.
NOW!
AW C'MON! NOT COOL!

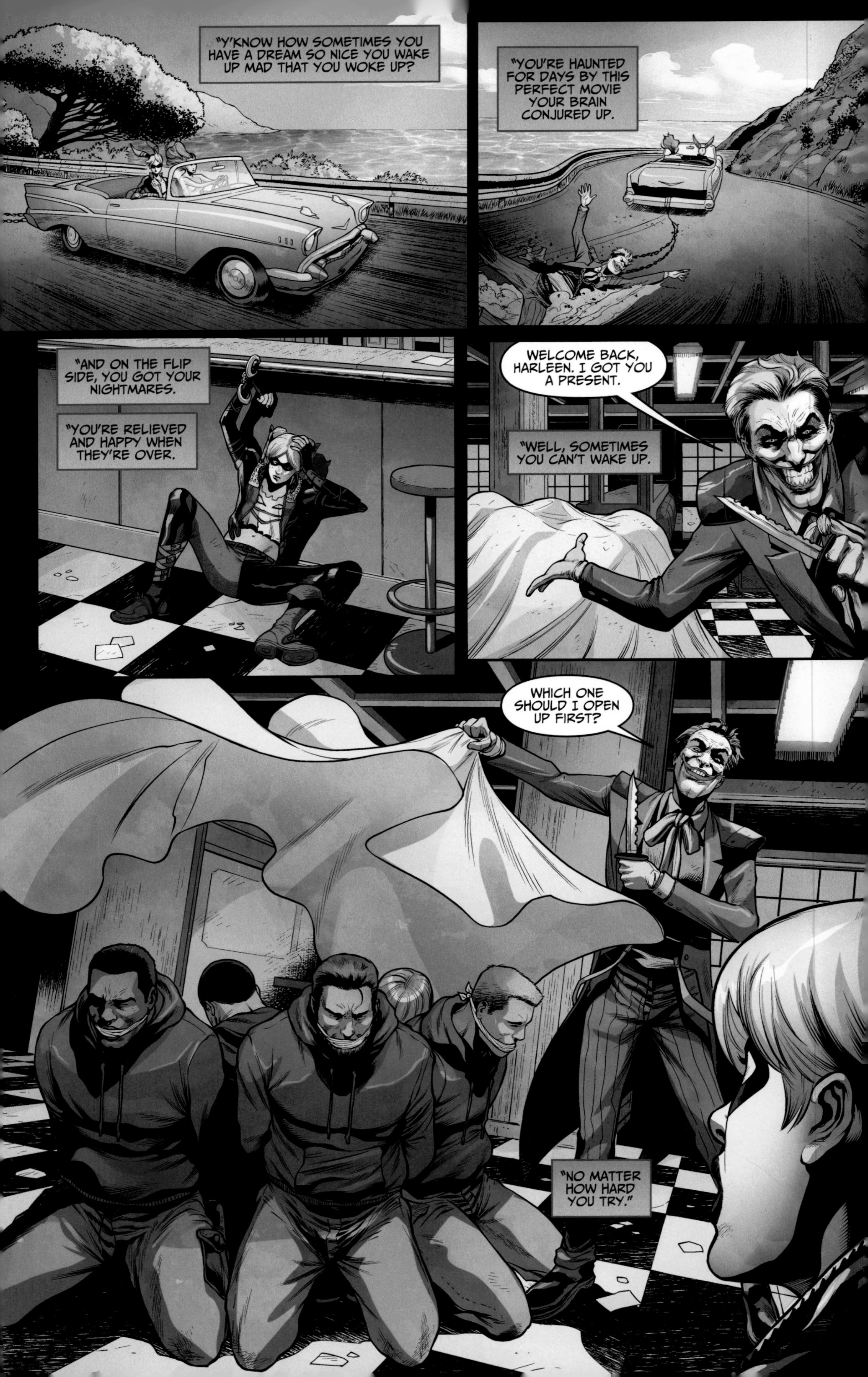
"Y'KNOW HOW SOMETIMES YOU HAVE A DREAM SO NICE YOU WAKE UP MAD THAT YOU WOKE UP?
"YOU'RE HAUNTED FOR DAYS BY THIS PERFECT MOVIE YOUR BRAIN CONJURED UP.
"AND ON THE FLIP SIDE, YOU GOT YOUR NIGHTMARES.
"YOU'RE RELIEVED AND HAPPY WHEN THEY'RE OVER.
WELCOME BACK, HARLEEN. I GOT YOU A PRESENT.
"WELL, SOMETIMES YOU CAN'T WAKE UP.
WHICH ONE SHOULD I OPEN UP FIRST?
"NO MATTER HOW HARD YOU TRY."

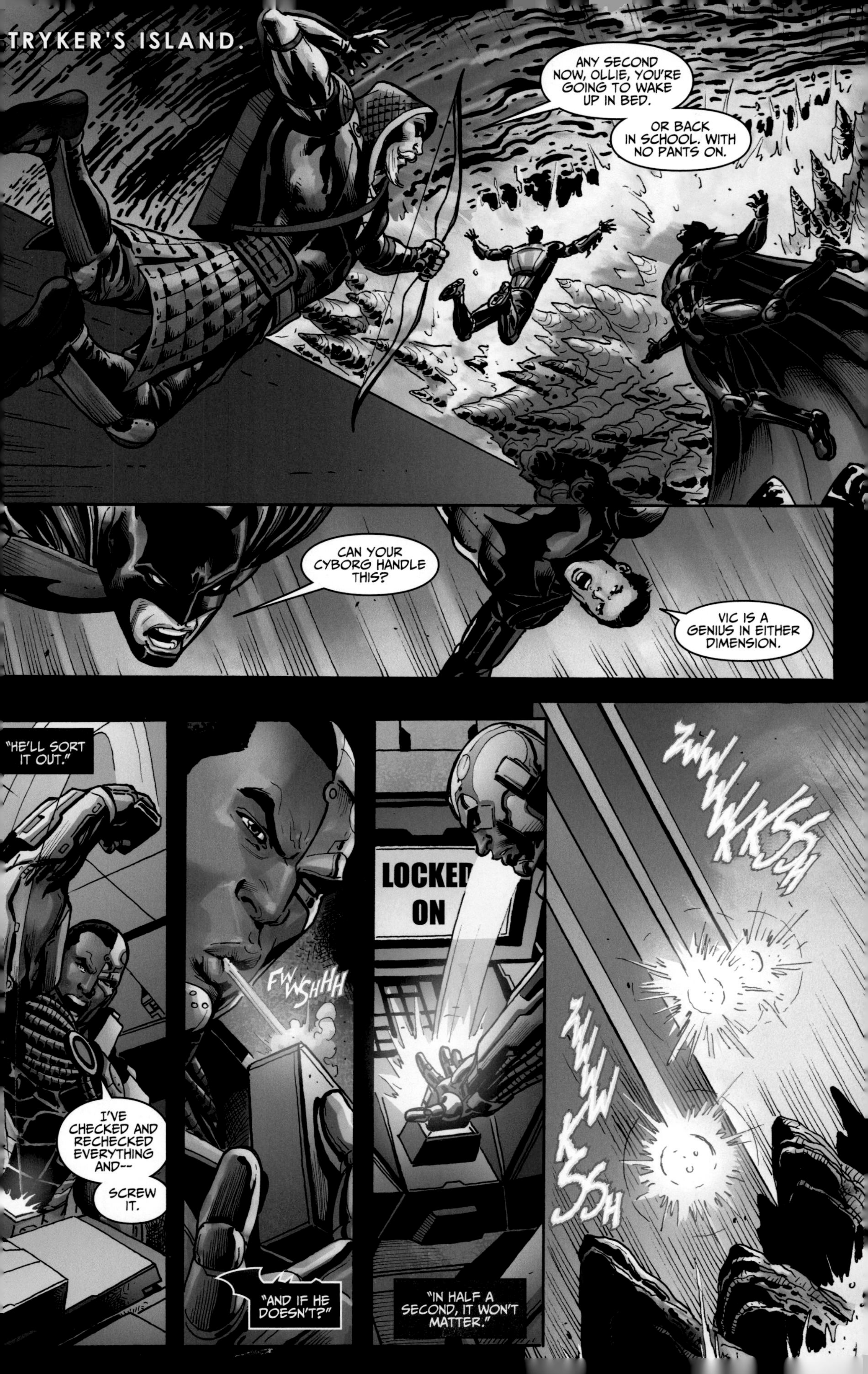
TRYKER'S ISLAND.
ANY SECOND NOW, OLLIE, YOU'RE GOING TO WAKE UP IN BED.
OR BACK IN SCHOOL. WITH NO PANTS ON.
CAN YOUR CYBORG HANDLE THIS?
VIC IS A GENIUS IN EITHER DIMENSION.
"HE'LL SORT IT OUT."
I'VE CHECKED AND RECHECKED EVERYTHING AND--
SCREW IT.
FWSHHH
"AND IF HE DOESN'T?"
LOCKED ON
"IN HALF A SECOND, IT WON'T MATTER."
ZWWWKKSSH
ZWWWKSSH

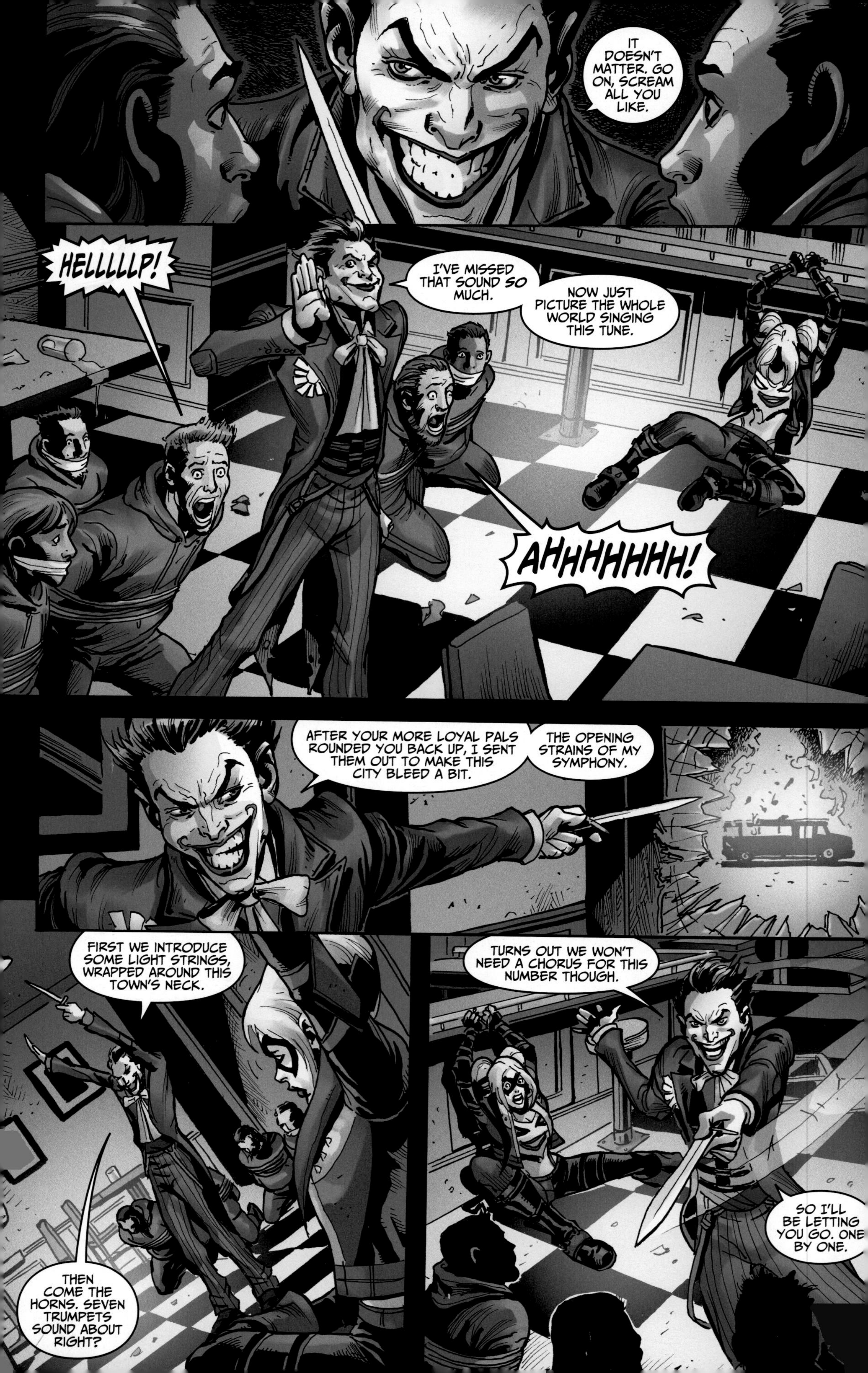

IT DOESN'T MATTER. GO ON, SCREAM ALL YOU LIKE.
HELLLLLP!
I'VE MISSED THAT SOUND SO MUCH.
NOW JUST PICTURE THE WHOLE WORLD SINGING THIS TUNE.
AHHHHHHH!
AFTER YOUR MORE LOYAL PALS ROUNDED YOU BACK UP, I SENT THEM OUT TO MAKE THIS CITY BLEED A BIT.
THE OPENING STRAINS OF MY SYMPHONY.
FIRST WE INTRODUCE SOME LIGHT STRINGS, WRAPPED AROUND THIS TOWN'S NECK.
THEN COME THE HORNS. SEVEN TRUMPETS SOUND ABOUT RIGHT?
TURNS OUT WE WON'T NEED A CHORUS FOR THIS NUMBER THOUGH.
SO I'LL BE LETTING YOU GO. ONE BY ONE.

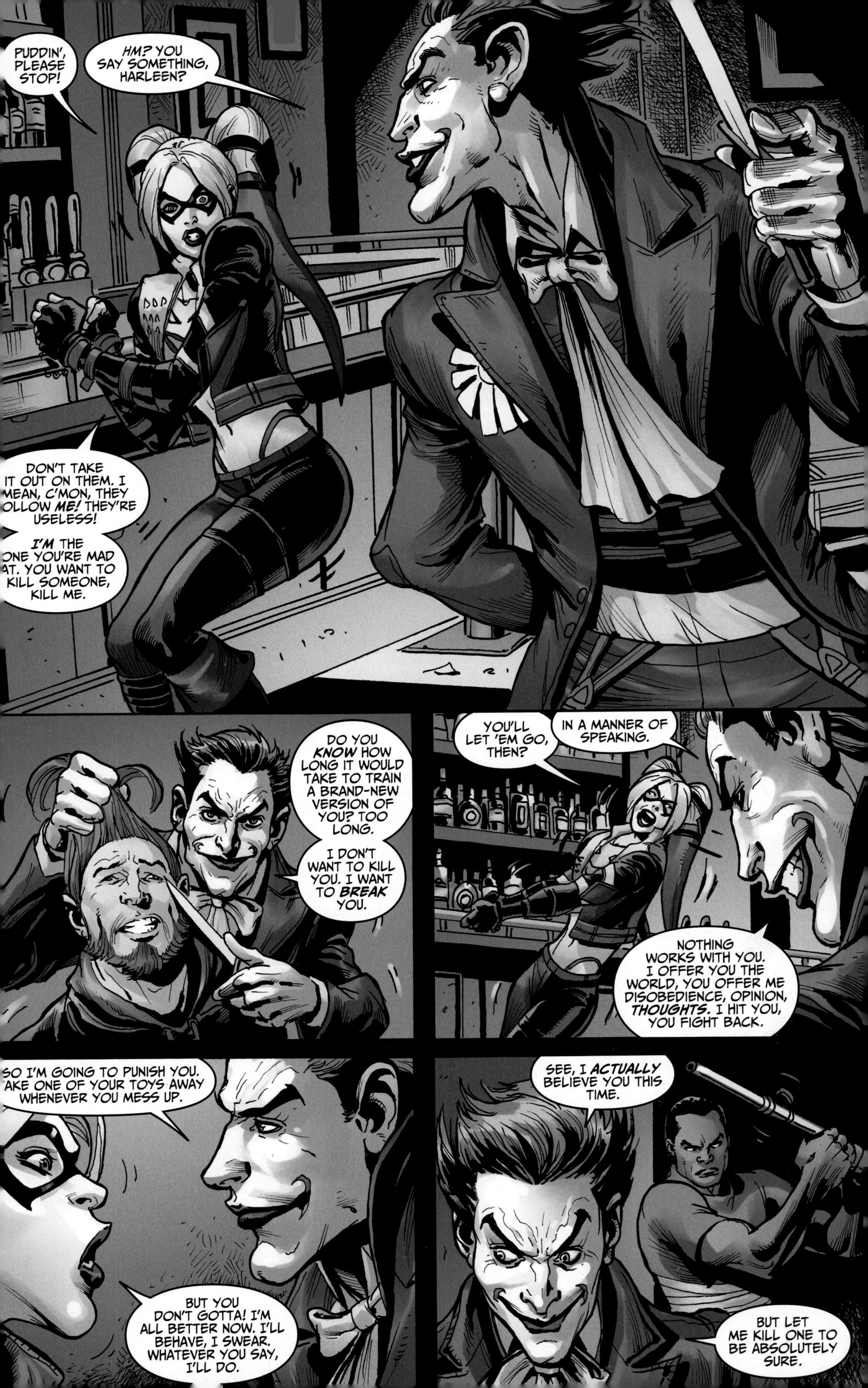
PUDDIN', PLEASE STOP!
HM? YOU SAY SOMETHING, HARLEEN?
DON'T TAKE IT OUT ON THEM. I MEAN, C'MON, THEY FOLLOW ME! THEY'RE USELESS!
I'M THE ONE YOU'RE MAD AT. YOU WANT TO KILL SOMEONE, KILL ME.
DO YOU KNOW HOW LONG IT WOULD TAKE TO TRAIN A BRAND-NEW VERSION OF YOU? TOO LONG.
I DON'T WANT TO KILL YOU. I WANT TO BREAK YOU.
YOU'LL LET 'EM GO, THEN?
IN A MANNER OF SPEAKING.
NOTHING WORKS WITH YOU. I OFFER YOU THE WORLD, YOU OFFER ME DISOBEDIENCE, OPINION, THOUGHTS. I HIT YOU, YOU FIGHT BACK.
SO I'M GOING TO PUNISH YOU. TAKE ONE OF YOUR TOYS AWAY WHENEVER YOU MESS UP.
BUT YOU DON'T GOTTA! I'M ALL BETTER NOW. I'LL BEHAVE, I SWEAR. WHATEVER YOU SAY, I'LL DO.
SEE, I ACTUALLY BELIEVE YOU THIS TIME.
BUT LET ME KILL ONE TO BE ABSOLUTELY SURE.

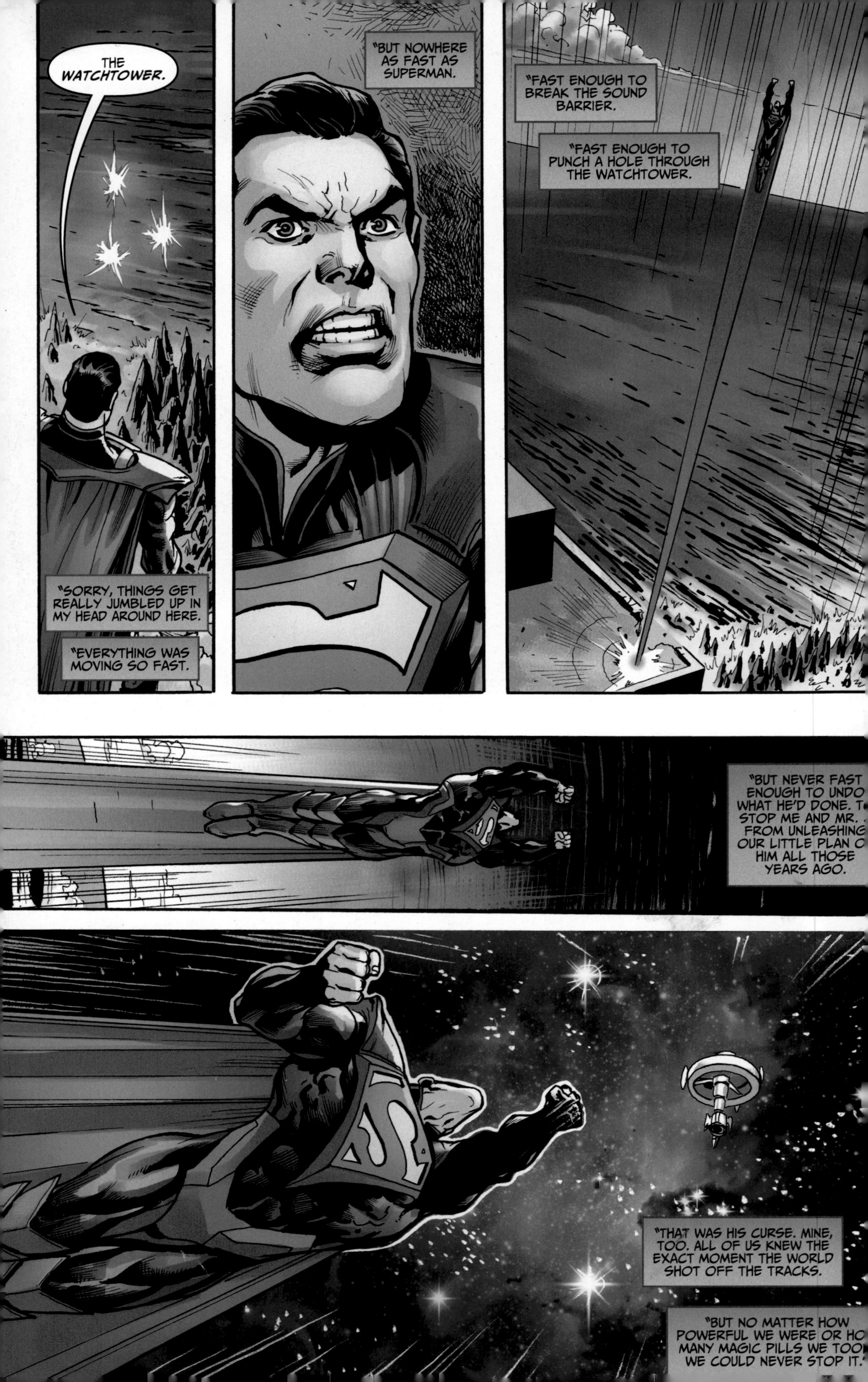
THE WATCHTOWER.
"SORRY, THINGS GET REALLY JUMBLED UP IN MY HEAD AROUND HERE.
"EVERYTHING WAS MOVING SO FAST.
"BUT NOWHERE AS FAST AS SUPERMAN.
"FAST ENOUGH TO BREAK THE SOUND BARRIER.
"FAST ENOUGH TO PUNCH A HOLE THROUGH THE WATCHTOWER.
"BUT NEVER FAST ENOUGH TO UNDO WHAT HE'D DONE. TO STOP ME AND MR. J FROM UNLEASHING OUR LITTLE PLAN ON HIM ALL THOSE YEARS AGO.
"THAT WAS HIS CURSE. MINE, TOO. ALL OF US KNEW THE EXACT MOMENT THE WORLD SHOT OFF THE TRACKS.
"BUT NO MATTER HOW POWERFUL WE WERE OR HOW MANY MAGIC PILLS WE TOOK, WE COULD NEVER STOP IT.

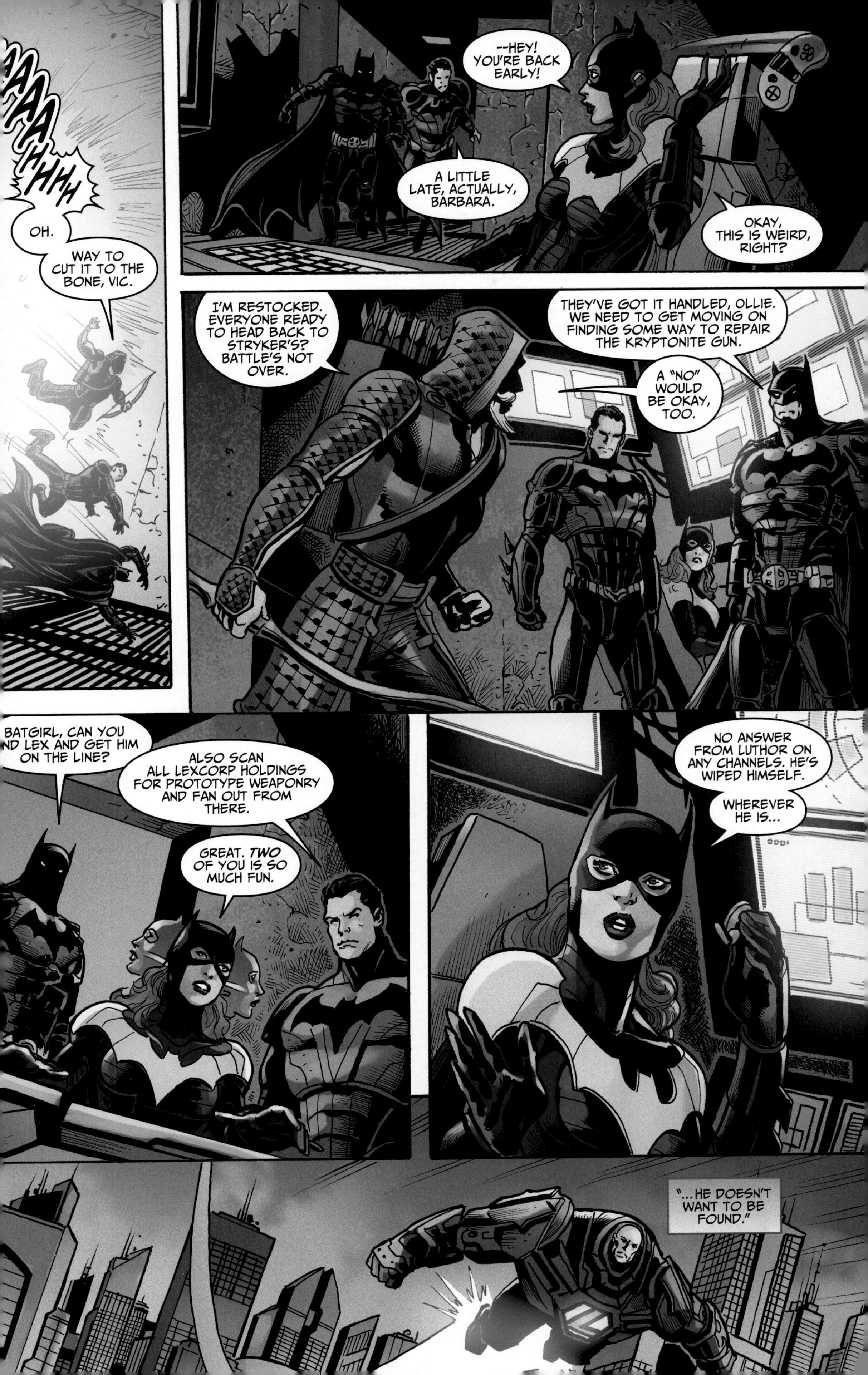
AAAAAAHHHH
OH.
WAY TO CUT IT TO THE BONE, VIC.
--HEY! YOU'RE BACK EARLY!
A LITTLE LATE, ACTUALLY, BARBARA.
OKAY, THIS IS WEIRD, RIGHT?
I'M RESTOCKED. EVERYONE READY TO HEAD BACK TO STRYKER'S? BATTLE'S NOT OVER.
THEY'VE GOT IT HANDLED, OLLIE. WE NEED TO GET MOVING ON FINDING SOME WAY TO REPAIR THE KRYPTONITE GUN.
A "NO" WOULD BE OKAY, TOO.
BATGIRL, CAN YOU ND LEX AND GET HIM ON THE LINE?
ALSO SCAN ALL LEXCORP HOLDINGS FOR PROTOTYPE WEAPONRY AND FAN OUT FROM THERE.
GREAT. *TWO* OF YOU IS SO MUCH FUN.
NO ANSWER FROM LUTHOR ON ANY CHANNELS. HE'S WIPED HIMSELF.
WHEREVER HE IS...
"...HE DOESN'T WANT TO BE FOUND."

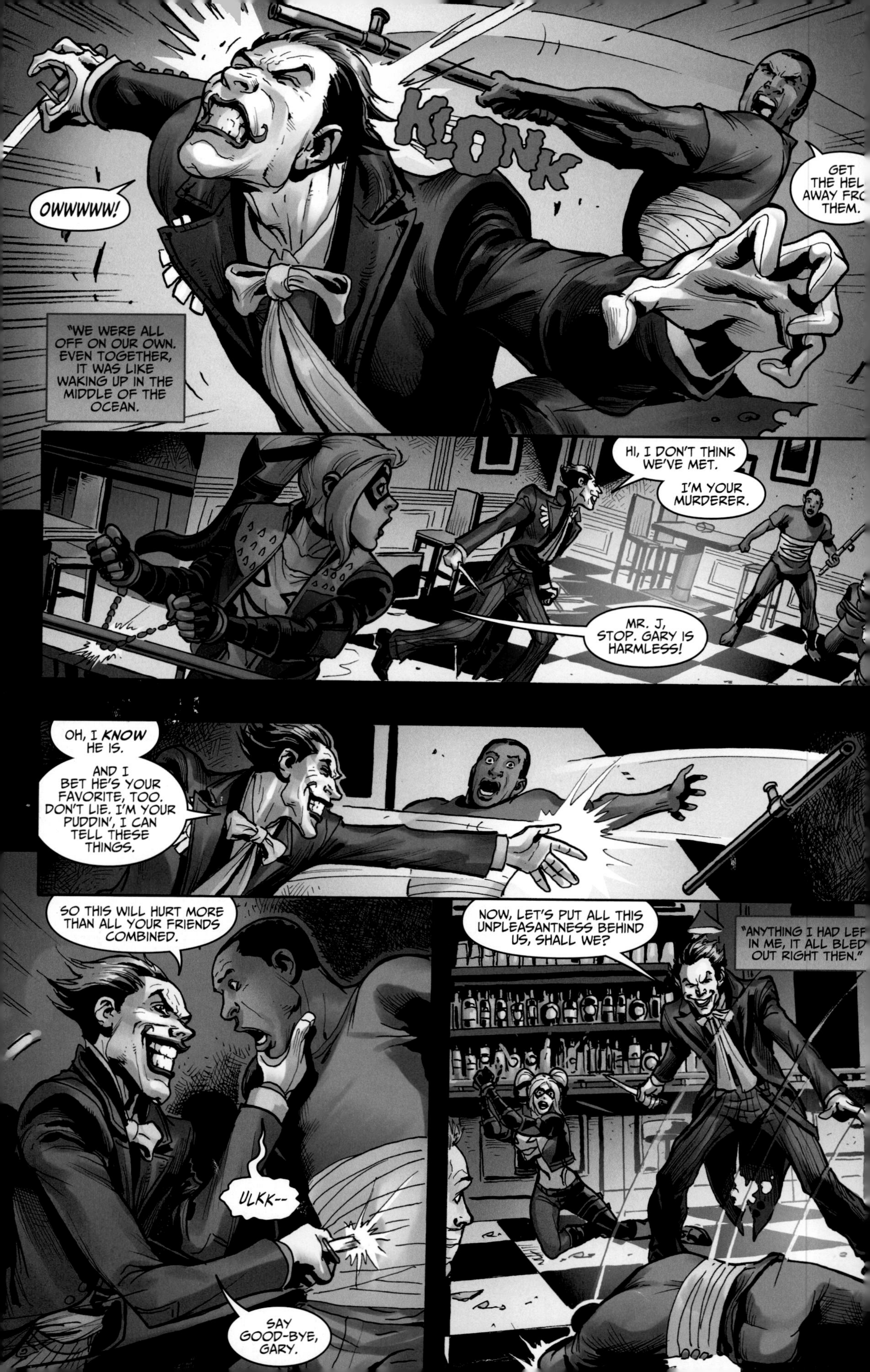
KLONK
GET THE HEL AWAY FRO THEM.
OWWWWW!
"WE WERE ALL OFF ON OUR OWN. EVEN TOGETHER, IT WAS LIKE WAKING UP IN THE MIDDLE OF THE OCEAN.
HI, I DON'T THINK WE'VE MET.
I'M YOUR MURDERER.
MR. J, STOP. GARY IS HARMLESS!
OH, I *KNOW* HE IS.
AND I BET HE'S YOUR FAVORITE, TOO. DON'T LIE. I'M YOUR PUDDIN', I CAN TELL THESE THINGS.
SO THIS WILL HURT MORE THAN ALL YOUR FRIENDS COMBINED.
ULKK--
SAY GOOD-BYE, GARY.
NOW, LET'S PUT ALL THIS UNPLEASANTNESS BEHIND US, SHALL WE?
"ANYTHING I HAD LEF IN ME, IT ALL BLED OUT RIGHT THEN."

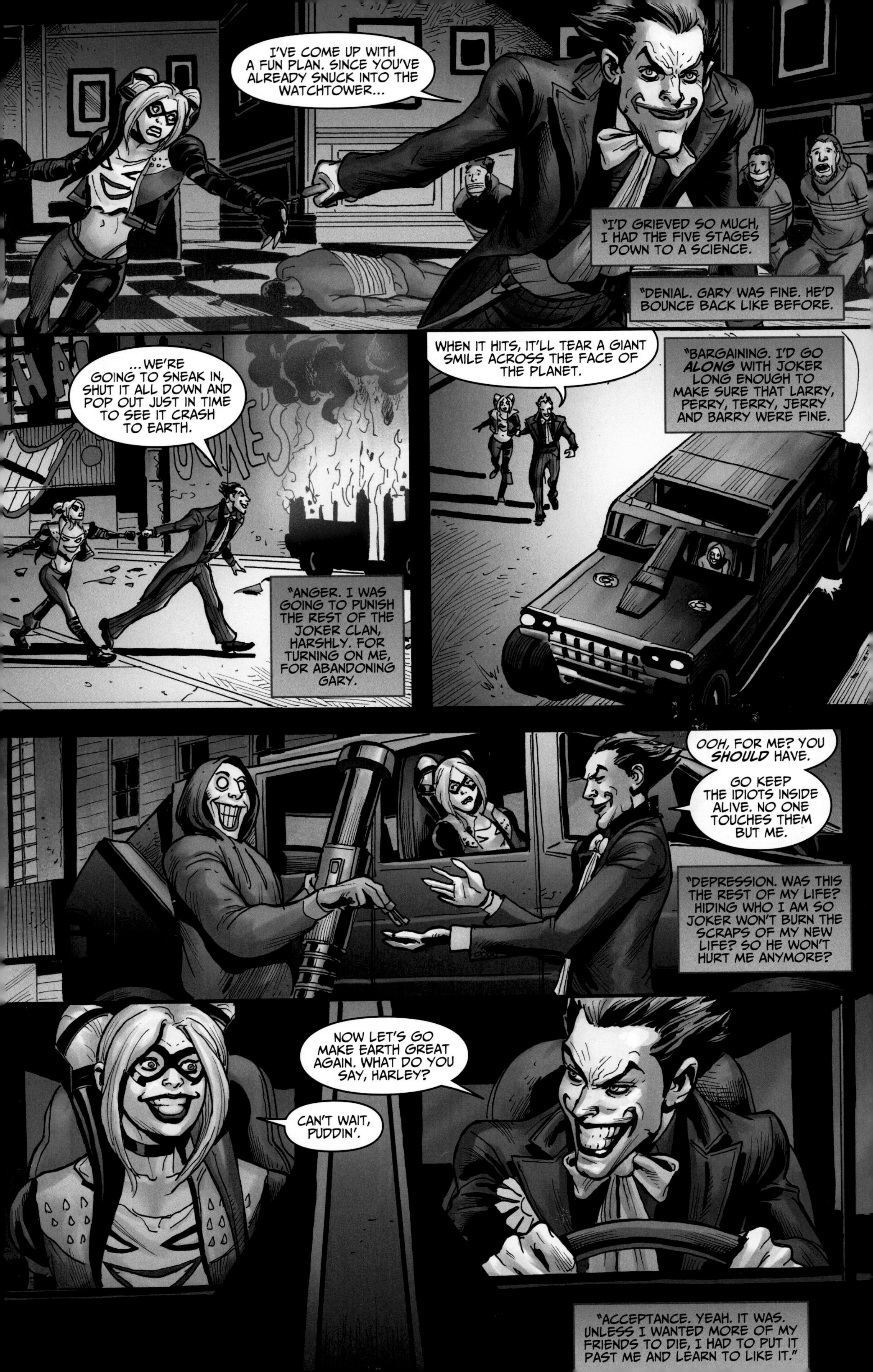
I'VE COME UP WITH A FUN PLAN. SINCE YOU'VE ALREADY SNUCK INTO THE WATCHTOWER...
"I'D GRIEVED SO MUCH, I HAD THE FIVE STAGES DOWN TO A SCIENCE.
"DENIAL. GARY WAS FINE. HE'D BOUNCE BACK LIKE BEFORE.
...WE'RE GOING TO SNEAK IN, SHUT IT ALL DOWN AND POP OUT JUST IN TIME TO SEE IT CRASH TO EARTH.
"ANGER. I WAS GOING TO PUNISH THE REST OF THE JOKER CLAN, HARSHLY. FOR TURNING ON ME, FOR ABANDONING GARY.
WHEN IT HITS, IT'LL TEAR A GIANT SMILE ACROSS THE FACE OF THE PLANET.
"BARGAINING. I'D GO *ALONG* WITH JOKER LONG ENOUGH TO MAKE SURE THAT LARRY, PERRY, TERRY, JERRY AND BARRY WERE FINE.
OOH, FOR ME? YOU *SHOULD* HAVE.
GO KEEP THE IDIOTS INSIDE ALIVE. NO ONE TOUCHES THEM BUT ME.
"DEPRESSION. WAS THIS THE REST OF MY LIFE? HIDING WHO I AM SO JOKER WON'T BURN THE SCRAPS OF MY NEW LIFE? SO HE WON'T HURT ME ANYMORE?
NOW LET'S GO MAKE EARTH GREAT AGAIN. WHAT DO YOU SAY, HARLEY?
CAN'T WAIT, PUDDIN'.
"ACCEPTANCE. YEAH. IT WAS. UNLESS I WANTED MORE OF MY FRIENDS TO DIE, I HAD TO PUT IT PAST ME AND LEARN TO LIKE IT."

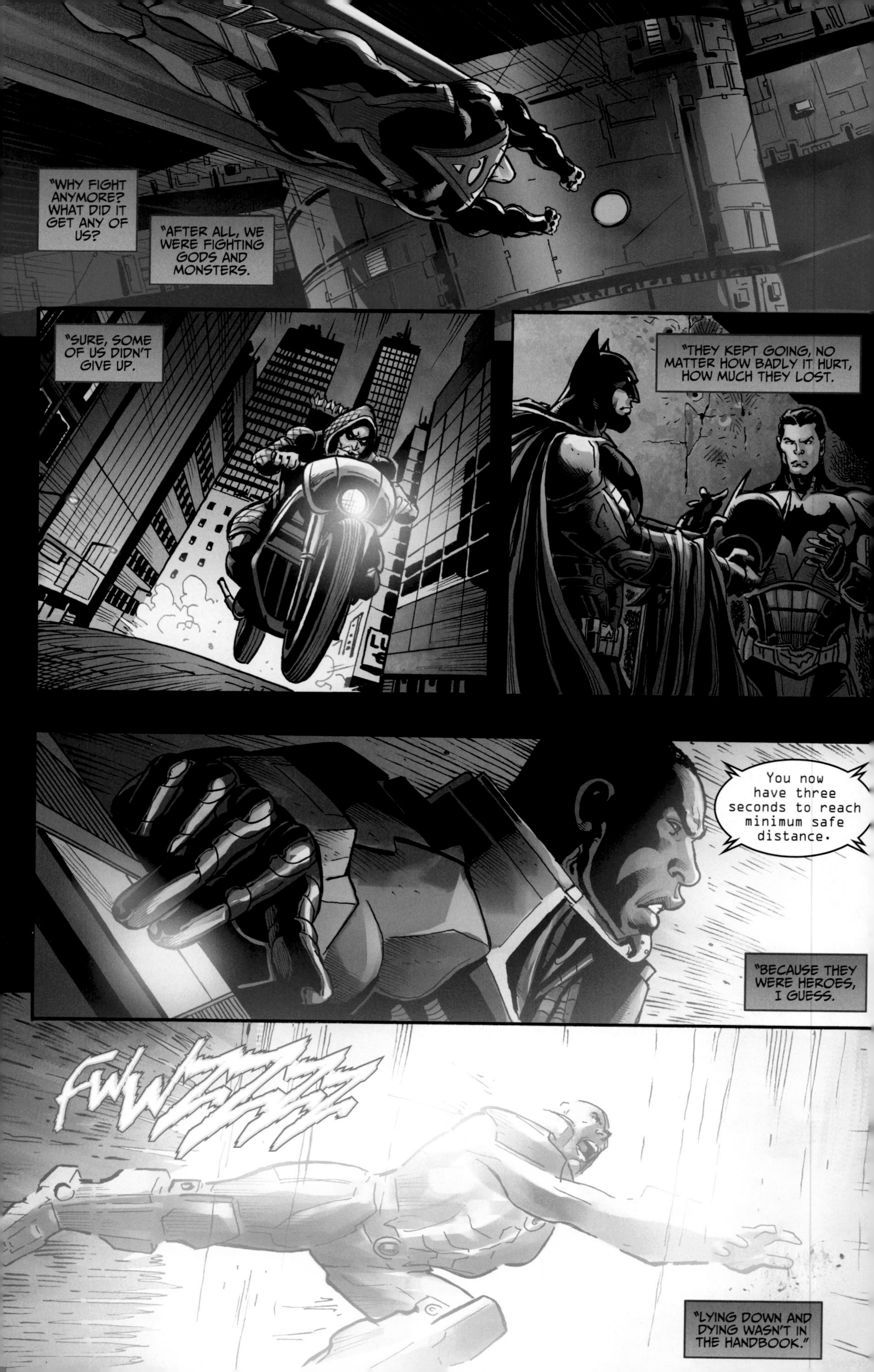
"WHY FIGHT ANYMORE? WHAT DID IT GET ANY OF US?
"AFTER ALL, WE WERE FIGHTING GODS AND MONSTERS.
"SURE, SOME OF US DIDN'T GIVE UP.
"THEY KEPT GOING, NO MATTER HOW BADLY IT HURT, HOW MUCH THEY LOST.
You now have three seconds to reach minimum safe distance.
"BECAUSE THEY WERE HEROES, I GUESS.
FWUSSSH
"LYING DOWN AND DYING WASN'T IN THE HANDBOOK."

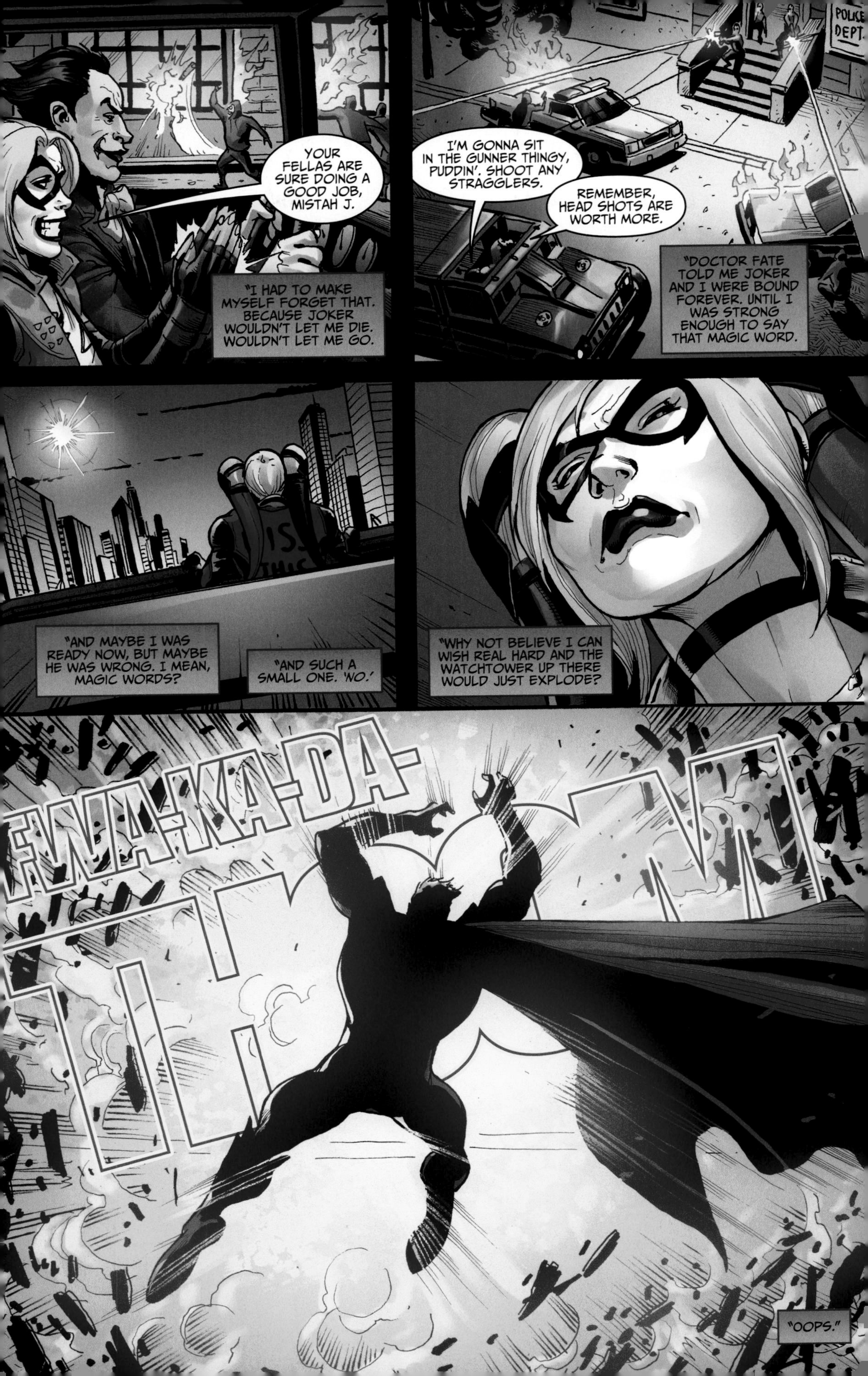
YOUR FELLAS ARE SURE DOING A GOOD JOB, MISTAH J.
"I HAD TO MAKE MYSELF FORGET THAT. BECAUSE JOKER WOULDN'T LET ME DIE. WOULDN'T LET ME GO.
POLICE DEPT.
I'M GONNA SIT IN THE GUNNER THINGY, PUDDIN'. SHOOT ANY STRAGGLERS.
REMEMBER, HEAD SHOTS ARE WORTH MORE.
"DOCTOR FATE TOLD ME JOKER AND I WERE BOUND FOREVER. UNTIL I WAS STRONG ENOUGH TO SAY THAT MAGIC WORD.
"AND MAYBE I WAS READY NOW, BUT MAYBE HE WAS WRONG. I MEAN, MAGIC WORDS?
"AND SUCH A SMALL ONE. 'NO.'
"WHY NOT BELIEVE I CAN WISH REAL HARD AND THE WATCHTOWER UP THERE WOULD JUST EXPLODE?
FWA-KA-DA-THOOM
"OOPS."

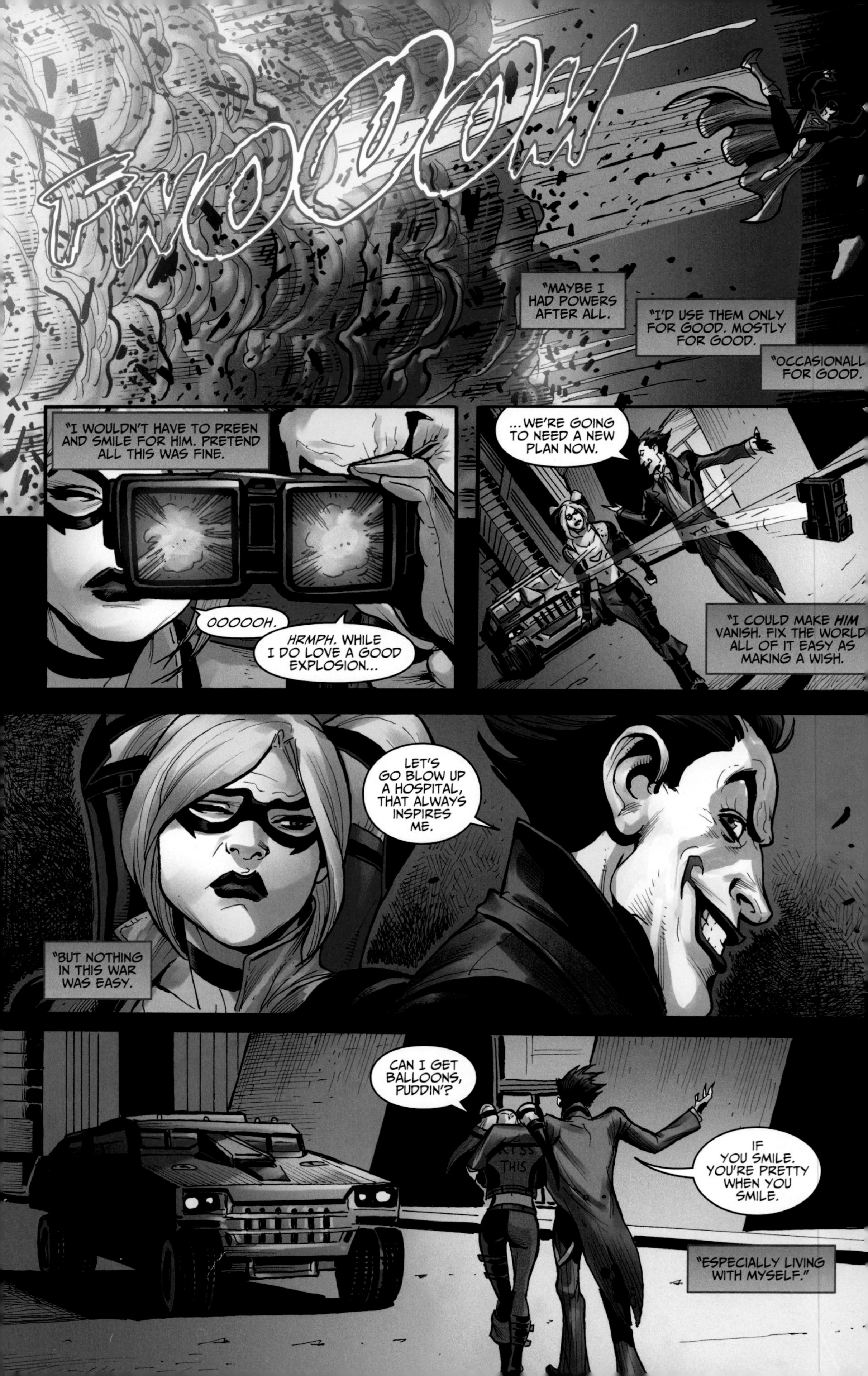

FWOOOOM
"MAYBE I HAD POWERS AFTER ALL.
"I'D USE THEM ONLY FOR GOOD. MOSTLY FOR GOOD.
"OCCASIONALL FOR GOOD.
"I WOULDN'T HAVE TO PREEN AND SMILE FOR HIM. PRETEND ALL THIS WAS FINE.
OOOOOH.
HRMPH. WHILE I DO LOVE A GOOD EXPLOSION...
...WE'RE GOING TO NEED A NEW PLAN NOW.
"I COULD MAKE HIM VANISH. FIX THE WORLD ALL OF IT EASY AS MAKING A WISH.
LET'S GO BLOW UP A HOSPITAL, THAT ALWAYS INSPIRES ME.
"BUT NOTHING IN THIS WAR WAS EASY.
CAN I GET BALLOONS, PUDDIN'?
IF YOU SMILE. YOU'RE PRETTY WHEN YOU SMILE.
"ESPECIALLY LIVING WITH MYSELF."

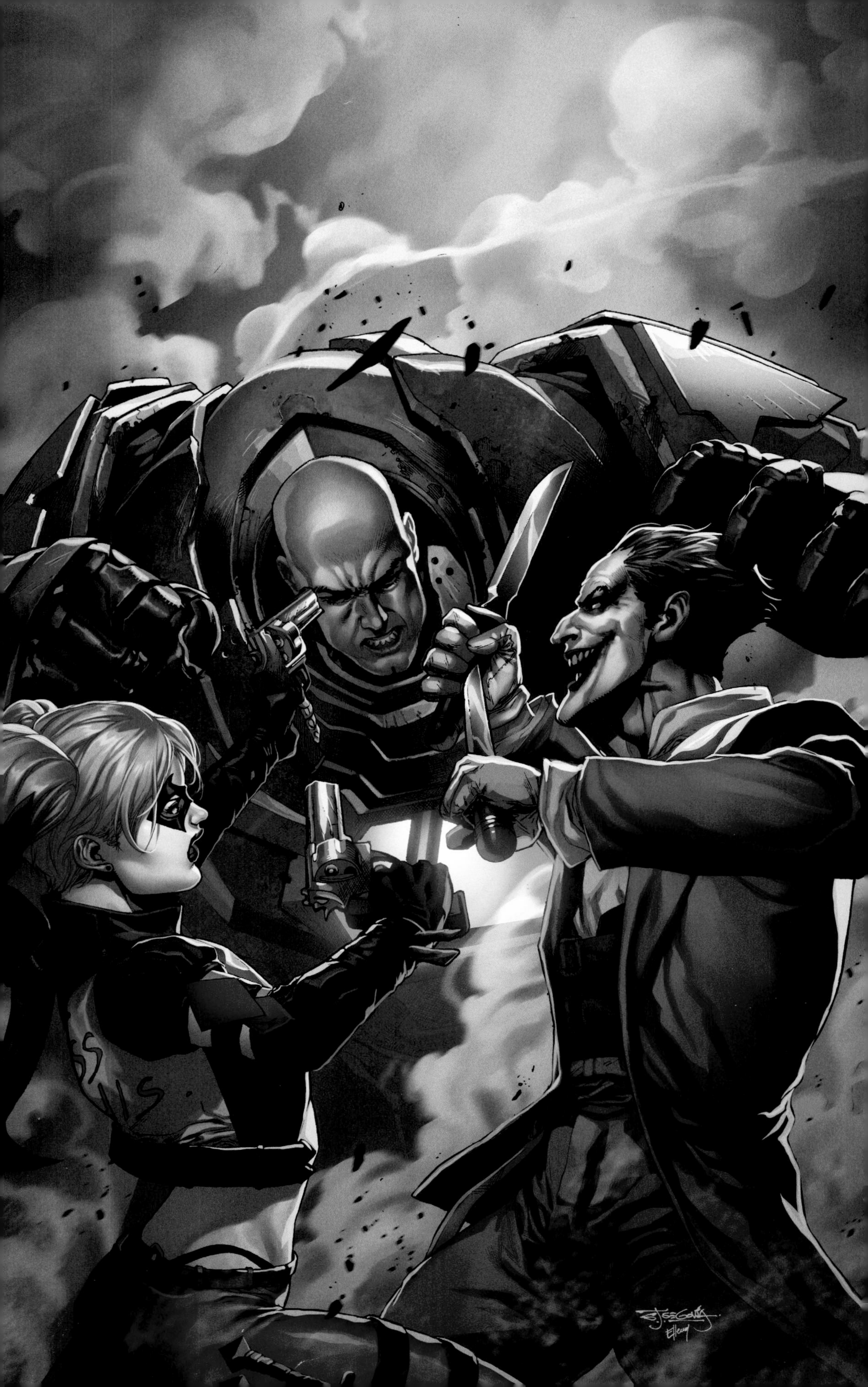

"Such Sweet Sorrow" **Jheremy Raapack Daniel Sampere Miguel Mendonca** Pencillers
Jheremy Raapack Juan Albarran Inkers **J. Nanjan** Colorist
Cover art by **Stephen Segovia** and **Elmer Santos**

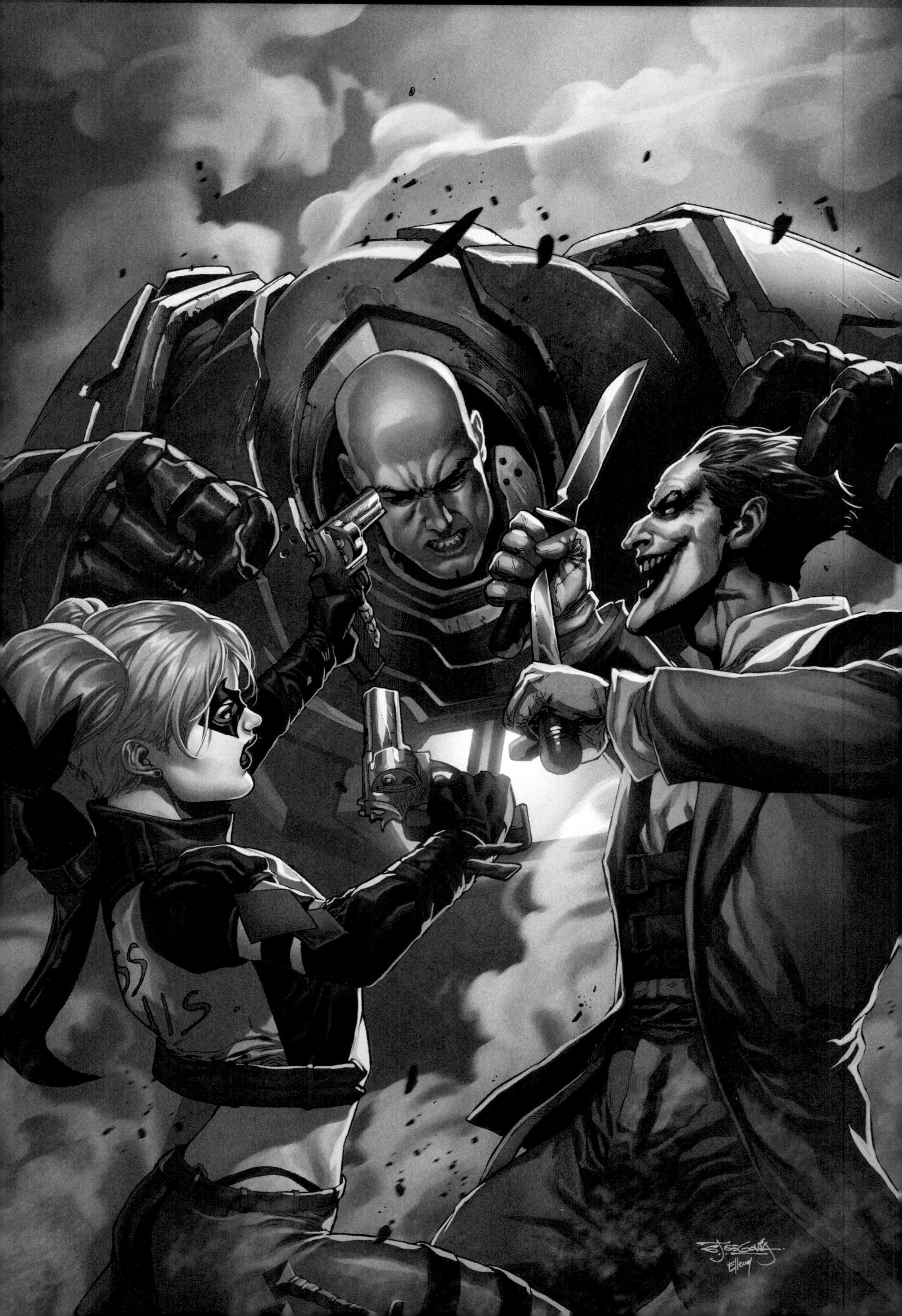

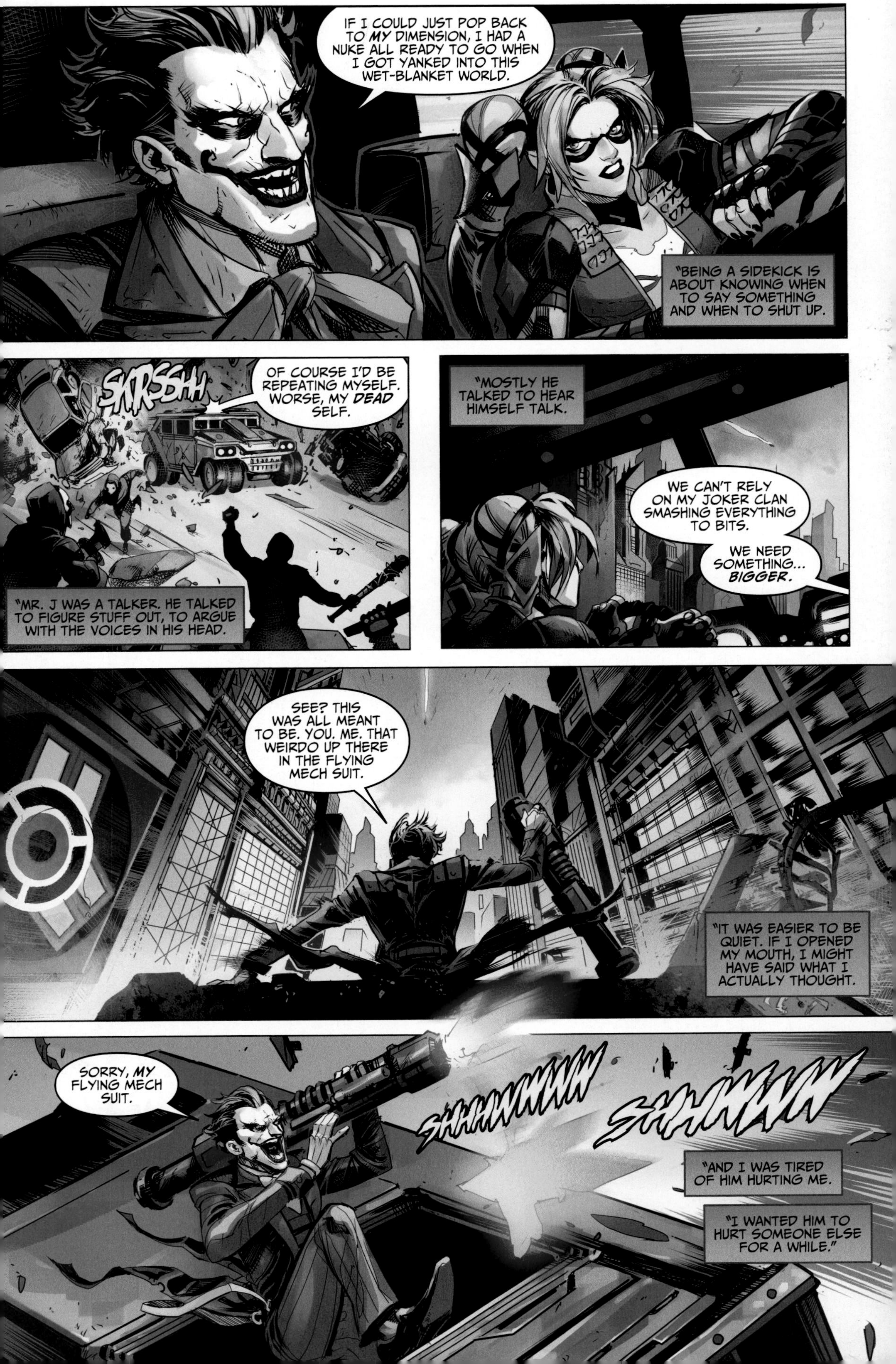
IF I COULD JUST POP BACK TO MY DIMENSION, I HAD A NUKE ALL READY TO GO WHEN I GOT YANKED INTO THIS WET-BLANKET WORLD.
"BEING A SIDEKICK IS ABOUT KNOWING WHEN TO SAY SOMETHING AND WHEN TO SHUT UP.
SKRSSHH
OF COURSE I'D BE REPEATING MYSELF. WORSE, MY DEAD SELF.
"MR. J WAS A TALKER. HE TALKED TO FIGURE STUFF OUT, TO ARGUE WITH THE VOICES IN HIS HEAD.
"MOSTLY HE TALKED TO HEAR HIMSELF TALK.
WE CAN'T RELY ON MY JOKER CLAN SMASHING EVERYTHING TO BITS.
WE NEED SOMETHING... BIGGER.
SEE? THIS WAS ALL MEANT TO BE. YOU. ME. THAT WEIRDO UP THERE IN THE FLYING MECH SUIT.
"IT WAS EASIER TO BE QUIET. IF I OPENED MY MOUTH, I MIGHT HAVE SAID WHAT I ACTUALLY THOUGHT.
SORRY, MY FLYING MECH SUIT.
SHHHWWWW
SHHWWW
"AND I WAS TIRED OF HIM HURTING ME.
"I WANTED HIM TO HURT SOMEONE ELSE FOR A WHILE."

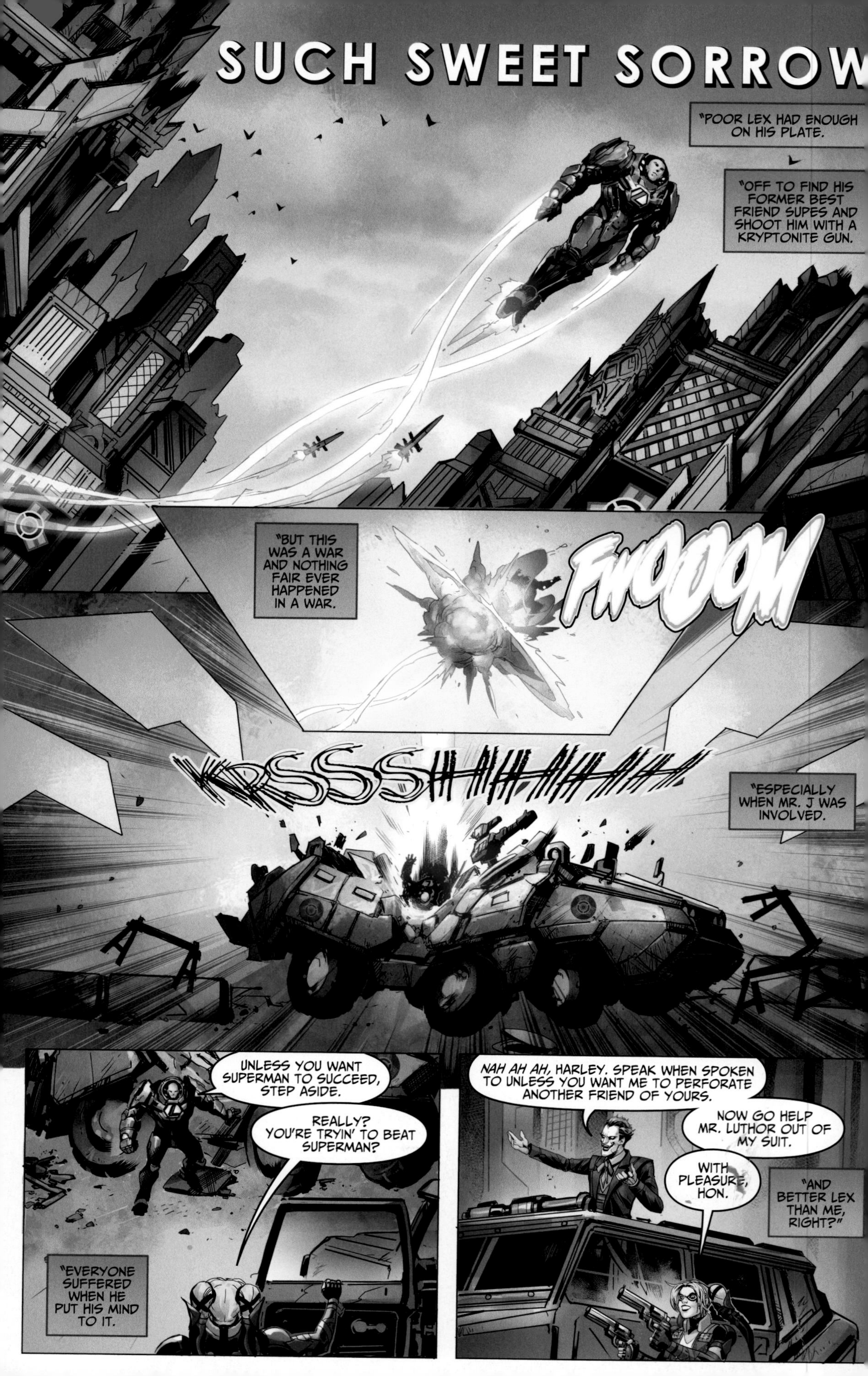
SUCH SWEET SORROW
"POOR LEX HAD ENOUGH ON HIS PLATE.
"OFF TO FIND HIS FORMER BEST FRIEND SUPES AND SHOOT HIM WITH A KRYPTONITE GUN.
"BUT THIS WAS A WAR AND NOTHING FAIR EVER HAPPENED IN A WAR.
FWOOOOM
"ESPECIALLY WHEN MR. J WAS INVOLVED.
UNLESS YOU WANT SUPERMAN TO SUCCEED, STEP ASIDE.
REALLY? YOU'RE TRYIN' TO BEAT SUPERMAN?
"EVERYONE SUFFERED WHEN HE PUT HIS MIND TO IT.
NAH AH AH, HARLEY. SPEAK WHEN SPOKEN TO UNLESS YOU WANT ME TO PERFORATE ANOTHER FRIEND OF YOURS.
NOW GO HELP MR. LUTHOR OUT OF MY SUIT.
WITH PLEASURE, HON.
"AND BETTER LEX THAN ME, RIGHT?"

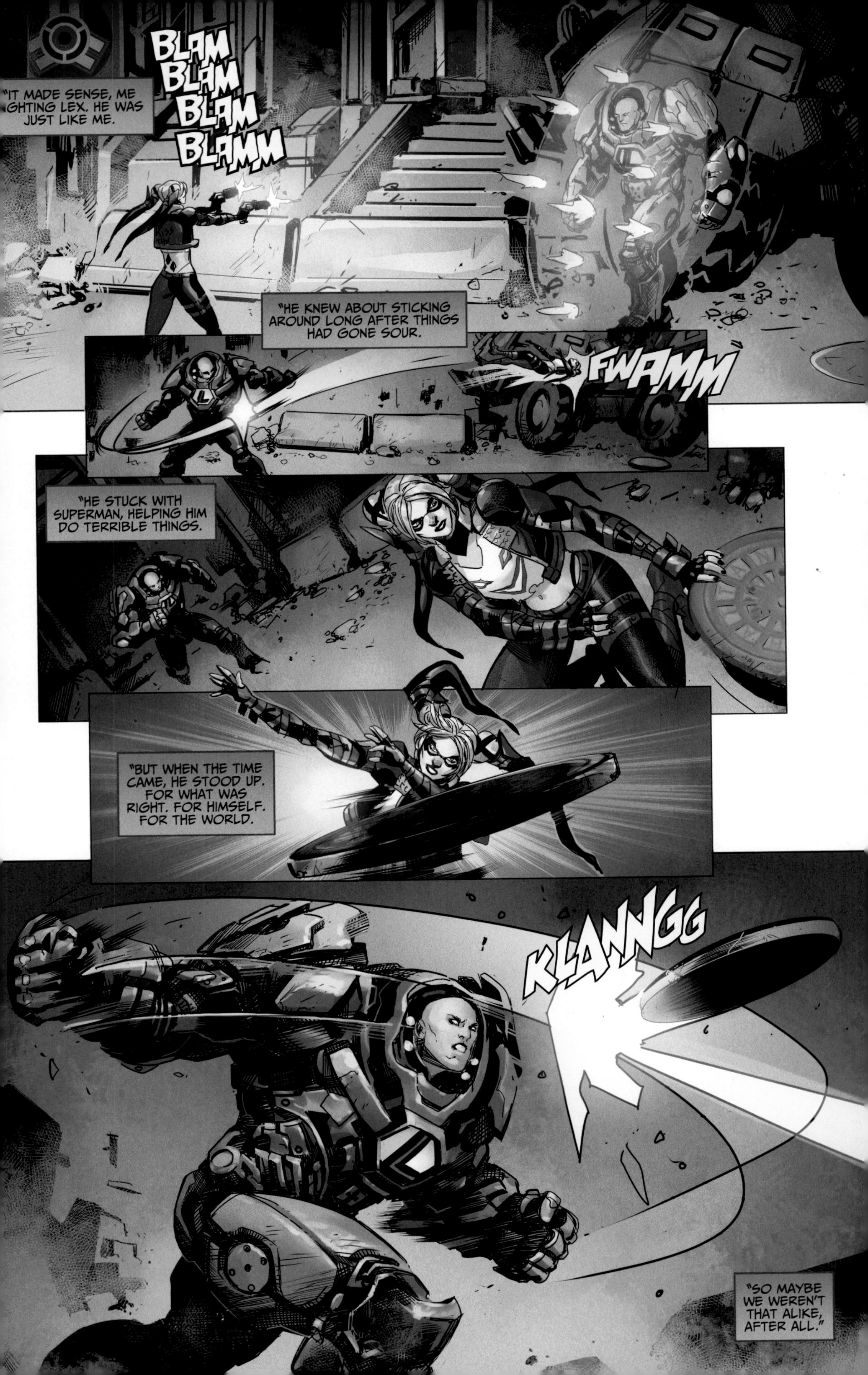
"IT MADE SENSE, ME
FIGHTING LEX. HE WAS
JUST LIKE ME.
BLAM
BLAM
BLAM
BLAMM
"HE KNEW ABOUT STICKING
AROUND LONG AFTER THINGS
HAD GONE SOUR.
FWAMM
"HE STUCK WITH
SUPERMAN, HELPING HIM
DO TERRIBLE THINGS.
"BUT WHEN THE TIME
CAME, HE STOOD UP.
FOR WHAT WAS
RIGHT. FOR HIMSELF.
FOR THE WORLD.
KLANNGG
"SO MAYBE
WE WEREN'T
THAT ALIKE,
AFTER ALL."

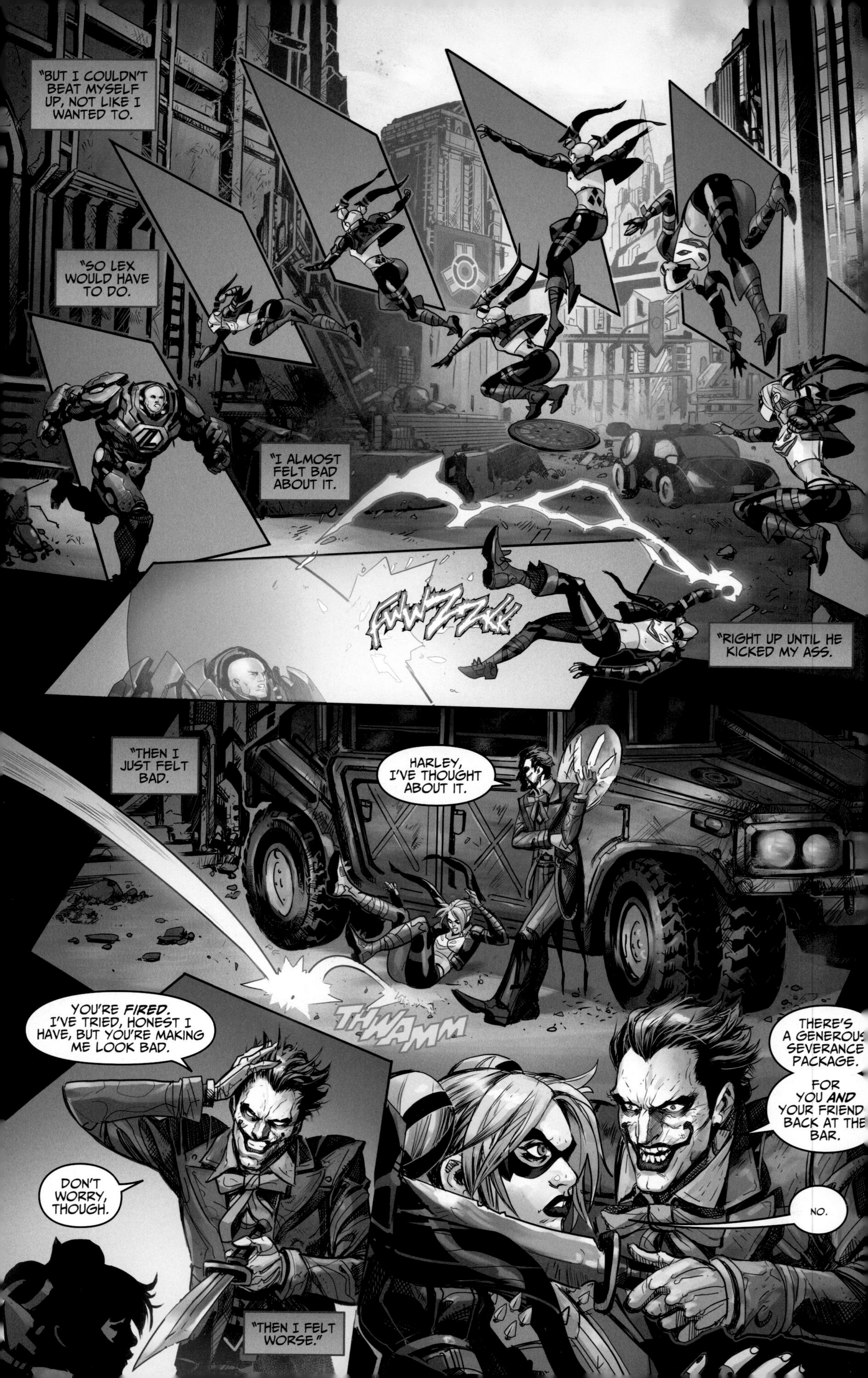

"BUT I COULDN'T BEAT MYSELF UP, NOT LIKE I WANTED TO.
"SO LEX WOULD HAVE TO DO.
"I ALMOST FELT BAD ABOUT IT.
FWWZZZKK
"RIGHT UP UNTIL HE KICKED MY ASS.
"THEN I JUST FELT BAD.
HARLEY, I'VE THOUGHT ABOUT IT.
THWAMM
YOU'RE *FIRED*. I'VE TRIED, HONEST I HAVE, BUT YOU'RE MAKING ME LOOK BAD.
DON'T WORRY, THOUGH.
THERE'S A GENEROUS SEVERANCE PACKAGE.
FOR YOU *AND* YOUR FRIEND BACK AT THE BAR.
NO.
"THEN I FELT WORSE."

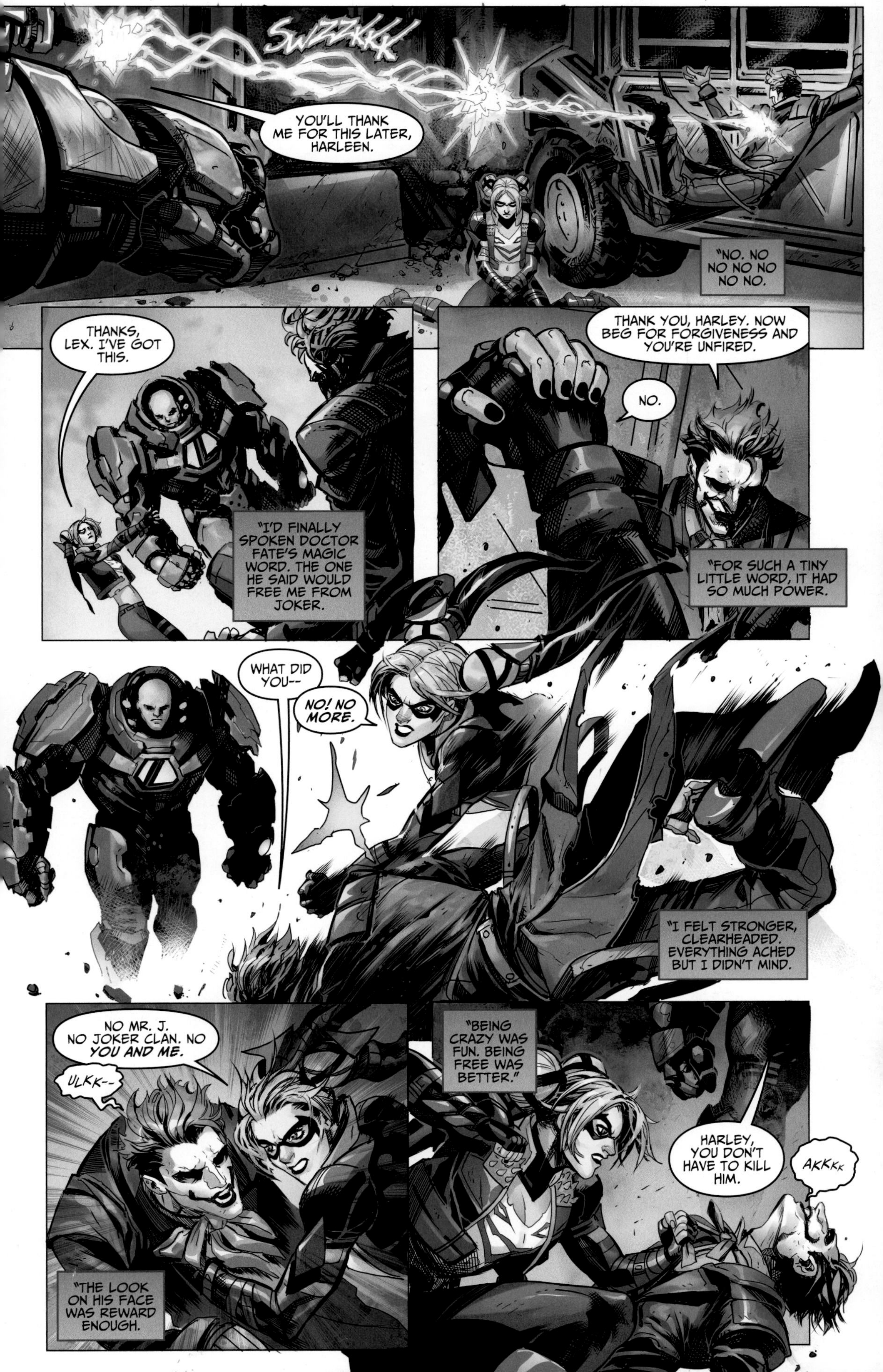
SWZZKKK
YOU'LL THANK ME FOR THIS LATER, HARLEEN.
"NO. NO NO NO NO NO NO.
THANKS, LEX. I'VE GOT THIS.
"I'D FINALLY SPOKEN DOCTOR FATE'S MAGIC WORD. THE ONE HE SAID WOULD FREE ME FROM JOKER.
THANK YOU, HARLEY. NOW BEG FOR FORGIVENESS AND YOU'RE UNFIRED.
NO.
"FOR SUCH A TINY LITTLE WORD, IT HAD SO MUCH POWER.
WHAT DID YOU--
NO! NO MORE.
"I FELT STRONGER, CLEARHEADED. EVERYTHING ACHED BUT I DIDN'T MIND.
NO MR. J. NO JOKER CLAN. NO YOU AND ME.
ULKK--
"THE LOOK ON HIS FACE WAS REWARD ENOUGH.
"BEING CRAZY WAS FUN. BEING FREE WAS BETTER."
HARLEY, YOU DON'T HAVE TO KILL HIM.
AKKKK

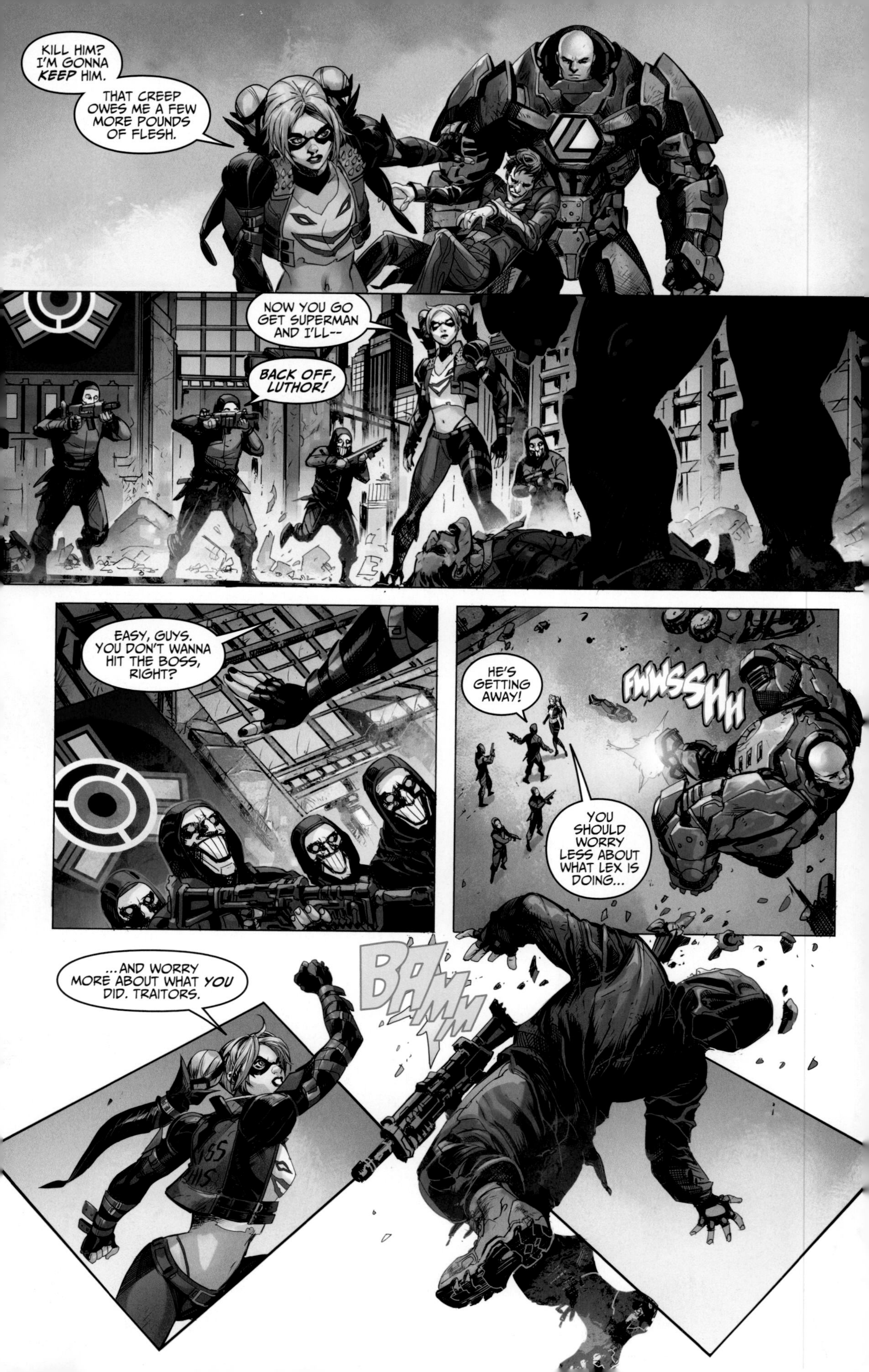
KILL HIM? I'M GONNA KEEP HIM.
THAT CREEP OWES ME A FEW MORE POUNDS OF FLESH.
NOW YOU GO GET SUPERMAN AND I'LL--
BACK OFF, LUTHOR!
EASY, GUYS. YOU DON'T WANNA HIT THE BOSS, RIGHT?
HE'S GETTING AWAY!
FWWSSHH
YOU SHOULD WORRY LESS ABOUT WHAT LEX IS DOING...
...AND WORRY MORE ABOUT WHAT YOU DID. TRAITORS.
BAMM

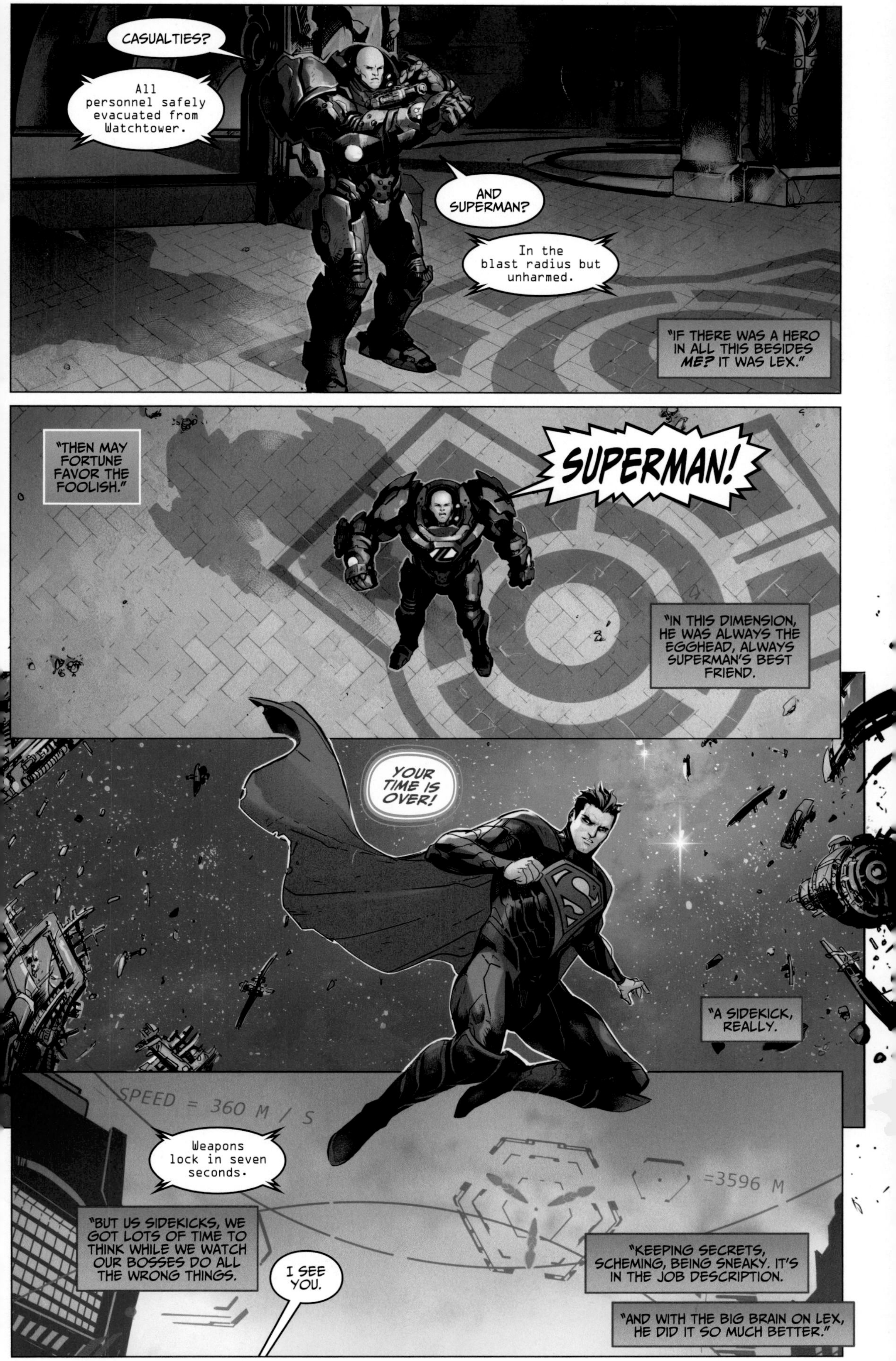
CASUALTIES?
All personnel safely evacuated from Watchtower.
AND SUPERMAN?
In the blast radius but unharmed.
"IF THERE WAS A HERO IN ALL THIS BESIDES ME? IT WAS LEX."
"THEN MAY FORTUNE FAVOR THE FOOLISH."
SUPERMAN!
"IN THIS DIMENSION, HE WAS ALWAYS THE EGGHEAD, ALWAYS SUPERMAN'S BEST FRIEND.
YOUR TIME IS OVER!
"A SIDEKICK, REALLY.
SPEED = 360 M / S
Weapons lock in seven seconds.
=3596 M
"BUT US SIDEKICKS, WE GOT LOTS OF TIME TO THINK WHILE WE WATCH OUR BOSSES DO ALL THE WRONG THINGS.
I SEE YOU.
"KEEPING SECRETS, SCHEMING, BEING SNEAKY. IT'S IN THE JOB DESCRIPTION.
"AND WITH THE BIG BRAIN ON LEX, HE DID IT SO MUCH BETTER."

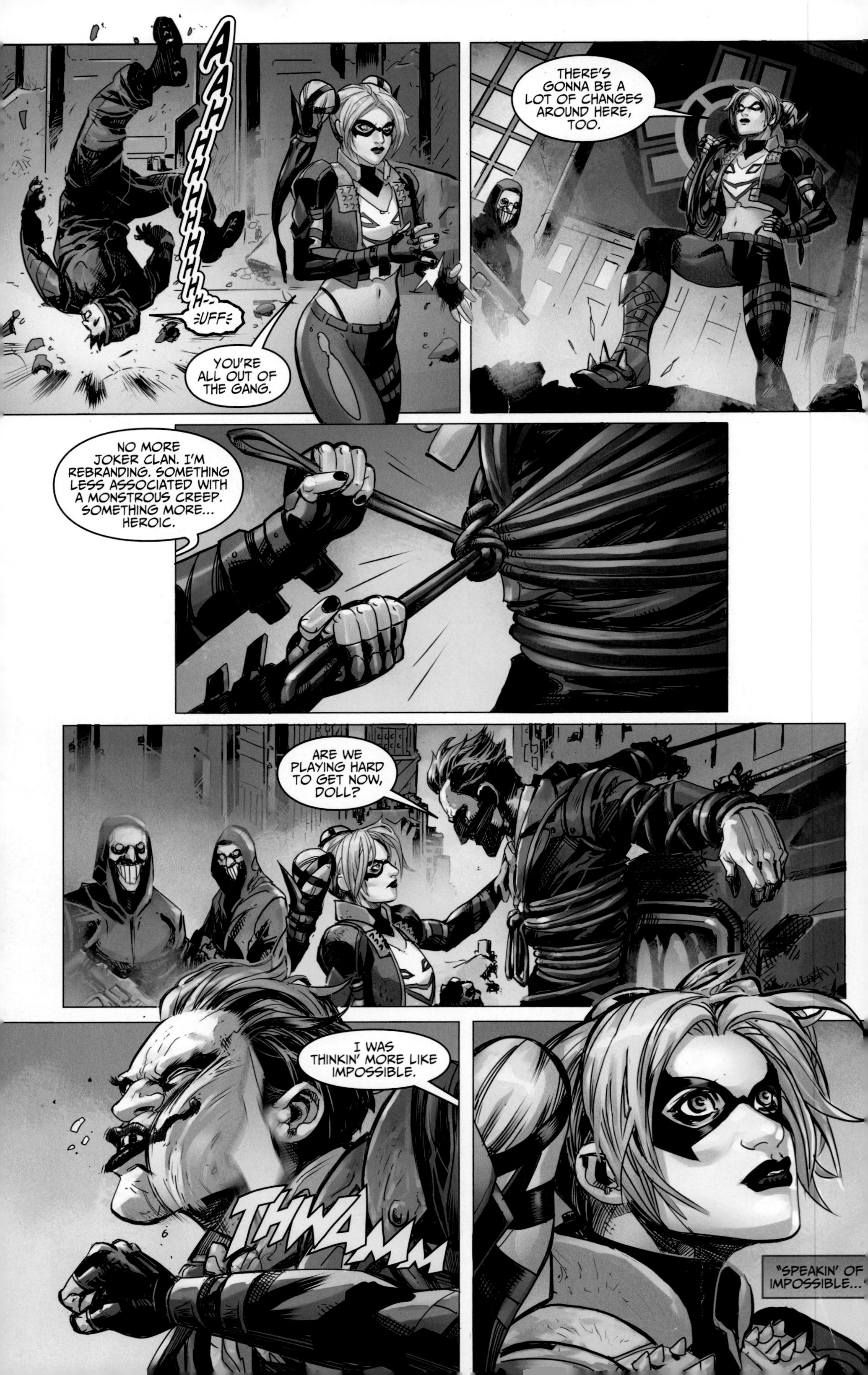
AAHHHHHHHHH--
-UFF-
YOU'RE ALL OUT OF THE GANG.
THERE'S GONNA BE A LOT OF CHANGES AROUND HERE, TOO.
NO MORE JOKER CLAN. I'M REBRANDING. SOMETHING LESS ASSOCIATED WITH A MONSTROUS CREEP. SOMETHING MORE... HEROIC.
ARE WE PLAYING HARD TO GET NOW, DOLL?
I WAS THINKIN' MORE LIKE IMPOSSIBLE.
THWAMM
"SPEAKIN' OF IMPOSSIBLE...

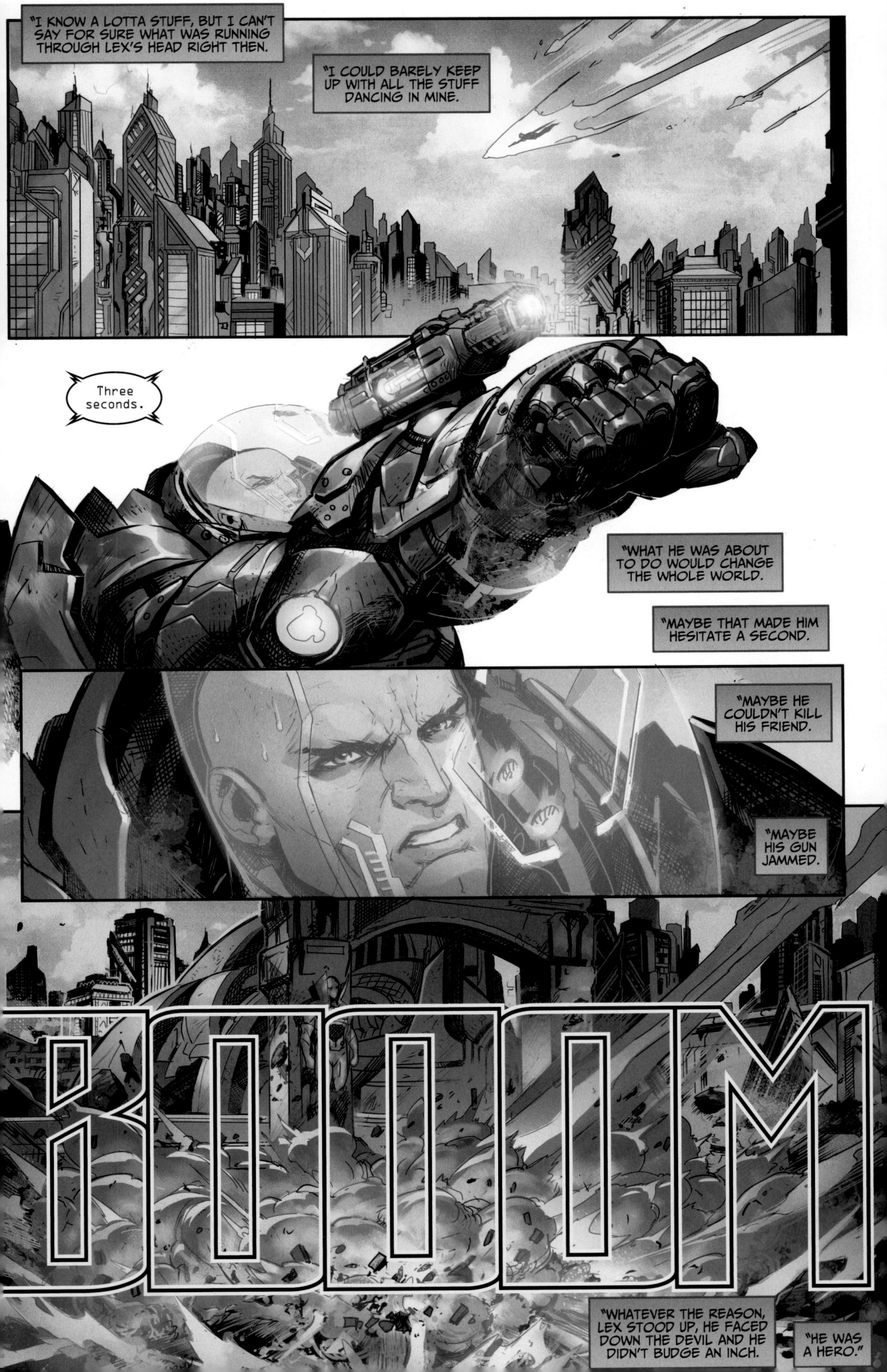
"I KNOW A LOTTA STUFF, BUT I CAN'T SAY FOR SURE WHAT WAS RUNNING THROUGH LEX'S HEAD RIGHT THEN.
"I COULD BARELY KEEP UP WITH ALL THE STUFF DANCING IN MINE.
Three seconds.
"WHAT HE WAS ABOUT TO DO WOULD CHANGE THE WHOLE WORLD.
"MAYBE THAT MADE HIM HESITATE A SECOND.
"MAYBE HE COULDN'T KILL HIS FRIEND.
"MAYBE HIS GUN JAMMED.
BOOOM
"WHATEVER THE REASON, LEX STOOD UP, HE FACED DOWN THE DEVIL AND HE DIDN'T BUDGE AN INCH.
"HE WAS A HERO."

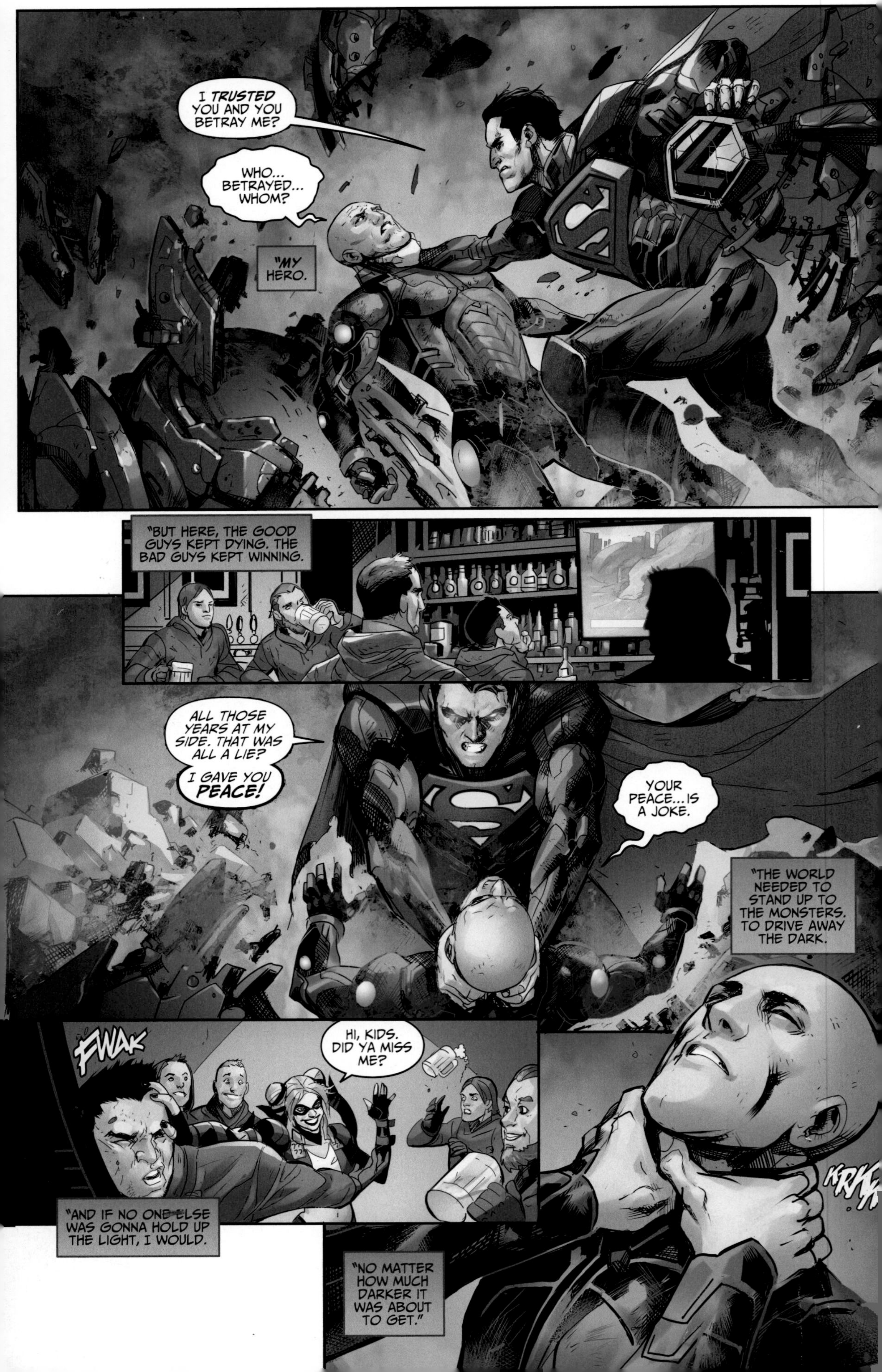

I TRUSTED YOU AND YOU BETRAY ME?
WHO... BETRAYED... WHOM?
"MY HERO.
"BUT HERE, THE GOOD GUYS KEPT DYING. THE BAD GUYS KEPT WINNING.
ALL THOSE YEARS AT MY SIDE. THAT WAS ALL A LIE?
I GAVE YOU PEACE!
YOUR PEACE...IS A JOKE.
"THE WORLD NEEDED TO STAND UP TO THE MONSTERS. TO DRIVE AWAY THE DARK.
FWAK
HI, KIDS. DID YA MISS ME?
"AND IF NO ONE ELSE WAS GONNA HOLD UP THE LIGHT, I WOULD.
KRAK
"NO MATTER HOW MUCH DARKER IT WAS ABOUT TO GET."

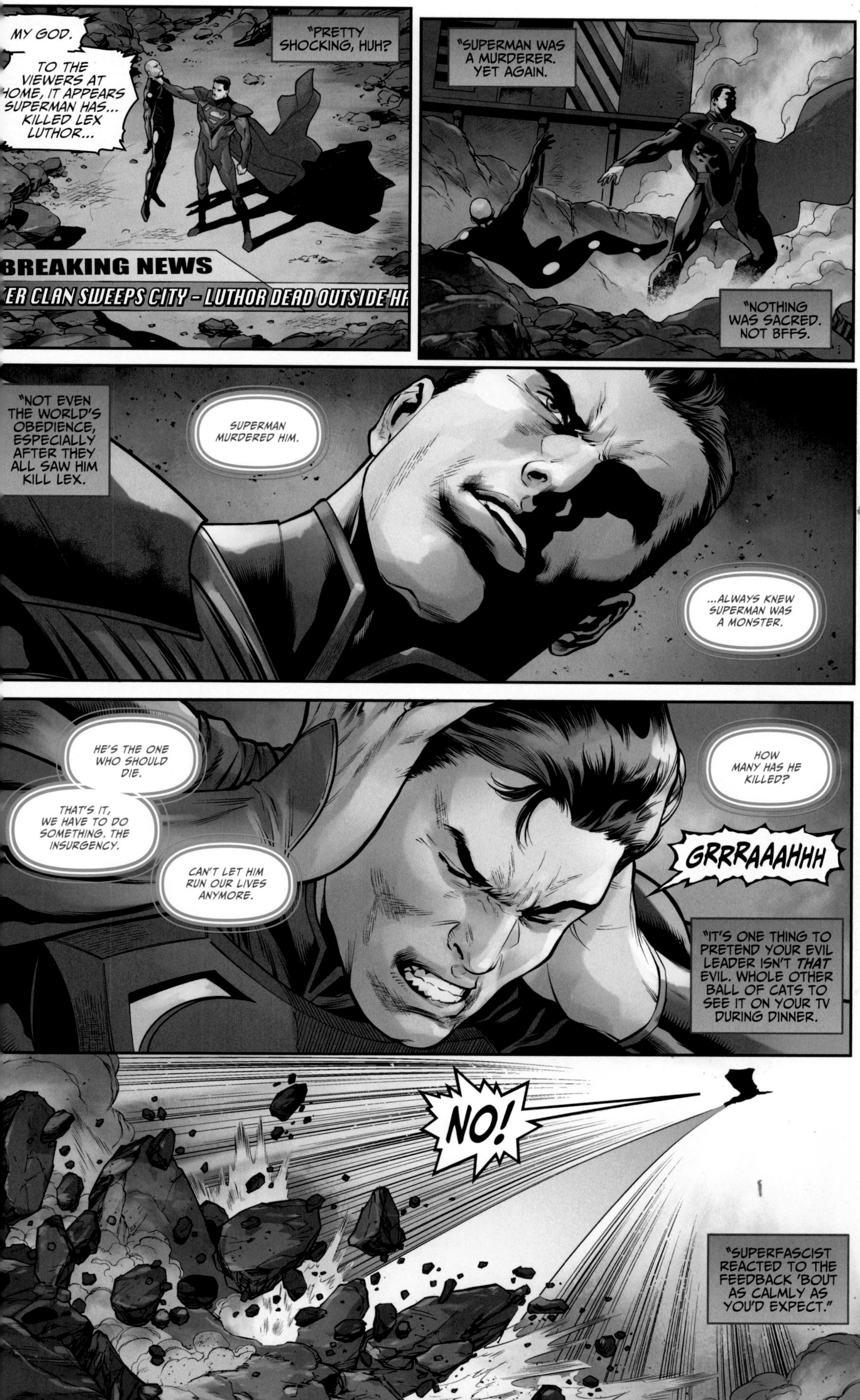
MY GOD.
TO THE VIEWERS AT HOME, IT APPEARS SUPERMAN HAS... KILLED LEX LUTHOR...
"PRETTY SHOCKING, HUH?
BREAKING NEWS
ER CLAN SWEEPS CITY – LUTHOR DEAD OUTSIDE H
"SUPERMAN WAS A MURDERER. YET AGAIN.
"NOTHING WAS SACRED. NOT BFFS.
"NOT EVEN THE WORLD'S OBEDIENCE, ESPECIALLY AFTER THEY ALL SAW HIM KILL LEX.
SUPERMAN MURDERED HIM.
...ALWAYS KNEW SUPERMAN WAS A MONSTER.
HE'S THE ONE WHO SHOULD DIE.
THAT'S IT, WE HAVE TO DO SOMETHING. THE INSURGENCY.
CAN'T LET HIM RUN OUR LIVES ANYMORE.
HOW MANY HAS HE KILLED?
GRRRAAAHHH
"IT'S ONE THING TO PRETEND YOUR EVIL LEADER ISN'T THAT EVIL. WHOLE OTHER BALL OF CATS TO SEE IT ON YOUR TV DURING DINNER.
NO!
"SUPERFASCIST REACTED TO THE FEEDBACK 'BOUT AS CALMLY AS YOU'D EXPECT."

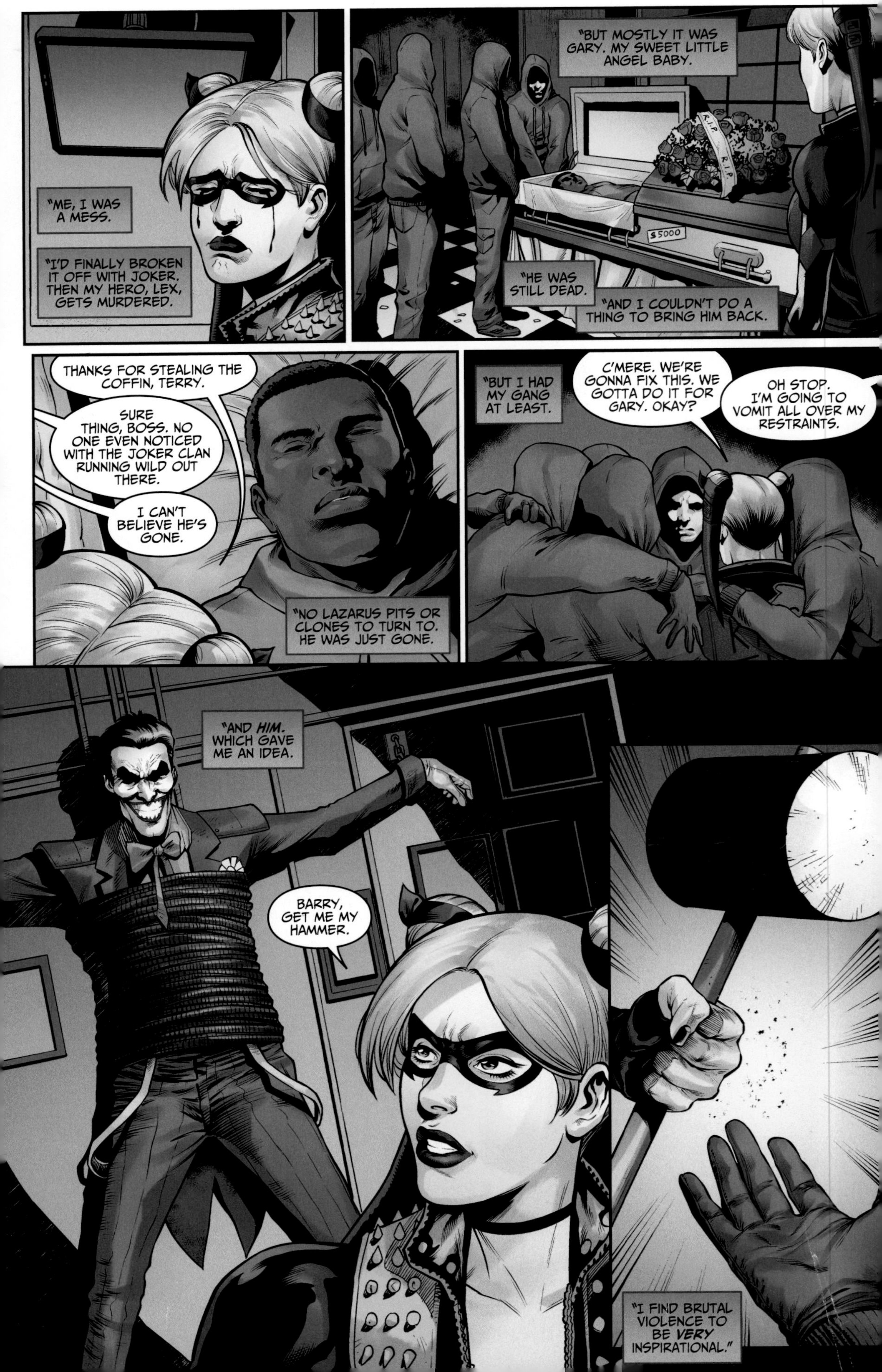
"ME, I WAS A MESS.
"I'D FINALLY BROKEN IT OFF WITH JOKER. THEN MY HERO, LEX, GETS MURDERED.
"BUT MOSTLY IT WAS GARY. MY SWEET LITTLE ANGEL BABY.
R.I.P.
R.I.P.
$5000
"HE WAS STILL DEAD.
"AND I COULDN'T DO A THING TO BRING HIM BACK.
THANKS FOR STEALING THE COFFIN, TERRY.
SURE THING, BOSS. NO ONE EVEN NOTICED WITH THE JOKER CLAN RUNNING WILD OUT THERE.
I CAN'T BELIEVE HE'S GONE.
"NO LAZARUS PITS OR CLONES TO TURN TO. HE WAS JUST GONE.
"BUT I HAD MY GANG AT LEAST.
C'MERE. WE'RE GONNA FIX THIS. WE GOTTA DO IT FOR GARY. OKAY?
OH STOP. I'M GOING TO VOMIT ALL OVER MY RESTRAINTS.
"AND *HIM*. WHICH GAVE ME AN IDEA.
BARRY, GET ME MY HAMMER.
"I FIND BRUTAL VIOLENCE TO BE *VERY* INSPIRATIONAL."

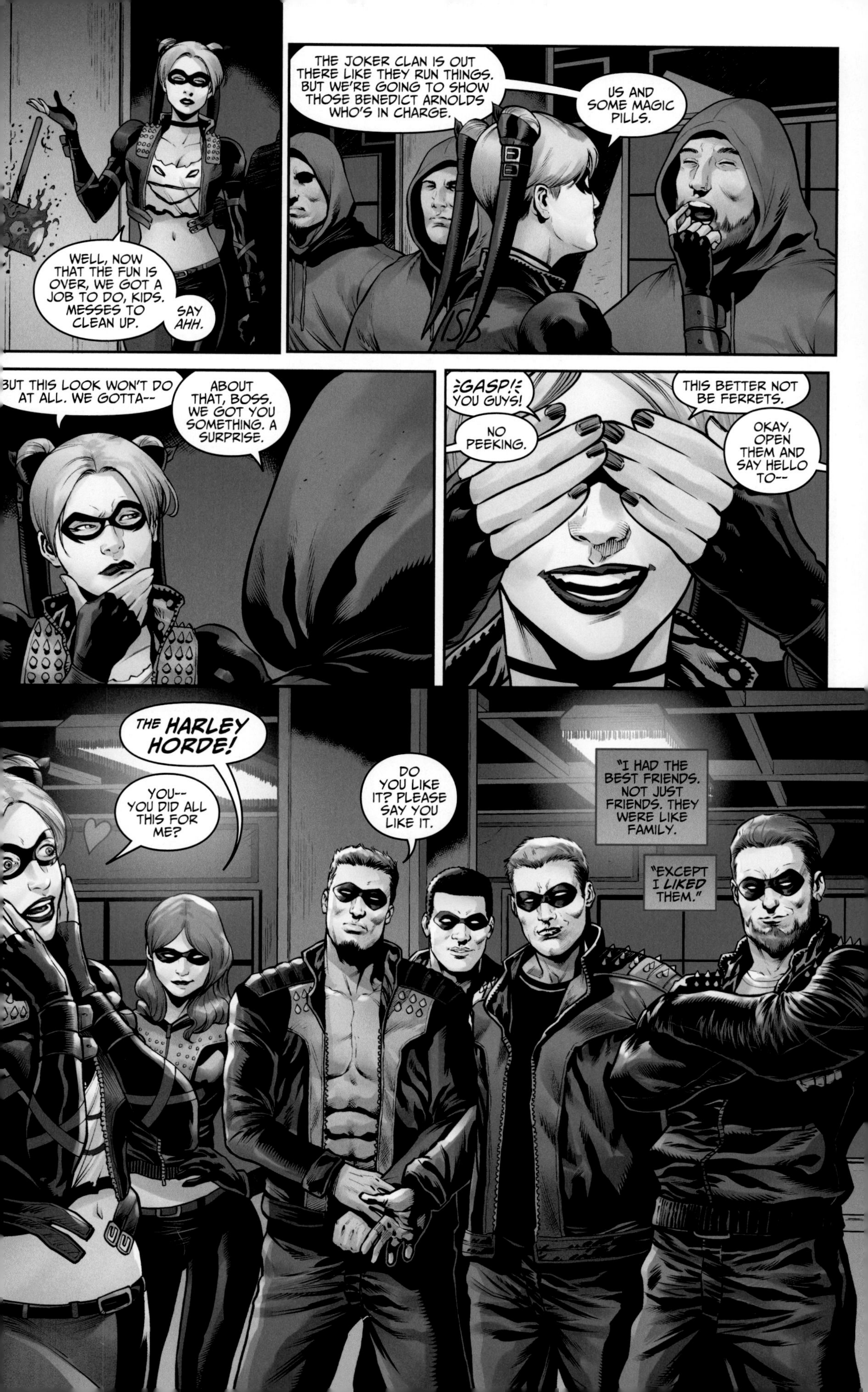

WELL, NOW THAT THE FUN IS OVER, WE GOT A JOB TO DO, KIDS. MESSES TO CLEAN UP.
SAY AHH.
THE JOKER CLAN IS OUT THERE LIKE THEY RUN THINGS. BUT WE'RE GOING TO SHOW THOSE BENEDICT ARNOLDS WHO'S IN CHARGE.
US AND SOME MAGIC PILLS.
BUT THIS LOOK WON'T DO AT ALL. WE GOTTA--
ABOUT THAT, BOSS. WE GOT YOU SOMETHING. A SURPRISE.
GASP! YOU GUYS!
THIS BETTER NOT BE FERRETS.
NO PEEKING.
OKAY, OPEN THEM AND SAY HELLO TO--
THE HARLEY HORDE!
YOU-- YOU DID ALL THIS FOR ME?
DO YOU LIKE IT? PLEASE SAY YOU LIKE IT.
"I HAD THE BEST FRIENDS. NOT JUST FRIENDS. THEY WERE LIKE FAMILY.
"EXCEPT I LIKED THEM."

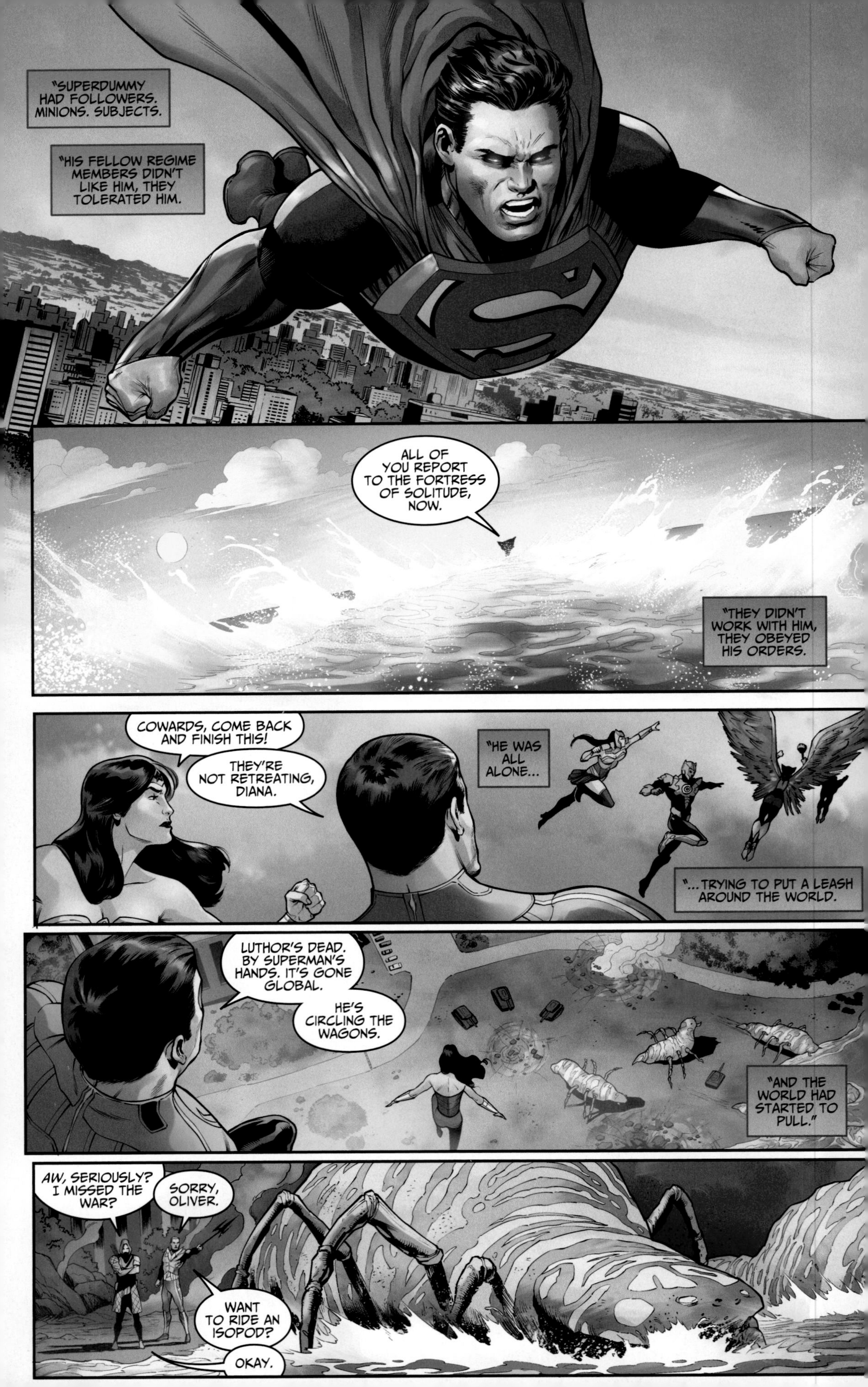
"SUPERDUMMY HAD FOLLOWERS. MINIONS. SUBJECTS.
"HIS FELLOW REGIME MEMBERS DIDN'T LIKE HIM, THEY TOLERATED HIM.
ALL OF YOU REPORT TO THE FORTRESS OF SOLITUDE, NOW.
"THEY DIDN'T WORK WITH HIM, THEY OBEYED HIS ORDERS.
COWARDS, COME BACK AND FINISH THIS!
THEY'RE NOT RETREATING, DIANA.
"HE WAS ALL ALONE...
"...TRYING TO PUT A LEASH AROUND THE WORLD.
LUTHOR'S DEAD. BY SUPERMAN'S HANDS. IT'S GONE GLOBAL.
HE'S CIRCLING THE WAGONS.
"AND THE WORLD HAD STARTED TO PULL."
AW, SERIOUSLY? I MISSED THE WAR?
SORRY, OLIVER.
WANT TO RIDE AN ISOPOD?
OKAY.

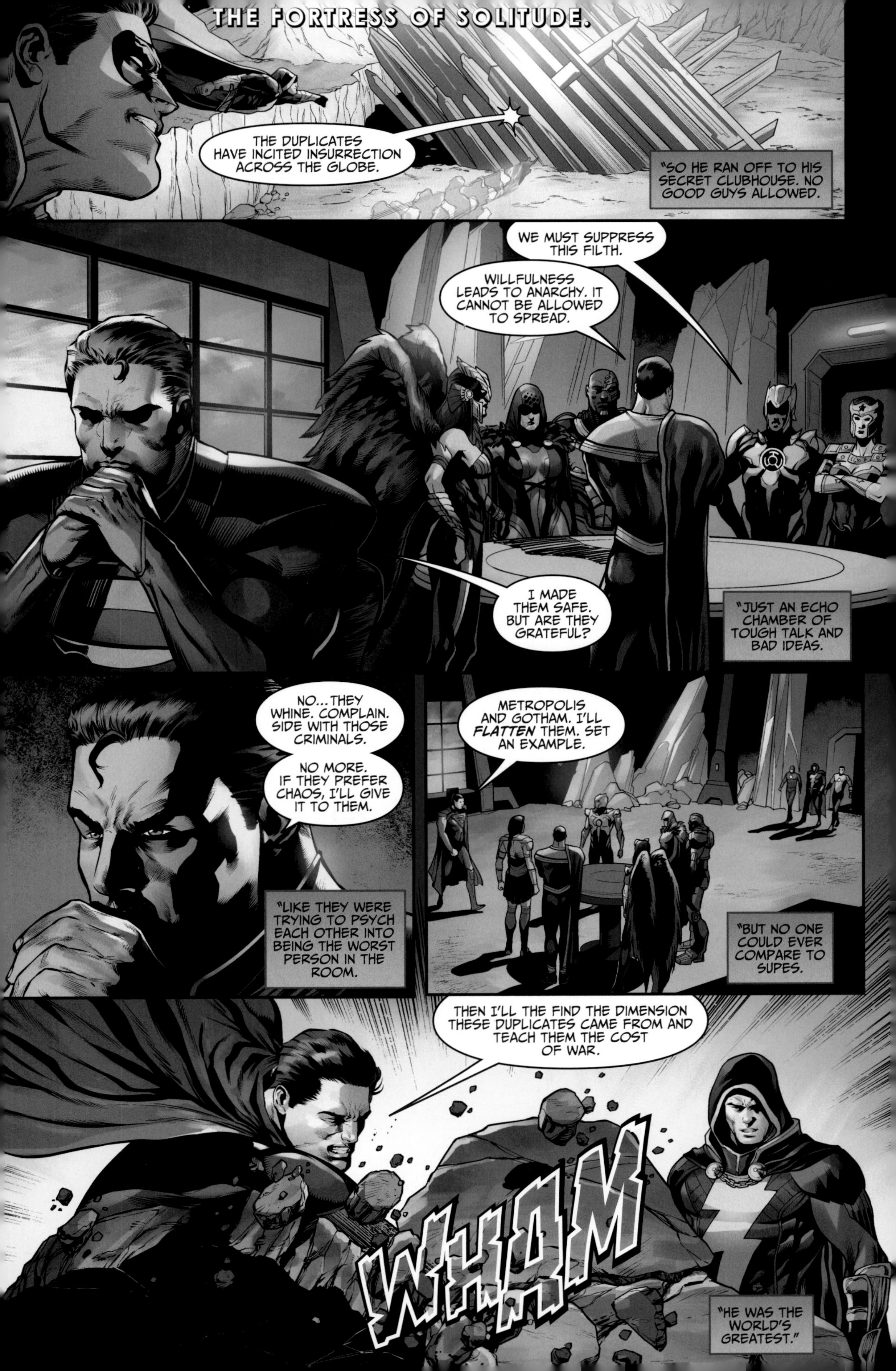
THE FORTRESS OF SOLITUDE.
THE DUPLICATES HAVE INCITED INSURRECTION ACROSS THE GLOBE.
"SO HE RAN OFF TO HIS SECRET CLUBHOUSE. NO GOOD GUYS ALLOWED.
WE MUST SUPPRESS THIS FILTH.
WILLFULNESS LEADS TO ANARCHY. IT CANNOT BE ALLOWED TO SPREAD.
I MADE THEM SAFE. BUT ARE THEY GRATEFUL?
"JUST AN ECHO CHAMBER OF TOUGH TALK AND BAD IDEAS.
NO...THEY WHINE. COMPLAIN. SIDE WITH THOSE CRIMINALS.
NO MORE. IF THEY PREFER CHAOS, I'LL GIVE IT TO THEM.
"LIKE THEY WERE TRYING TO PSYCH EACH OTHER INTO BEING THE WORST PERSON IN THE ROOM.
METROPOLIS AND GOTHAM. I'LL *FLATTEN* THEM. SET AN EXAMPLE.
"BUT NO ONE COULD EVER COMPARE TO SUPES.
THEN I'LL THE FIND THE DIMENSION THESE DUPLICATES CAME FROM AND TEACH THEM THE COST OF WAR.
WHAM
"HE WAS THE WORLD'S GREATEST."

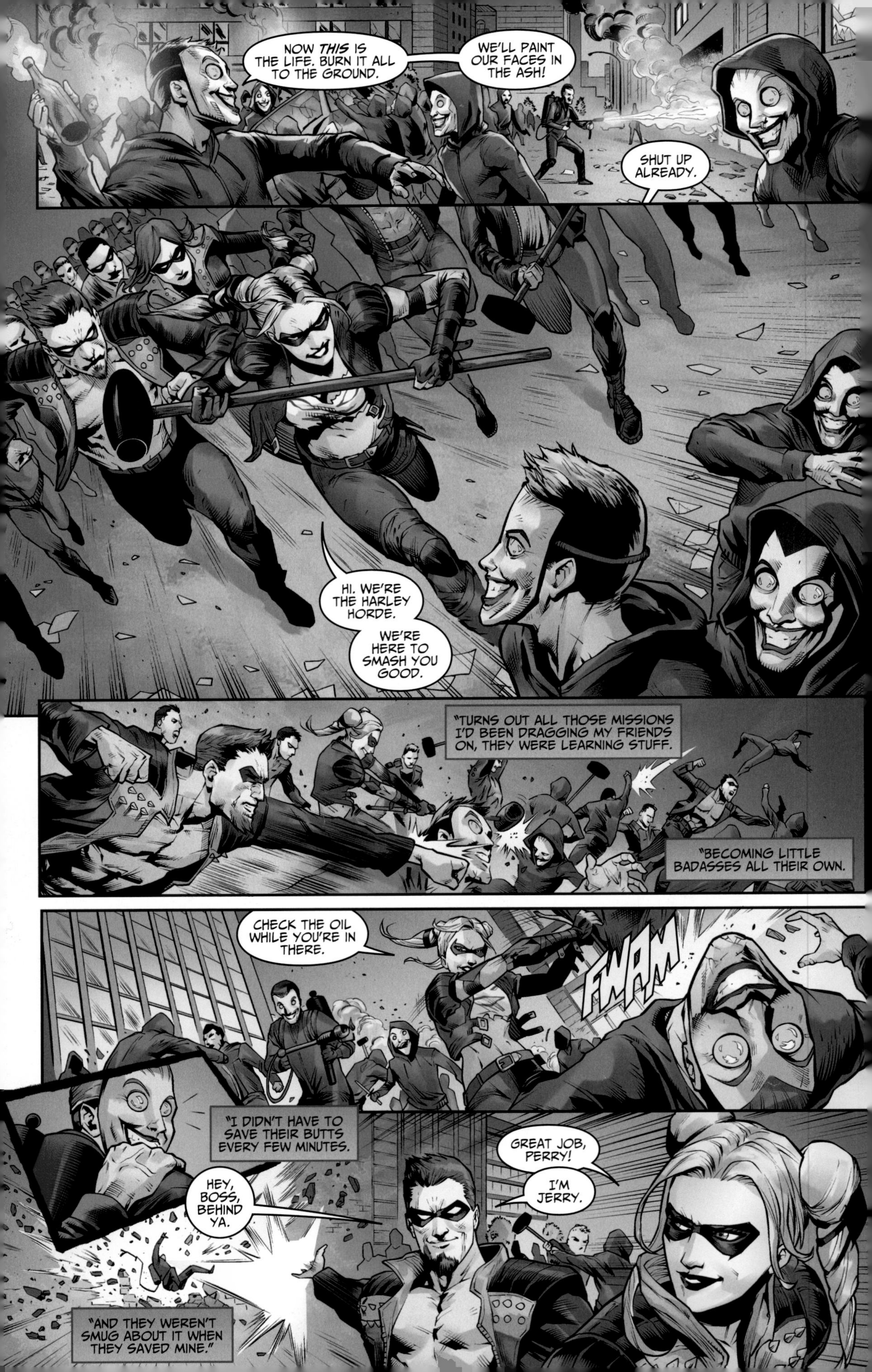
NOW THIS IS THE LIFE. BURN IT ALL TO THE GROUND.
WE'LL PAINT OUR FACES IN THE ASH!
SHUT UP ALREADY.
HI. WE'RE THE HARLEY HORDE.
WE'RE HERE TO SMASH YOU GOOD.
"TURNS OUT ALL THOSE MISSIONS I'D BEEN DRAGGING MY FRIENDS ON, THEY WERE LEARNING STUFF.
"BECOMING LITTLE BADASSES ALL THEIR OWN.
CHECK THE OIL WHILE YOU'RE IN THERE.
FWAM
"I DIDN'T HAVE TO SAVE THEIR BUTTS EVERY FEW MINUTES.
GREAT JOB, PERRY!
I'M JERRY.
HEY, BOSS, BEHIND YA.
"AND THEY WEREN'T SMUG ABOUT IT WHEN THEY SAVED MINE."

DON'T PLAY WITH YOUR FOOD, KIDS.

"I WAS PROUD. OF ALL OF US.

BEEP BEEP!

"OUR FIRST HOUR ON THE JOB AND WE'D SWEPT THROUGH THE CITY, DEFLECTING BULLETS AND TAKING DOWN JOKER CLAN MEMBERS.

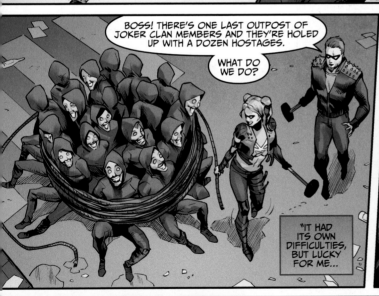

BOSS! THERE'S ONE LAST OUTPOST OF JOKER CLAN MEMBERS AND THEY'RE HOLED UP WITH A DOZEN HOSTAGES.

WHAT DO WE DO?

"IT HAD ITS OWN DIFFICULTIES, BUT LUCKY FOR ME...

HM. NOT ENOUGH OF US TO STOP THEM AND SAVE EVERYONE. WE'D NEED A LOT MORE BODIES.

BOSS, IF I MAY?

"...TURNS OUT MY FRIENDS WEREN'T JUST SERVING IN MY ARMY.

I THINK I KNOW A FEW PEOPLE WILLING TO HELP.

"THEY WERE GONNA HELP ME LEAD IT."

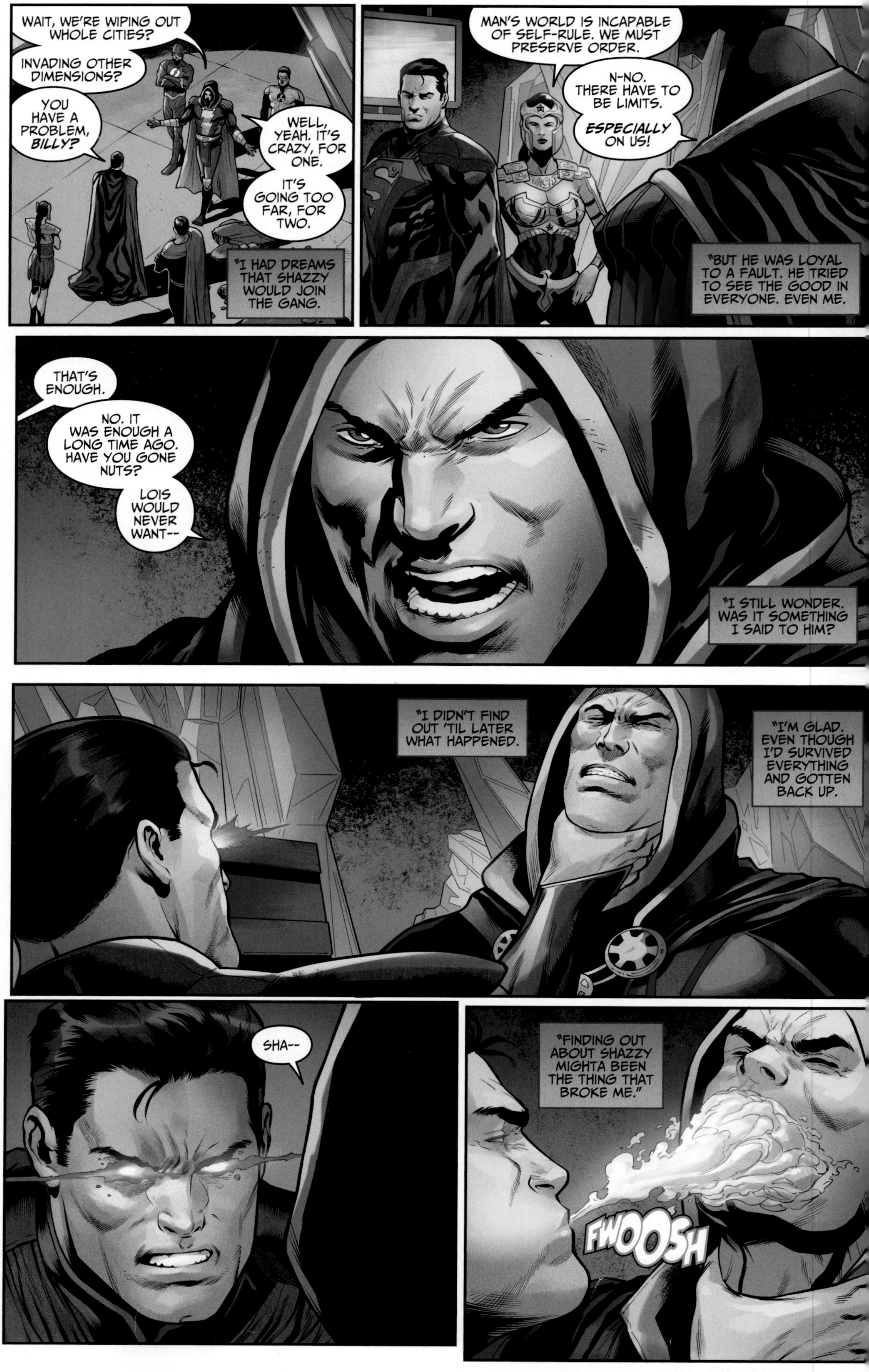
WAIT, WE'RE WIPING OUT WHOLE CITIES?
INVADING OTHER DIMENSIONS?
YOU HAVE A PROBLEM, BILLY?
WELL, YEAH. IT'S CRAZY, FOR ONE.
IT'S GOING TOO FAR, FOR TWO.
"I HAD DREAMS THAT SHAZZY WOULD JOIN THE GANG.
MAN'S WORLD IS INCAPABLE OF SELF-RULE. WE MUST PRESERVE ORDER.
N-NO. THERE HAVE TO BE LIMITS.
ESPECIALLY ON US!
"BUT HE WAS LOYAL TO A FAULT. HE TRIED TO SEE THE GOOD IN EVERYONE. EVEN ME.
THAT'S ENOUGH.
NO. IT WAS ENOUGH A LONG TIME AGO. HAVE YOU GONE NUTS?
LOIS WOULD NEVER WANT--
"I STILL WONDER. WAS IT SOMETHING I SAID TO HIM?
"I DIDN'T FIND OUT 'TIL LATER WHAT HAPPENED.
"I'M GLAD. EVEN THOUGH I'D SURVIVED EVERYTHING AND GOTTEN BACK UP.
SHA--
"FINDING OUT ABOUT SHAZZY MIGHTA BEEN THE THING THAT BROKE ME."
FWOOSH

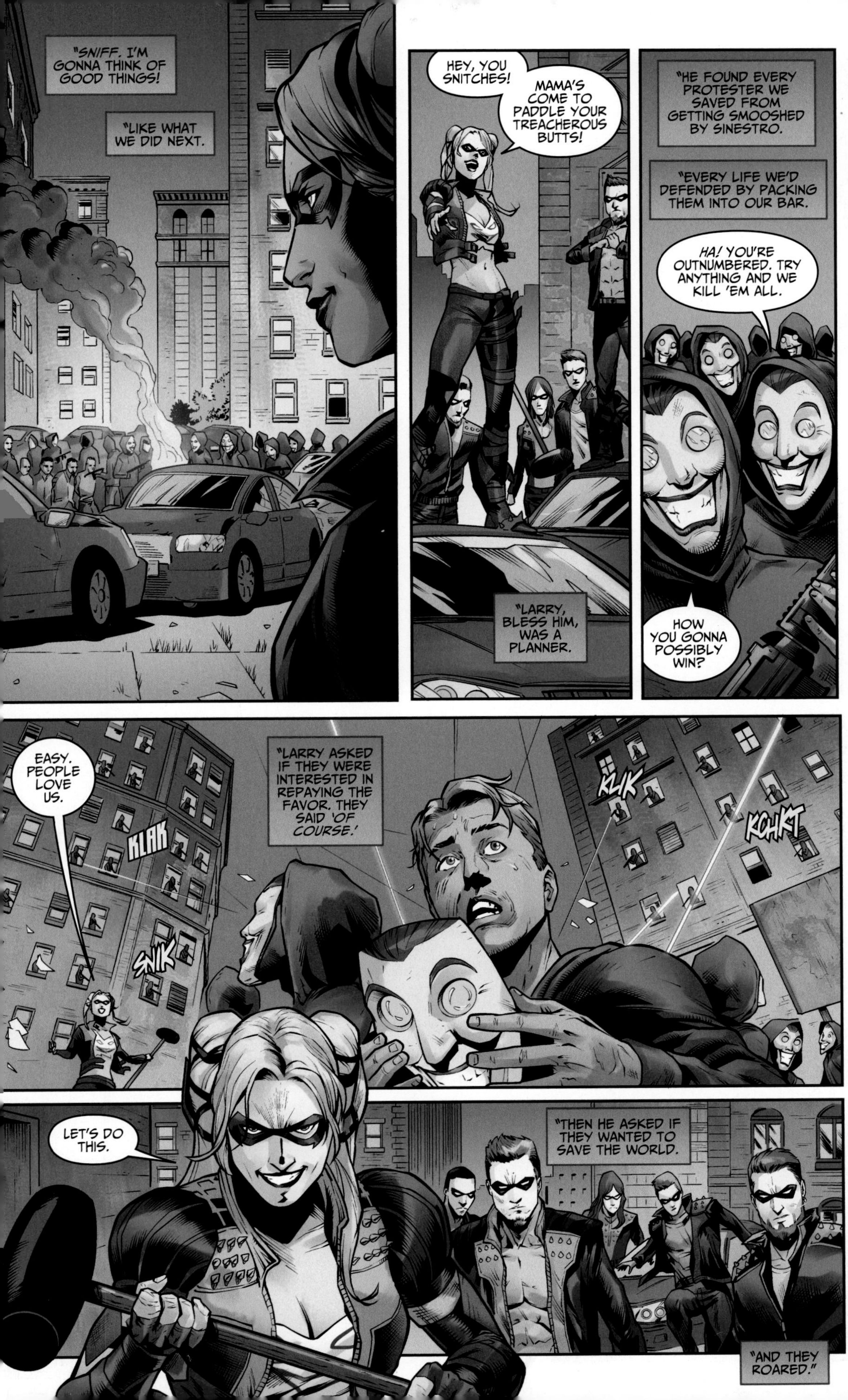
"SNIFF. I'M GONNA THINK OF GOOD THINGS!
"LIKE WHAT WE DID NEXT.
HEY, YOU SNITCHES!
MAMA'S COME TO PADDLE YOUR TREACHEROUS BUTTS!
"LARRY, BLESS HIM, WAS A PLANNER.
"HE FOUND EVERY PROTESTER WE SAVED FROM GETTING SMOOSHED BY SINESTRO.
"EVERY LIFE WE'D DEFENDED BY PACKING THEM INTO OUR BAR.
HA! YOU'RE OUTNUMBERED. TRY ANYTHING AND WE KILL 'EM ALL.
HOW YOU GONNA POSSIBLY WIN?
EASY. PEOPLE LOVE US.
"LARRY ASKED IF THEY WERE INTERESTED IN REPAYING THE FAVOR. THEY SAID 'OF COURSE.'
KLAK
KLIK
KCHKT
SNIK
LET'S DO THIS.
"THEN HE ASKED IF THEY WANTED TO SAVE THE WORLD.
"AND THEY ROARED."

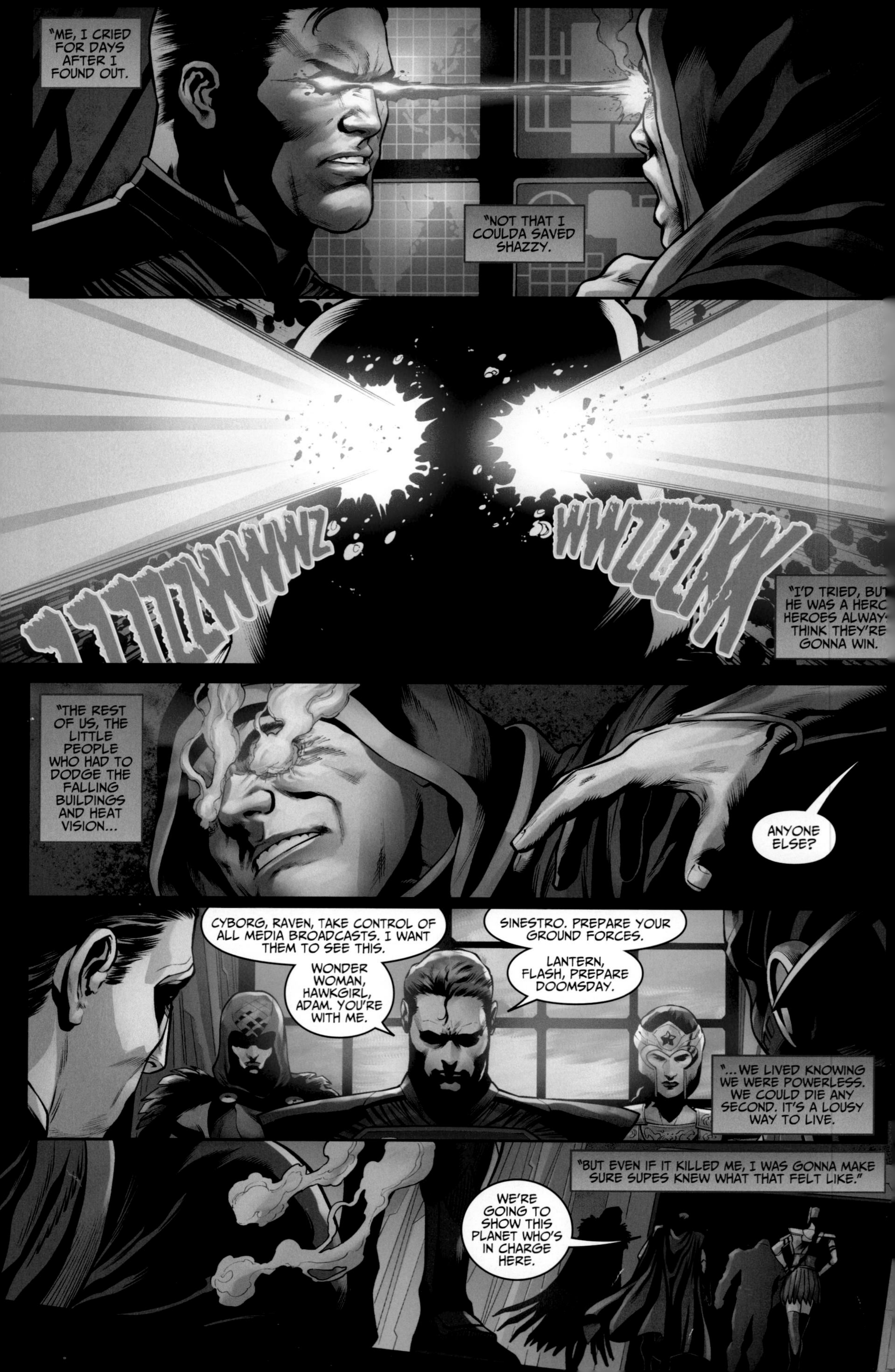
"ME, I CRIED FOR DAYS AFTER I FOUND OUT.
"NOT THAT I COULDA SAVED SHAZZY.
"I'D TRIED, BUT HE WAS A HERO HEROES ALWAY THINK THEY'RE GONNA WIN.
"THE REST OF US, THE LITTLE PEOPLE WHO HAD TO DODGE THE FALLING BUILDINGS AND HEAT VISION...
ANYONE ELSE?
CYBORG, RAVEN, TAKE CONTROL OF ALL MEDIA BROADCASTS. I WANT THEM TO SEE THIS.
WONDER WOMAN, HAWKGIRL, ADAM. YOU'RE WITH ME.
SINESTRO. PREPARE YOUR GROUND FORCES.
LANTERN, FLASH, PREPARE DOOMSDAY.
"...WE LIVED KNOWING WE WERE POWERLESS. WE COULD DIE ANY SECOND. IT'S A LOUSY WAY TO LIVE.
"BUT EVEN IF IT KILLED ME, I WAS GONNA MAKE SURE SUPES KNEW WHAT THAT FELT LIKE."
WE'RE GOING TO SHOW THIS PLANET WHO'S IN CHARGE HERE.

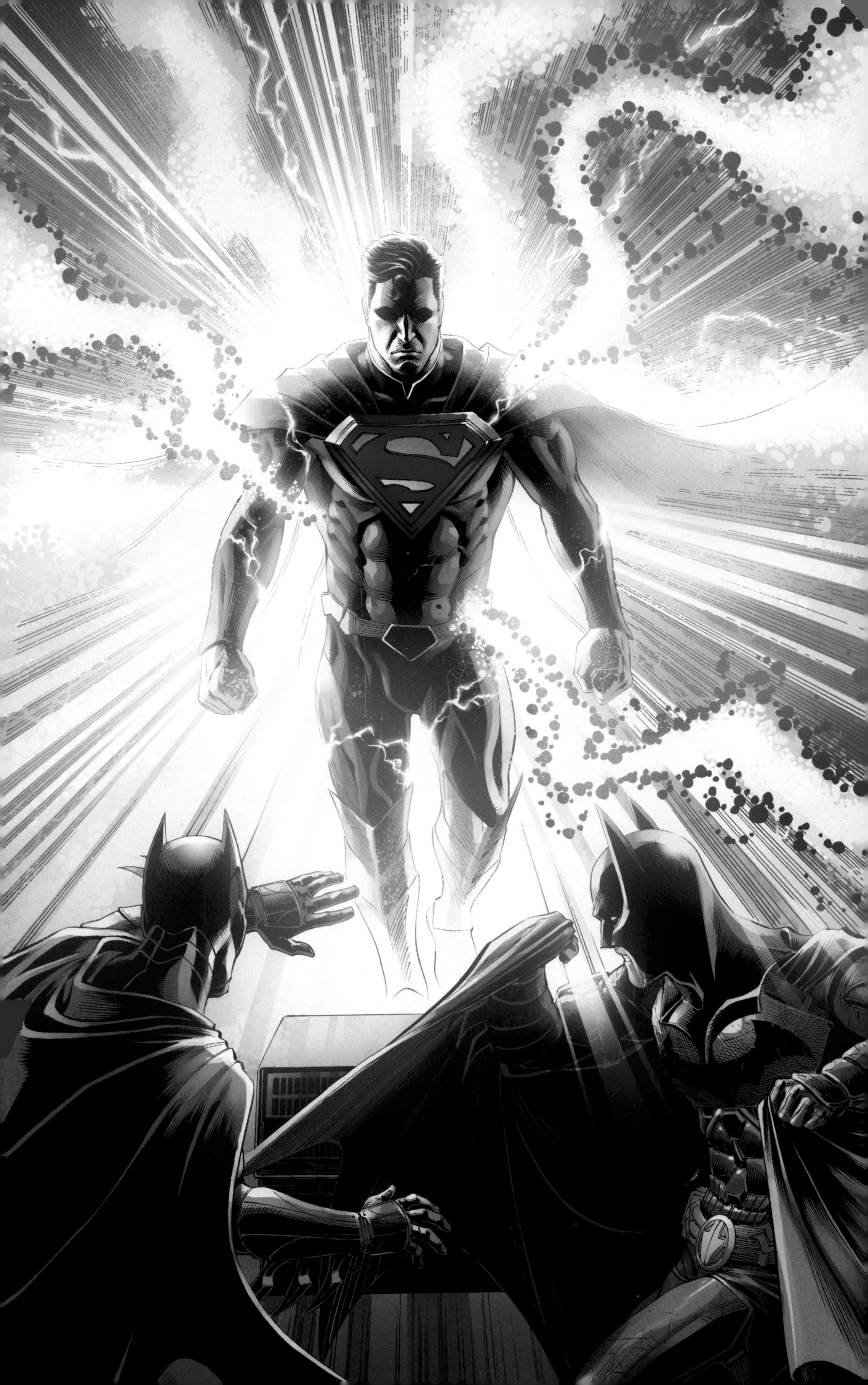

"Apocalypse Now-ish" **Marco Santucci** **Tom Derenick** Artists **J. Nanjan** Colorist
Cover art by **Mike S. Miller** and **J. Nanjan**

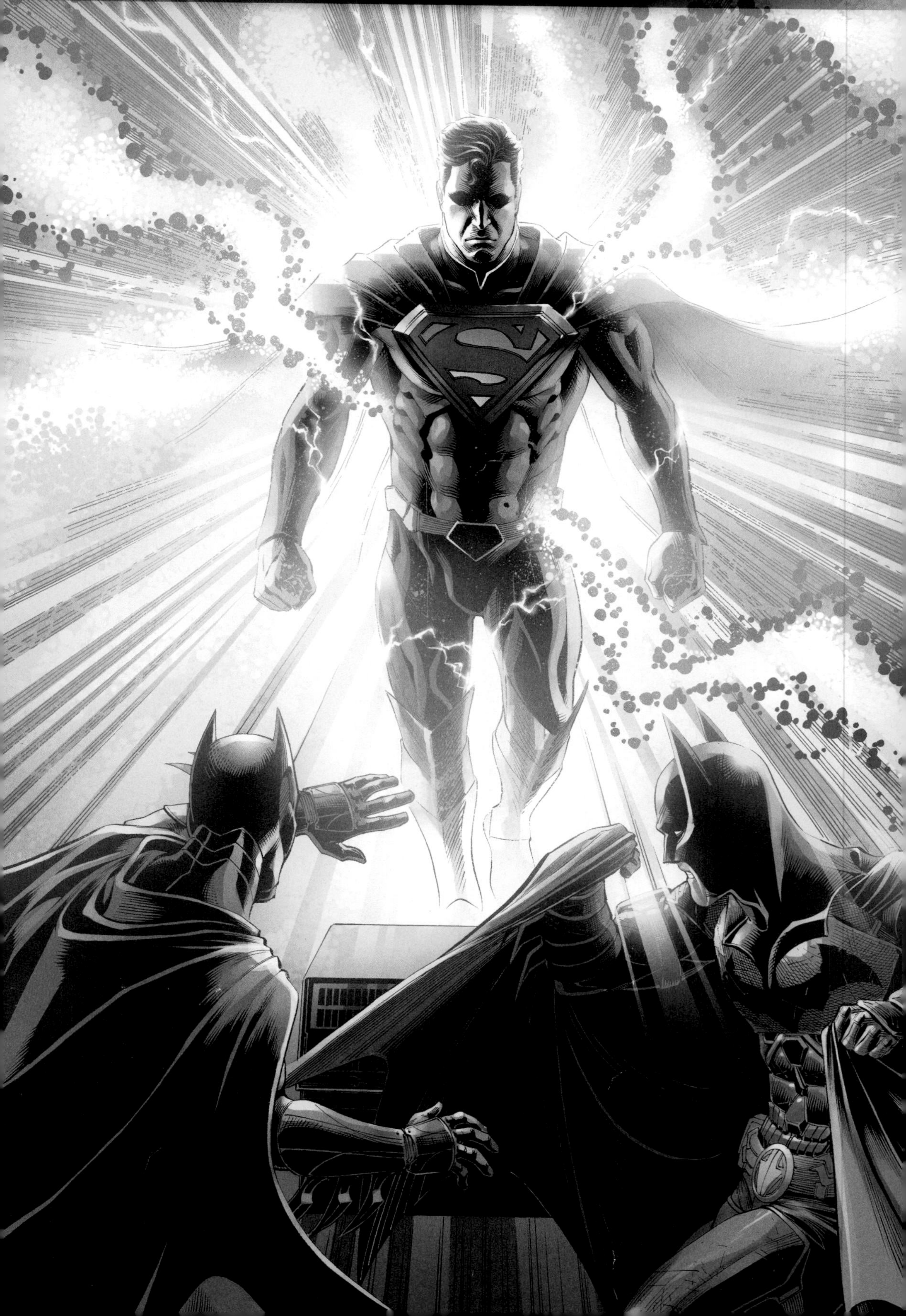

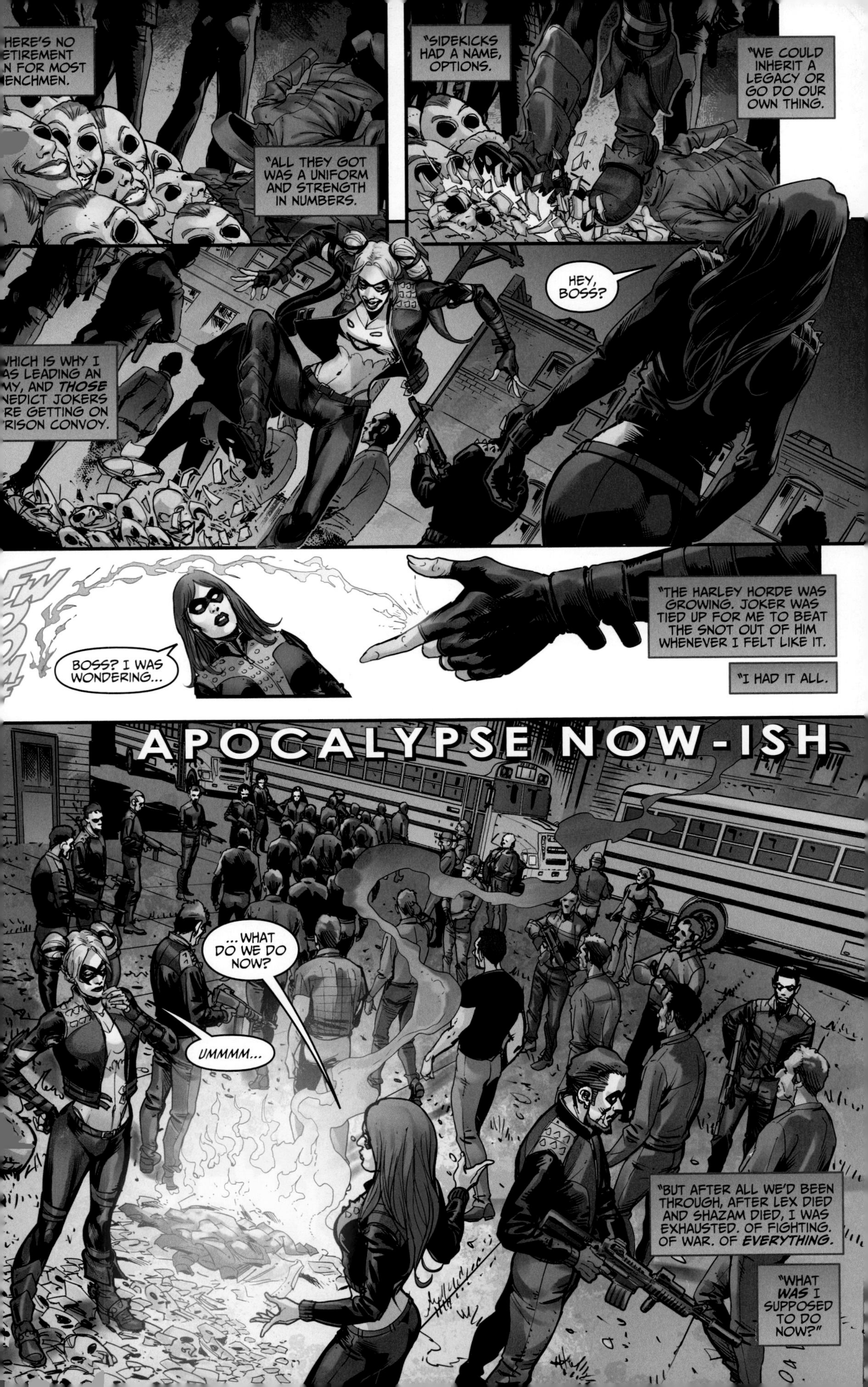

HERE'S NO ETIREMENT N FOR MOST ENCHMEN.
"ALL THEY GOT WAS A UNIFORM AND STRENGTH IN NUMBERS.
"SIDEKICKS HAD A NAME, OPTIONS.
"WE COULD INHERIT A LEGACY OR GO DO OUR OWN THING.
HICH IS WHY I AS LEADING AN MY, AND *THOSE* NEDICT JOKERS RE GETTING ON RISON CONVOY.
HEY, BOSS?
BOSS? I WAS WONDERING...
"THE HARLEY HORDE WAS GROWING. JOKER WAS TIED UP FOR ME TO BEAT THE SNOT OUT OF HIM WHENEVER I FELT LIKE IT.
"I HAD IT ALL.
APOCALYPSE NOW-ISH
...WHAT DO WE DO NOW?
UMMMM...
"BUT AFTER ALL WE'D BEEN THROUGH, AFTER LEX DIED AND SHAZAM DIED, I WAS EXHAUSTED. OF FIGHTING. OF WAR. OF *EVERYTHING*.
"WHAT *WAS* I SUPPOSED TO DO NOW?"

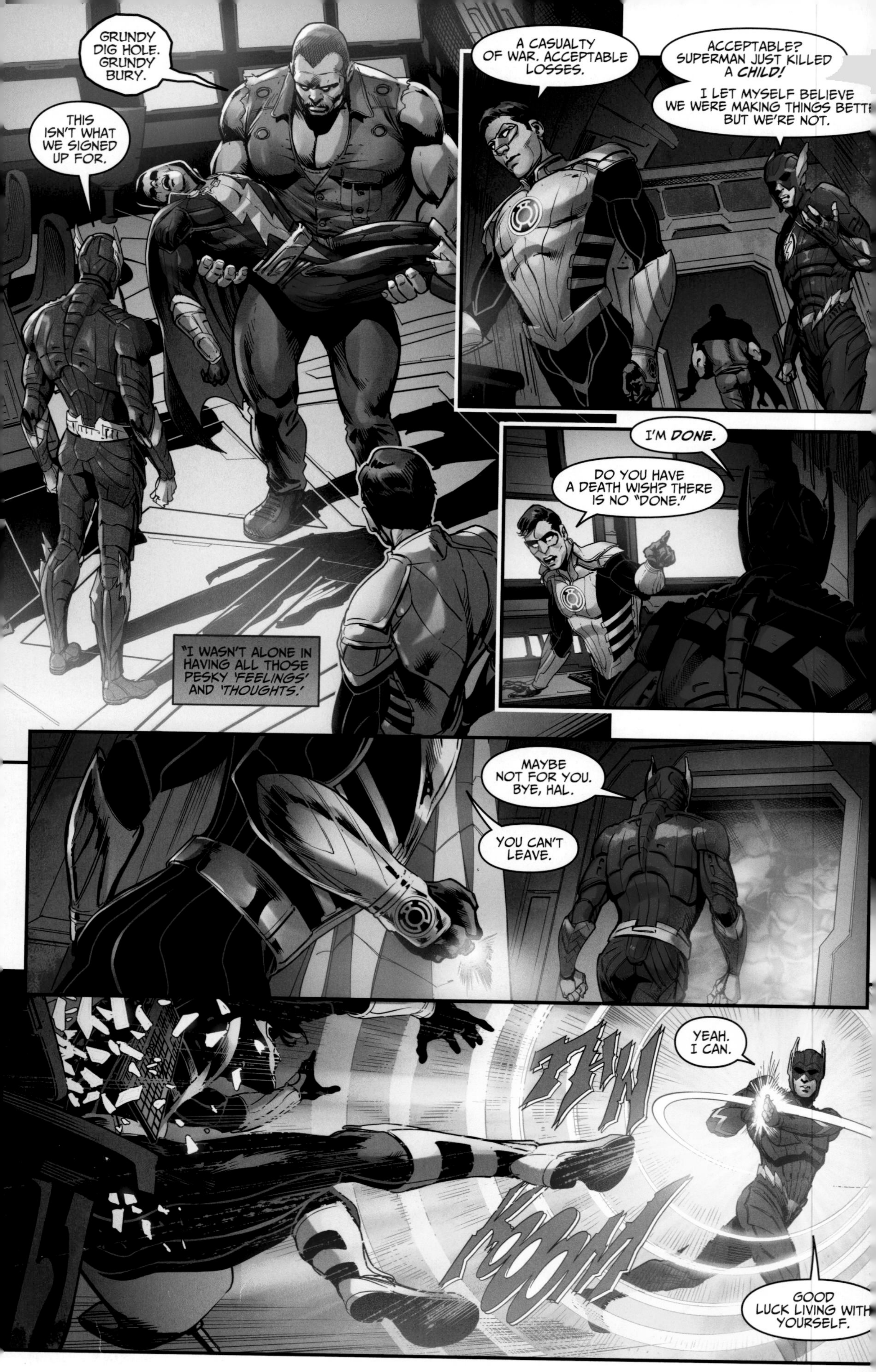
GRUNDY DIG HOLE. GRUNDY BURY.
THIS ISN'T WHAT WE SIGNED UP FOR.
A CASUALTY OF WAR. ACCEPTABLE LOSSES.
ACCEPTABLE? SUPERMAN JUST KILLED A CHILD!
I LET MYSELF BELIEVE WE WERE MAKING THINGS BETT BUT WE'RE NOT.
I'M DONE.
DO YOU HAVE A DEATH WISH? THERE IS NO "DONE."
"I WASN'T ALONE IN HAVING ALL THOSE PESKY 'FEELINGS' AND 'THOUGHTS.'
MAYBE NOT FOR YOU. BYE, HAL.
YOU CAN'T LEAVE.
YEAH. I CAN.
FZWM
KRAKOOM
GOOD LUCK LIVING WITH YOURSELF.

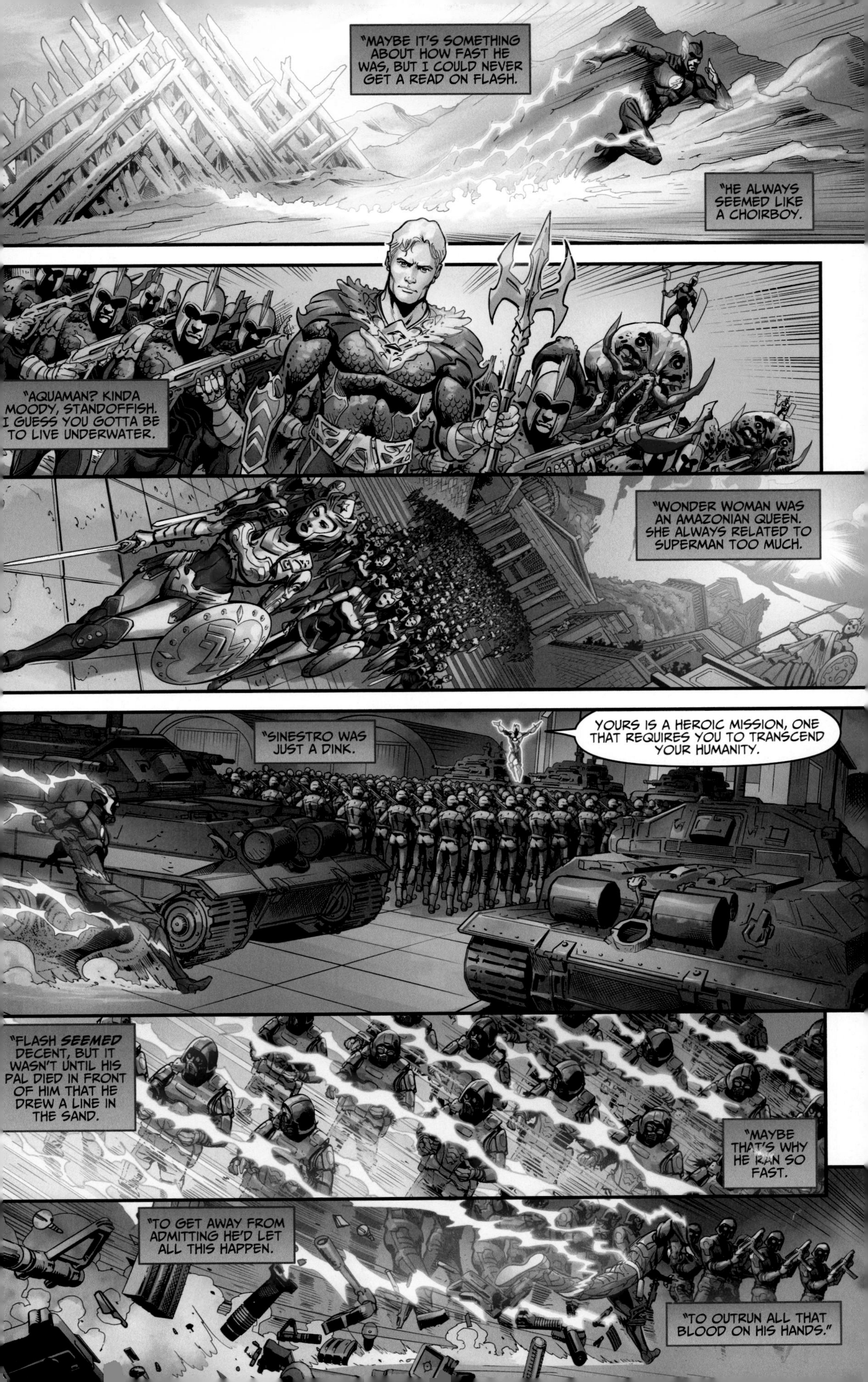
"MAYBE IT'S SOMETHING ABOUT HOW FAST HE WAS, BUT I COULD NEVER GET A READ ON FLASH.
"HE ALWAYS SEEMED LIKE A CHOIRBOY.
"AQUAMAN? KINDA MOODY, STANDOFFISH. I GUESS YOU GOTTA BE TO LIVE UNDERWATER.
"WONDER WOMAN WAS AN AMAZONIAN QUEEN. SHE ALWAYS RELATED TO SUPERMAN TOO MUCH.
"SINESTRO WAS JUST A DINK.
YOURS IS A HEROIC MISSION, ONE THAT REQUIRES YOU TO TRANSCEND YOUR HUMANITY.
"FLASH *SEEMED* DECENT, BUT IT WASN'T UNTIL HIS PAL DIED IN FRONT OF HIM THAT HE DREW A LINE IN THE SAND.
"MAYBE THAT'S WHY HE RAN SO FAST.
"TO GET AWAY FROM ADMITTING HE'D LET ALL THIS HAPPEN.
"TO OUTRUN ALL THAT BLOOD ON HIS HANDS."

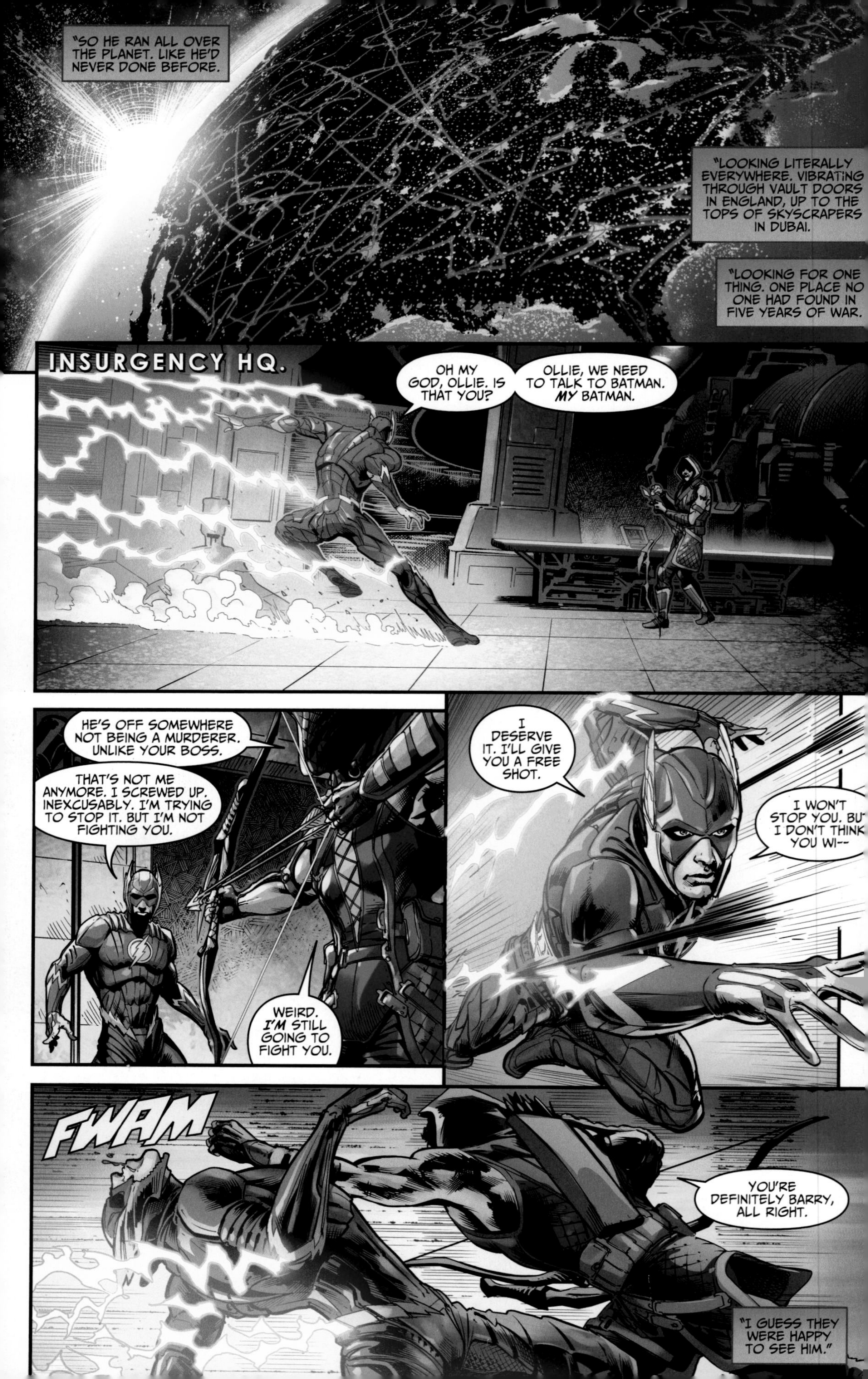

"SO HE RAN ALL OVER THE PLANET. LIKE HE'D NEVER DONE BEFORE.
"LOOKING LITERALLY EVERYWHERE. VIBRATING THROUGH VAULT DOORS IN ENGLAND, UP TO THE TOPS OF SKYSCRAPERS IN DUBAI.
"LOOKING FOR ONE THING. ONE PLACE NO ONE HAD FOUND IN FIVE YEARS OF WAR.
INSURGENCY HQ.
OH MY GOD, OLLIE. IS THAT YOU?
OLLIE, WE NEED TO TALK TO BATMAN. *MY* BATMAN.
HE'S OFF SOMEWHERE NOT BEING A MURDERER. UNLIKE YOUR BOSS.
THAT'S NOT ME ANYMORE. I SCREWED UP. INEXCUSABLY. I'M TRYING TO STOP IT. BUT I'M NOT FIGHTING YOU.
WEIRD. *I'M* STILL GOING TO FIGHT YOU.
I DESERVE IT. I'LL GIVE YOU A FREE SHOT.
I WON'T STOP YOU. BU' I DON'T THINK YOU WI--
FWAM
YOU'RE DEFINITELY BARRY, ALL RIGHT.
"I GUESS THEY WERE HAPPY TO SEE HIM."

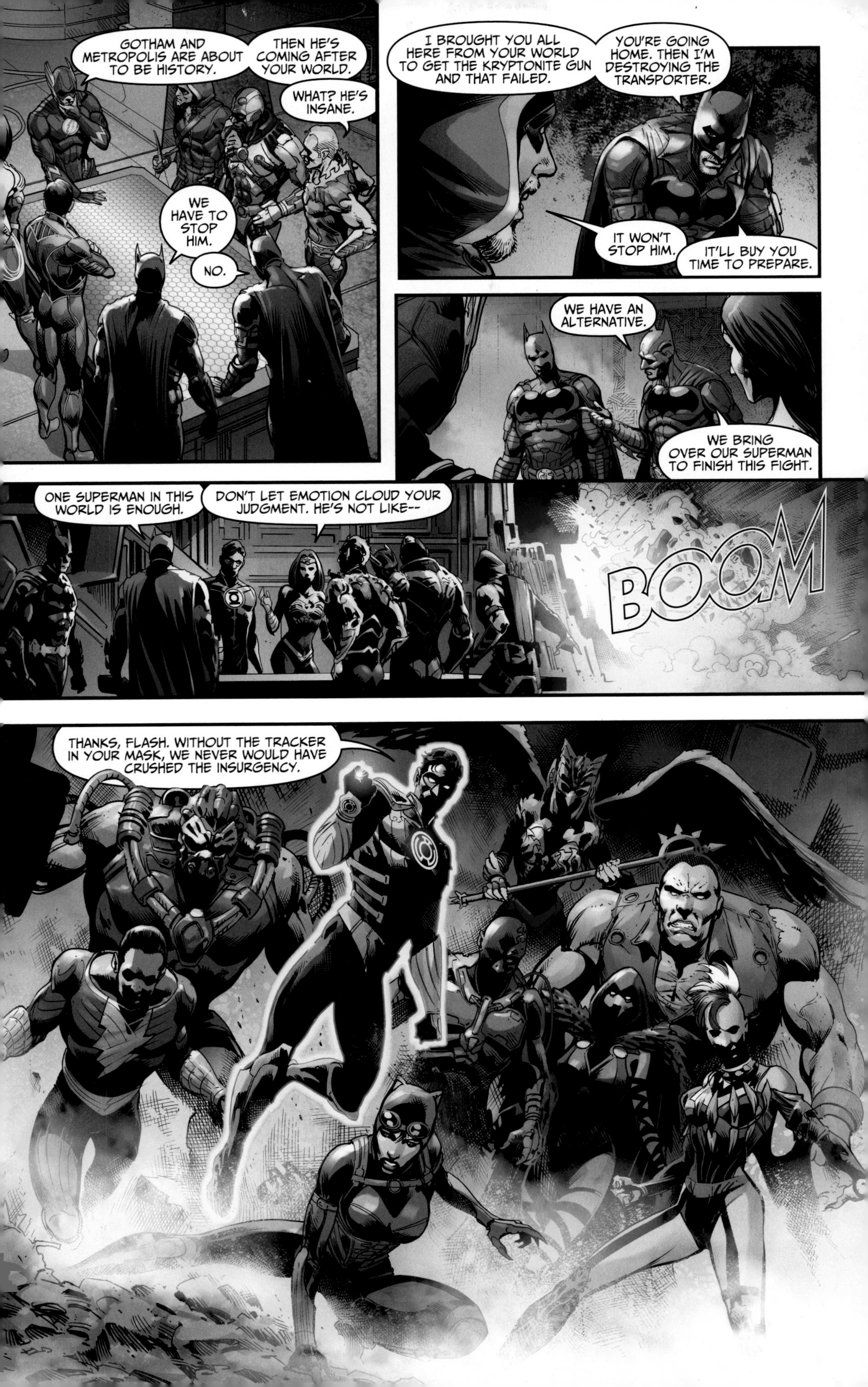
GOTHAM AND METROPOLIS ARE ABOUT TO BE HISTORY.
THEN HE'S COMING AFTER YOUR WORLD.
WHAT? HE'S INSANE.
WE HAVE TO STOP HIM.
NO.
I BROUGHT YOU ALL HERE FROM YOUR WORLD TO GET THE KRYPTONITE GUN AND THAT FAILED.
YOU'RE GOING HOME. THEN I'M DESTROYING THE TRANSPORTER.
IT WON'T STOP HIM.
IT'LL BUY YOU TIME TO PREPARE.
WE HAVE AN ALTERNATIVE.
WE BRING OVER OUR SUPERMAN TO FINISH THIS FIGHT.
ONE SUPERMAN IN THIS WORLD IS ENOUGH.
DON'T LET EMOTION CLOUD YOUR JUDGMENT. HE'S NOT LIKE--
BOOM
THANKS, FLASH. WITHOUT THE TRACKER IN YOUR MASK, WE NEVER WOULD HAVE CRUSHED THE INSURGENCY.

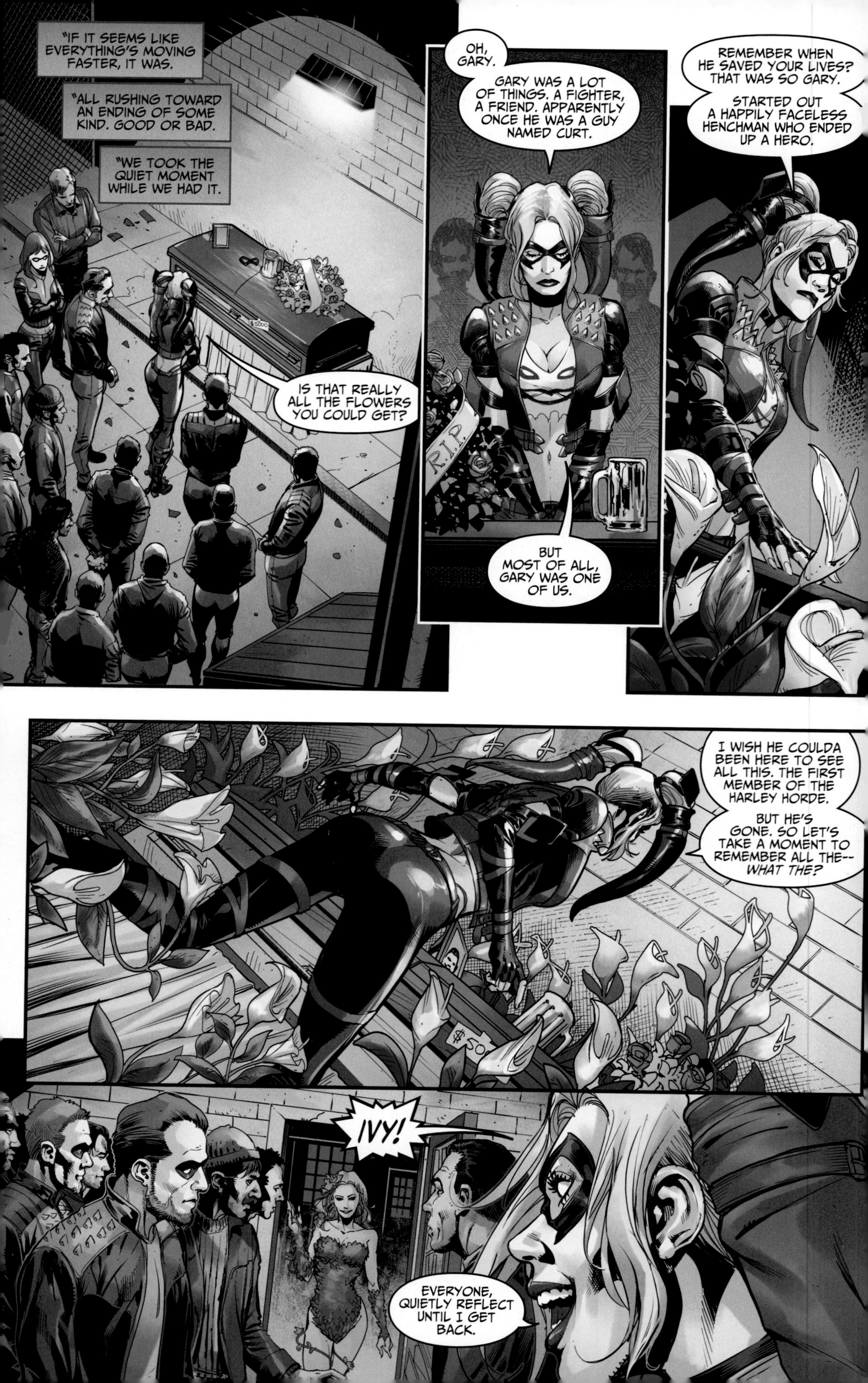
"IF IT SEEMS LIKE EVERYTHING'S MOVING FASTER, IT WAS.
"ALL RUSHING TOWARD AN ENDING OF SOME KIND. GOOD OR BAD.
"WE TOOK THE QUIET MOMENT WHILE WE HAD IT.
IS THAT REALLY ALL THE FLOWERS YOU COULD GET?
OH, GARY.
GARY WAS A LOT OF THINGS. A FIGHTER, A FRIEND. APPARENTLY ONCE HE WAS A GUY NAMED CURT.
R.I.P.
BUT MOST OF ALL, GARY WAS ONE OF US.
REMEMBER WHEN HE SAVED YOUR LIVES? THAT WAS SO GARY.
STARTED OUT A HAPPILY FACELESS HENCHMAN WHO ENDED UP A HERO.
I WISH HE COULDA BEEN HERE TO SEE ALL THIS. THE FIRST MEMBER OF THE HARLEY HORDE.
BUT HE'S GONE. SO LET'S TAKE A MOMENT TO REMEMBER ALL THE-- *WHAT THE?*
IVY!
EVERYONE, QUIETLY REFLECT UNTIL I GET BACK.

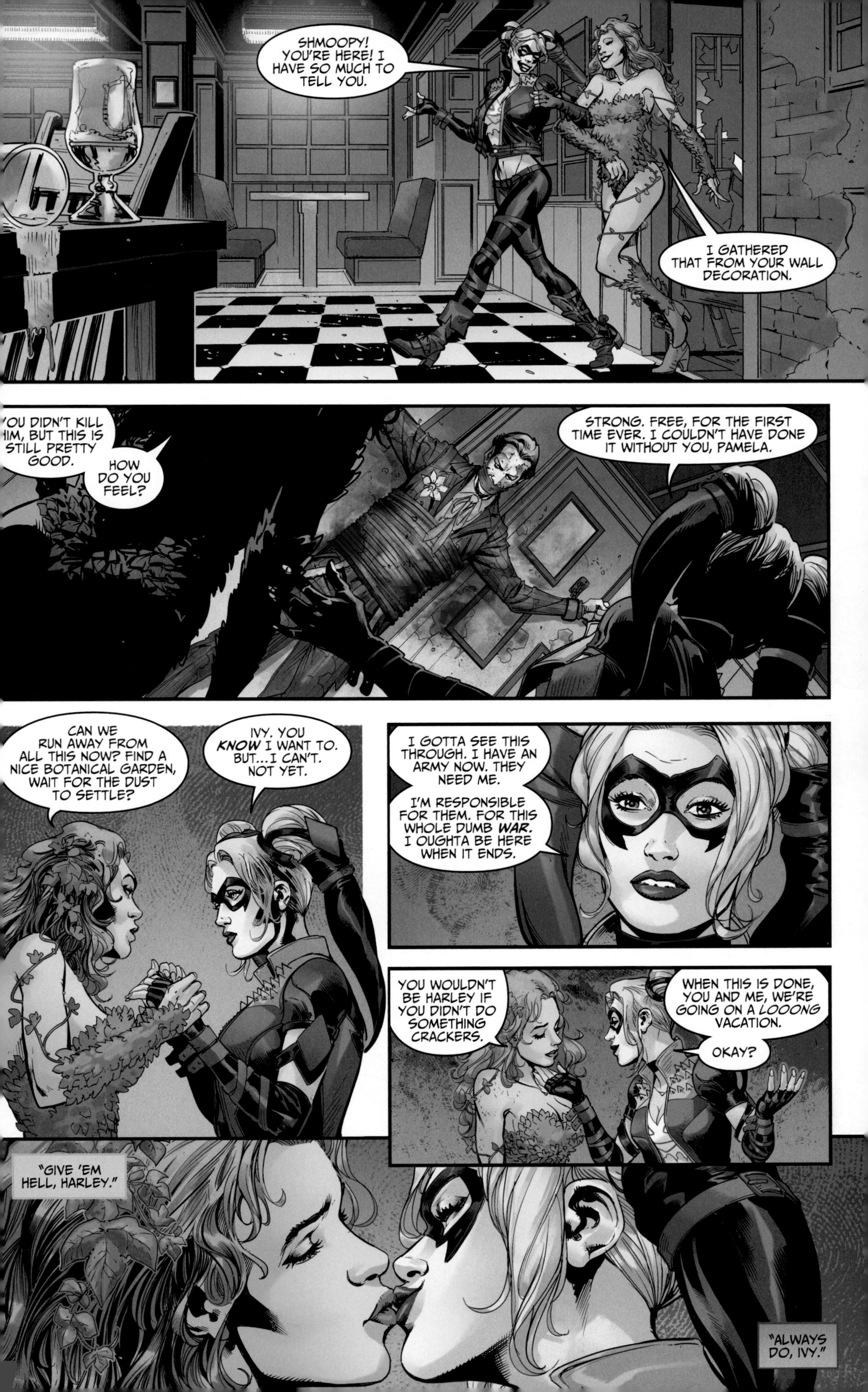

SHMOOPY! YOU'RE HERE! I HAVE SO MUCH TO TELL YOU.
I GATHERED THAT FROM YOUR WALL DECORATION.
YOU DIDN'T KILL HIM, BUT THIS IS STILL PRETTY GOOD.
HOW DO YOU FEEL?
STRONG. FREE, FOR THE FIRST TIME EVER. I COULDN'T HAVE DONE IT WITHOUT YOU, PAMELA.
CAN WE RUN AWAY FROM ALL THIS NOW? FIND A NICE BOTANICAL GARDEN, WAIT FOR THE DUST TO SETTLE?
IVY. YOU *KNOW* I WANT TO. BUT...I CAN'T. NOT YET.
I GOTTA SEE THIS THROUGH. I HAVE AN ARMY NOW. THEY NEED ME.
I'M RESPONSIBLE FOR THEM. FOR THIS WHOLE DUMB *WAR.* I OUGHTA BE HERE WHEN IT ENDS.
YOU WOULDN'T BE HARLEY IF YOU DIDN'T DO SOMETHING CRACKERS.
WHEN THIS IS DONE, YOU AND ME, WE'RE GOING ON A *LOOONG* VACATION.
OKAY?
"GIVE 'EM HELL, HARLEY."
"ALWAYS DO, IVY."

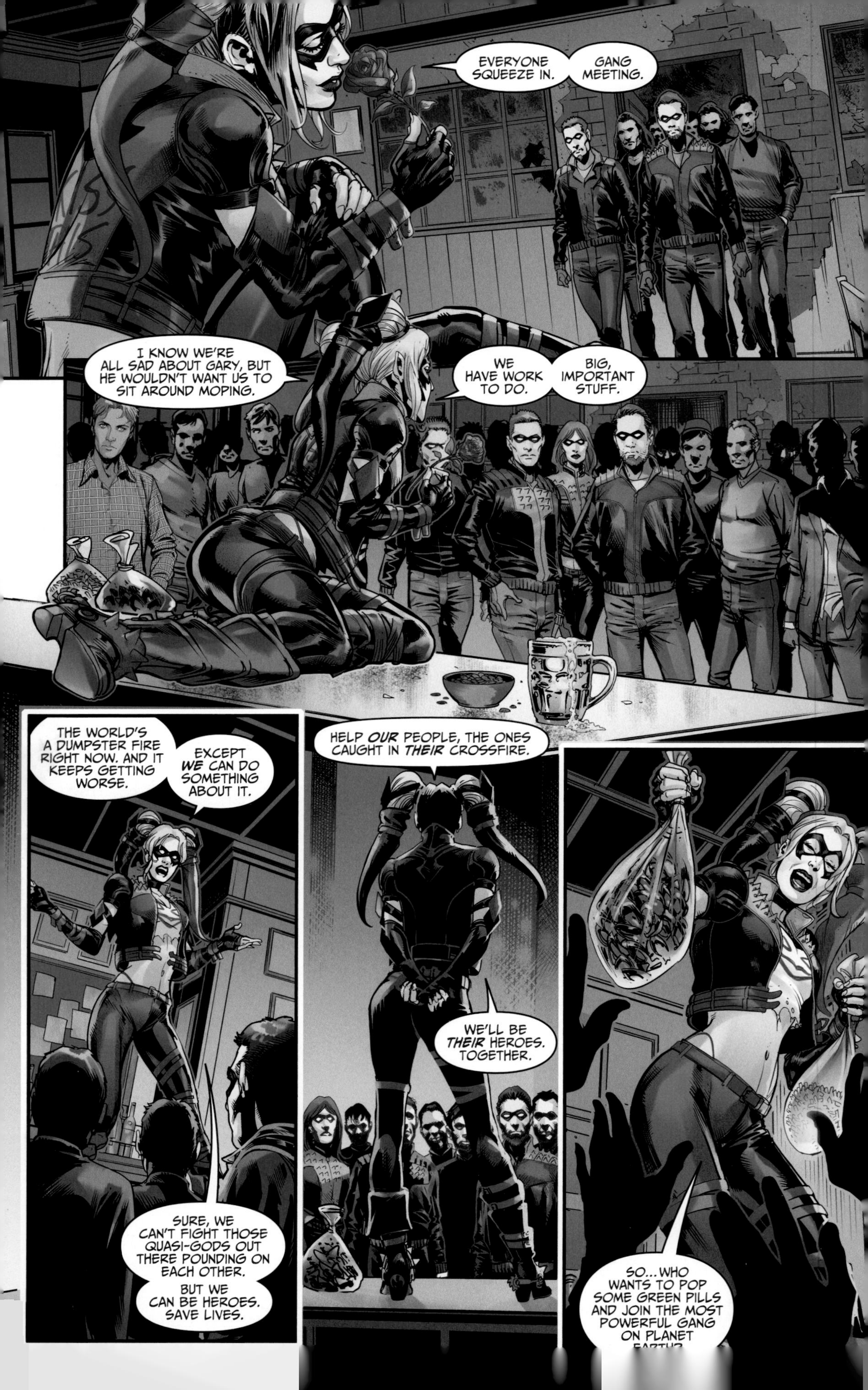
EVERYONE SQUEEZE IN.
GANG MEETING.
I KNOW WE'RE ALL SAD ABOUT GARY, BUT HE WOULDN'T WANT US TO SIT AROUND MOPING.
WE HAVE WORK TO DO.
BIG, IMPORTANT STUFF.
THE WORLD'S A DUMPSTER FIRE RIGHT NOW. AND IT KEEPS GETTING WORSE.
EXCEPT WE CAN DO SOMETHING ABOUT IT.
SURE, WE CAN'T FIGHT THOSE QUASI-GODS OUT THERE POUNDING ON EACH OTHER.
BUT WE CAN BE HEROES. SAVE LIVES.
HELP OUR PEOPLE, THE ONES CAUGHT IN THEIR CROSSFIRE.
WE'LL BE THEIR HEROES. TOGETHER.
SO...WHO WANTS TO POP SOME GREEN PILLS AND JOIN THE MOST POWERFUL GANG ON PLANET

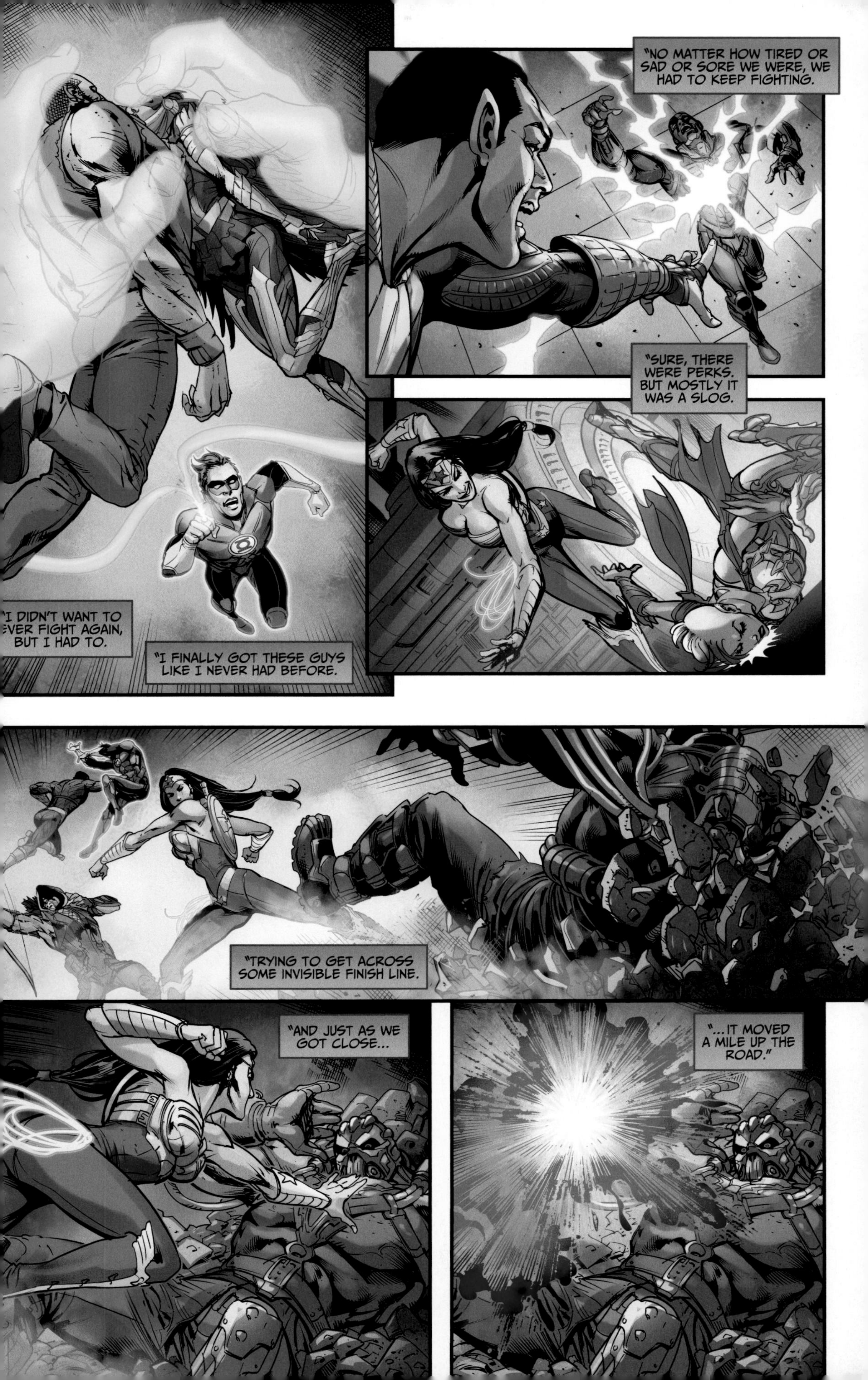

"NO MATTER HOW TIRED OR SAD OR SORE WE WERE, WE HAD TO KEEP FIGHTING.
"I DIDN'T WANT TO EVER FIGHT AGAIN, BUT I HAD TO.
"I FINALLY GOT THESE GUYS LIKE I NEVER HAD BEFORE.
"SURE, THERE WERE PERKS. BUT MOSTLY IT WAS A SLOG.
"TRYING TO GET ACROSS SOME INVISIBLE FINISH LINE.
"AND JUST AS WE GOT CLOSE...
"...IT MOVED A MILE UP THE ROAD."

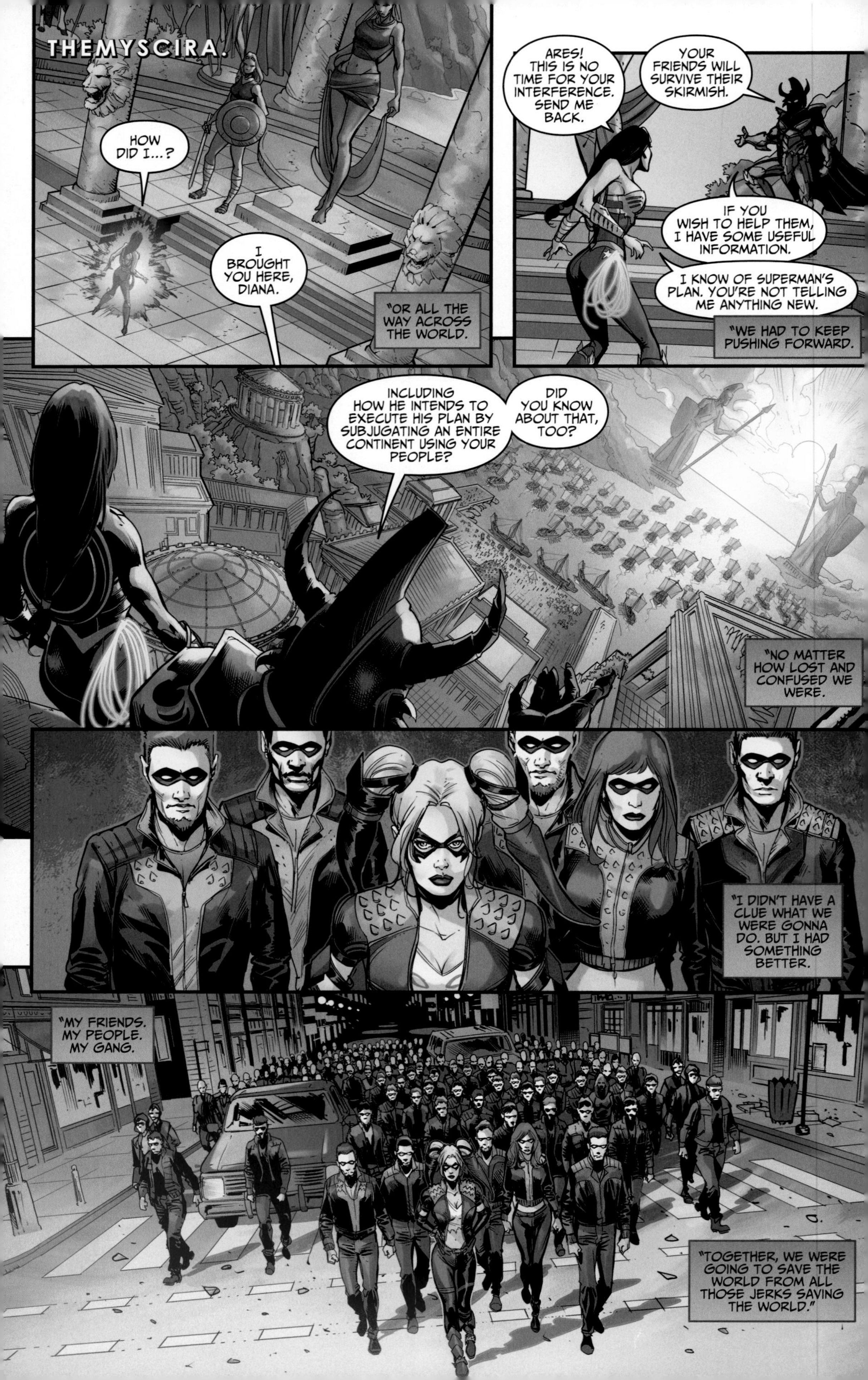
THEMYSCIRA.
HOW DID I...?
I BROUGHT YOU HERE, DIANA.
"OR ALL THE WAY ACROSS THE WORLD.
ARES! THIS IS NO TIME FOR YOUR INTERFERENCE. SEND ME BACK.
YOUR FRIENDS WILL SURVIVE THEIR SKIRMISH.
IF YOU WISH TO HELP THEM, I HAVE SOME USEFUL INFORMATION.
I KNOW OF SUPERMAN'S PLAN. YOU'RE NOT TELLING ME ANYTHING NEW.
"WE HAD TO KEEP PUSHING FORWARD.
INCLUDING HOW HE INTENDS TO EXECUTE HIS PLAN BY SUBJUGATING AN ENTIRE CONTINENT USING YOUR PEOPLE?
DID YOU KNOW ABOUT THAT, TOO?
"NO MATTER HOW LOST AND CONFUSED WE WERE.
"I DIDN'T HAVE A CLUE WHAT WE WERE GONNA DO. BUT I HAD SOMETHING BETTER.
"MY FRIENDS. MY PEOPLE. MY GANG.
"TOGETHER, WE WERE GOING TO SAVE THE WORLD FROM ALL THOSE JERKS SAVING THE WORLD."

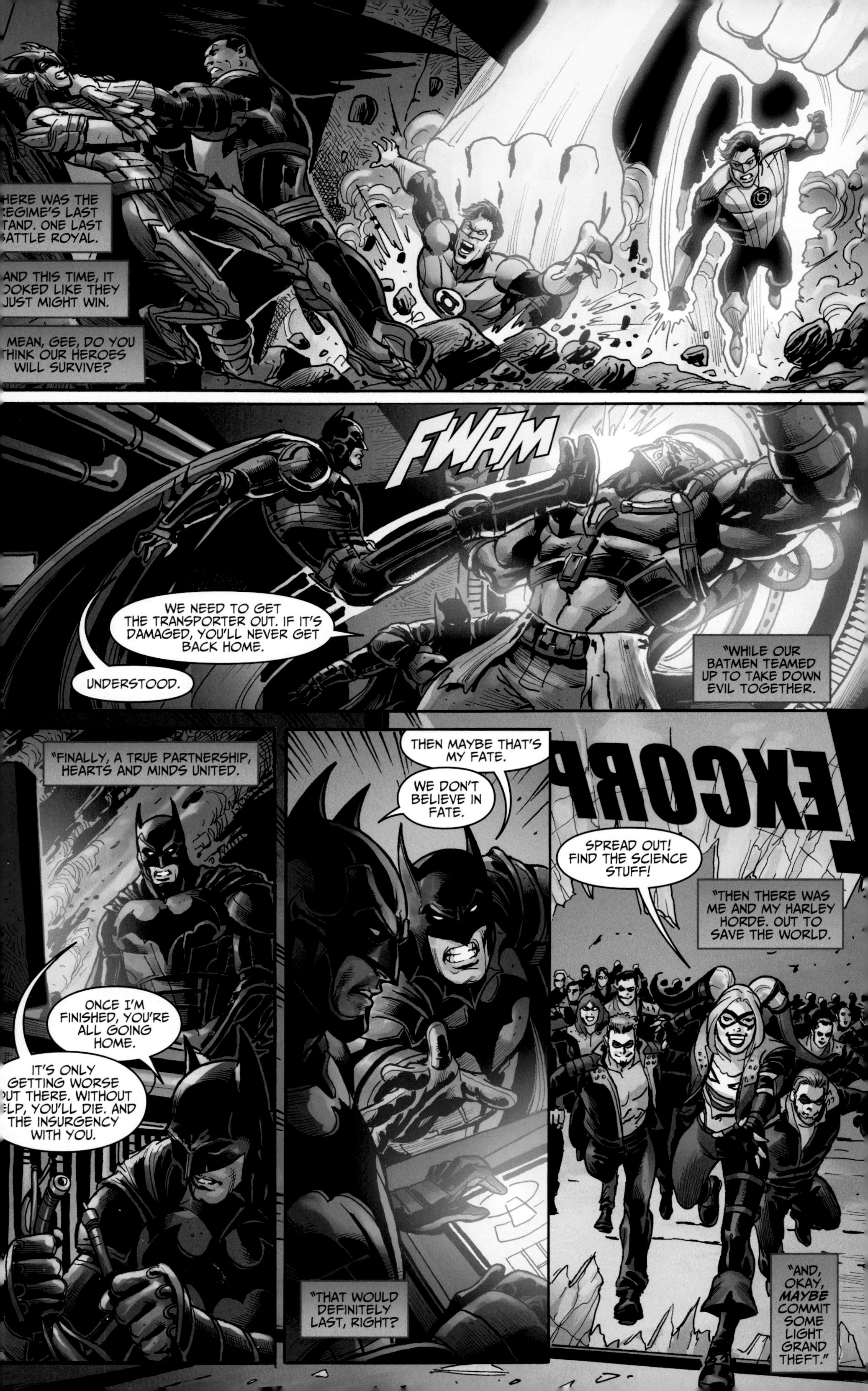
HERE WAS THE REGIME'S LAST STAND. ONE LAST BATTLE ROYAL.
AND THIS TIME, IT LOOKED LIKE THEY JUST MIGHT WIN.
MEAN, GEE, DO YOU THINK OUR HEROES WILL SURVIVE?
FWAM
WE NEED TO GET THE TRANSPORTER OUT. IF IT'S DAMAGED, YOU'LL NEVER GET BACK HOME.
UNDERSTOOD.
"WHILE OUR BATMEN TEAMED UP TO TAKE DOWN EVIL TOGETHER.
"FINALLY, A TRUE PARTNERSHIP, HEARTS AND MINDS UNITED.
ONCE I'M FINISHED, YOU'RE ALL GOING HOME.
IT'S ONLY GETTING WORSE OUT THERE. WITHOUT HELP, YOU'LL DIE. AND THE INSURGENCY WITH YOU.
THEN MAYBE THAT'S MY FATE.
WE DON'T BELIEVE IN FATE.
"THAT WOULD DEFINITELY LAST, RIGHT?
EXCORP
SPREAD OUT! FIND THE SCIENCE STUFF!
"THEN THERE WAS ME AND MY HARLEY HORDE. OUT TO SAVE THE WORLD.
"AND, OKAY, *MAYBE* COMMIT SOME LIGHT GRAND THEFT."

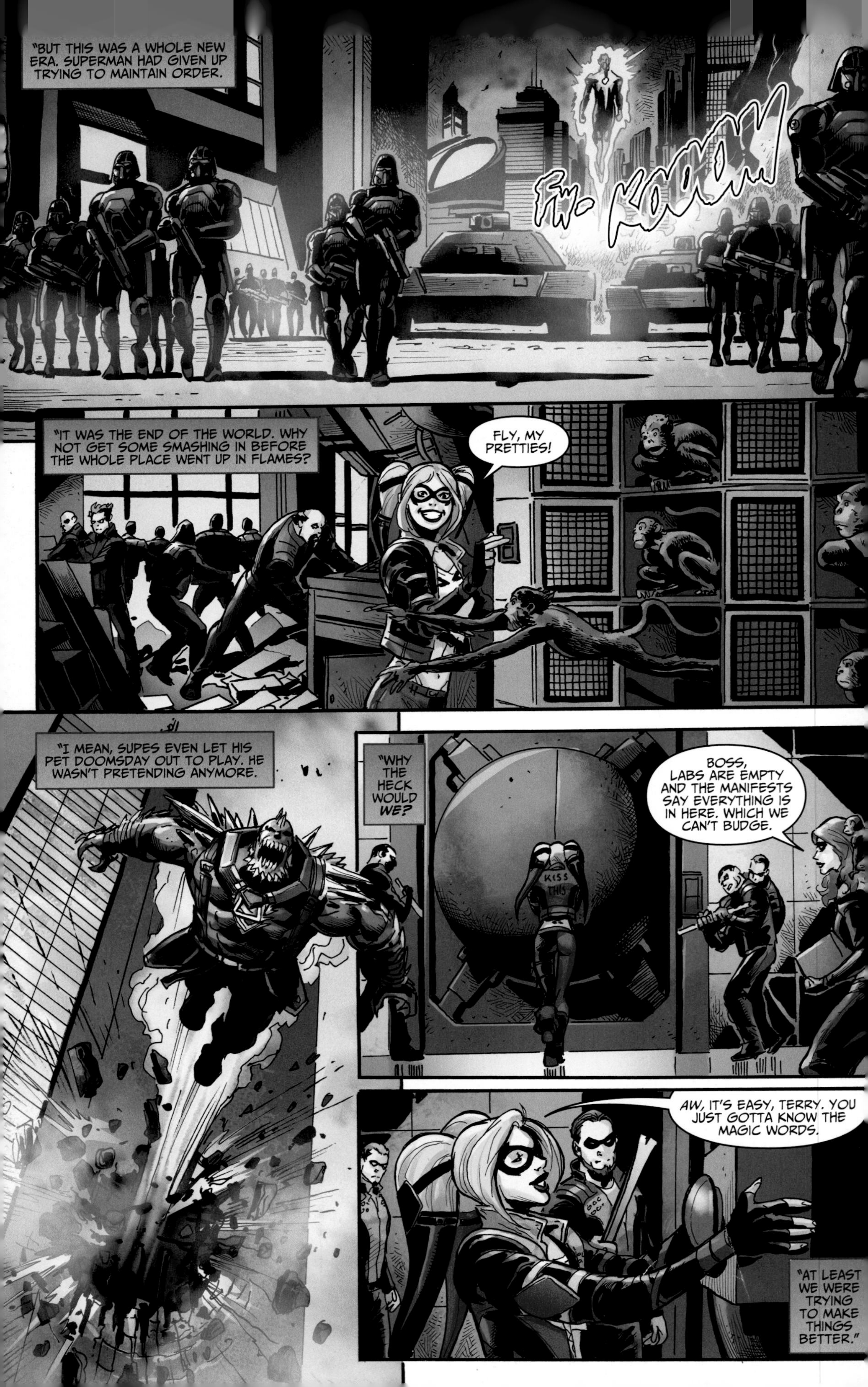
"BUT THIS WAS A WHOLE NEW ERA. SUPERMAN HAD GIVEN UP TRYING TO MAINTAIN ORDER.
FW-KOOOM
"IT WAS THE END OF THE WORLD. WHY NOT GET SOME SMASHING IN BEFORE THE WHOLE PLACE WENT UP IN FLAMES?
FLY, MY PRETTIES!
"I MEAN, SUPES EVEN LET HIS PET DOOMSDAY OUT TO PLAY. HE WASN'T PRETENDING ANYMORE.
"WHY THE HECK WOULD *WE*?
BOSS, LABS ARE EMPTY AND THE MANIFESTS SAY EVERYTHING IS IN HERE. WHICH WE CAN'T BUDGE.
KISS THIS
AW, IT'S EASY, TERRY. YOU JUST GOTTA KNOW THE MAGIC WORDS.
"AT LEAST WE WERE TRYING TO MAKE THINGS BETTER."

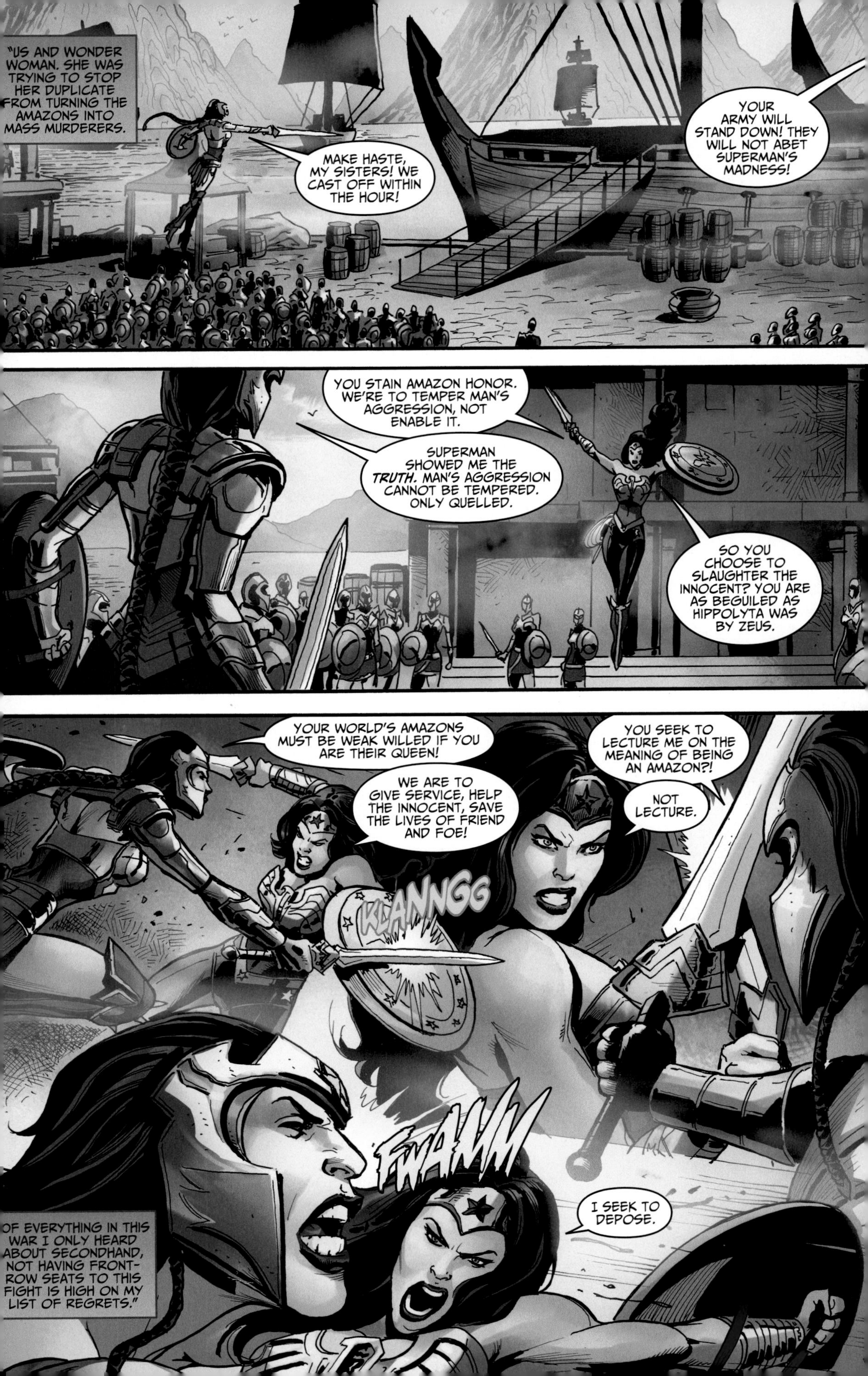
"US AND WONDER WOMAN. SHE WAS TRYING TO STOP HER DUPLICATE FROM TURNING THE AMAZONS INTO MASS MURDERERS.
MAKE HASTE, MY SISTERS! WE CAST OFF WITHIN THE HOUR!
YOUR ARMY WILL STAND DOWN! THEY WILL NOT ABET SUPERMAN'S MADNESS!
YOU STAIN AMAZON HONOR. WE'RE TO TEMPER MAN'S AGGRESSION, NOT ENABLE IT.
SUPERMAN SHOWED ME THE *TRUTH*. MAN'S AGGRESSION CANNOT BE TEMPERED. ONLY QUELLED.
SO YOU CHOOSE TO SLAUGHTER THE INNOCENT? YOU ARE AS BEGUILED AS HIPPOLYTA WAS BY ZEUS.
YOUR WORLD'S AMAZONS MUST BE WEAK WILLED IF YOU ARE THEIR QUEEN!
WE ARE TO GIVE SERVICE, HELP THE INNOCENT, SAVE THE LIVES OF FRIEND AND FOE!
YOU SEEK TO LECTURE ME ON THE MEANING OF BEING AN AMAZON?!
NOT LECTURE.
KLANNGG
FWAMM
I SEEK TO DEPOSE.
OF EVERYTHING IN THIS WAR I ONLY HEARD ABOUT SECONDHAND, NOT HAVING FRONT-ROW SEATS TO THIS FIGHT IS HIGH ON MY LIST OF REGRETS."

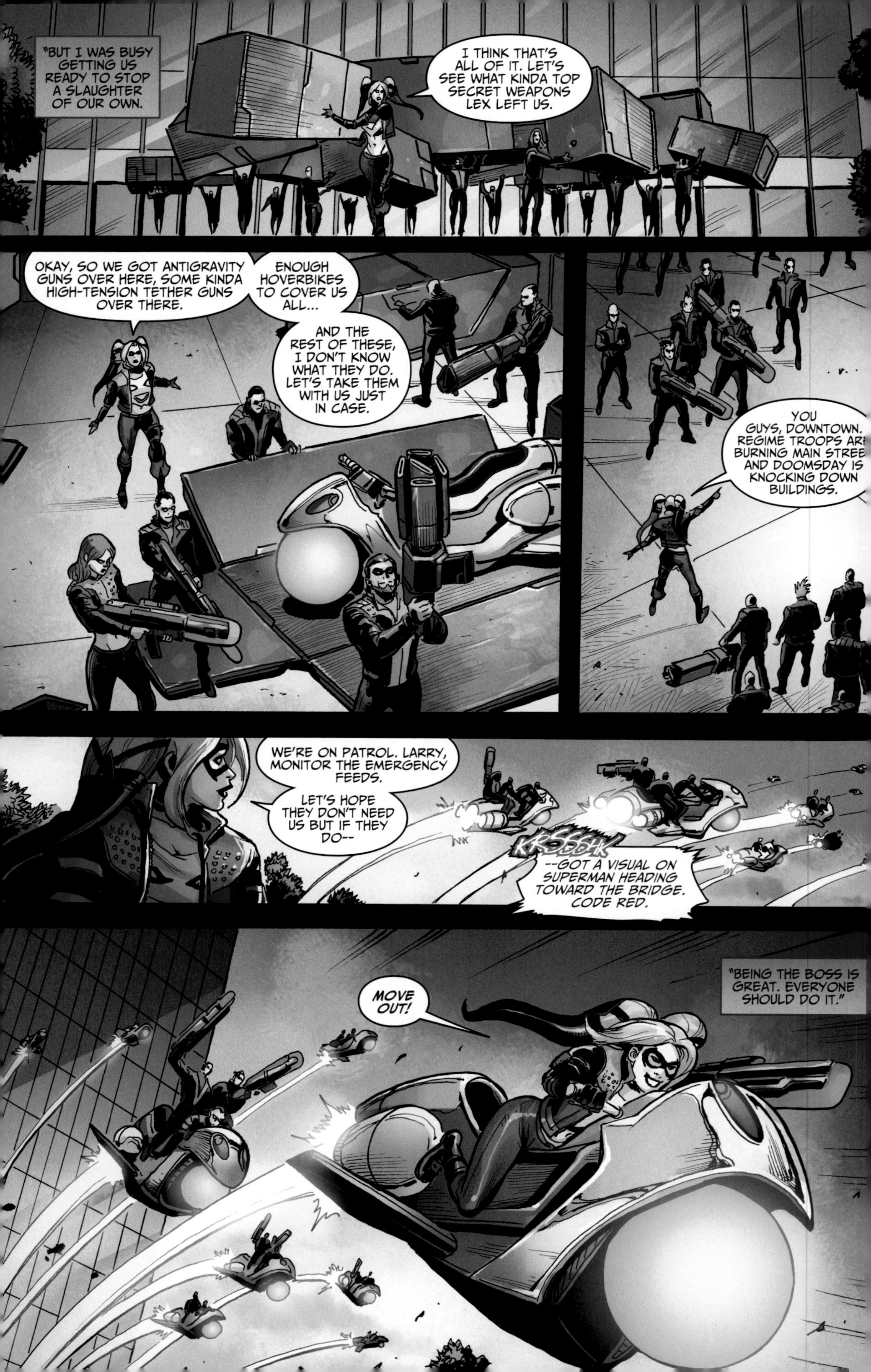
"BUT I WAS BUSY GETTING US READY TO STOP A SLAUGHTER OF OUR OWN.
I THINK THAT'S ALL OF IT. LET'S SEE WHAT KINDA TOP SECRET WEAPONS LEX LEFT US.
OKAY, SO WE GOT ANTIGRAVITY GUNS OVER HERE, SOME KINDA HIGH-TENSION TETHER GUNS OVER THERE.
ENOUGH HOVERBIKES TO COVER US ALL...
AND THE REST OF THESE, I DON'T KNOW WHAT THEY DO. LET'S TAKE THEM WITH US JUST IN CASE.
YOU GUYS, DOWNTOWN. REGIME TROOPS ARE BURNING MAIN STREET AND DOOMSDAY IS KNOCKING DOWN BUILDINGS.
WE'RE ON PATROL. LARRY, MONITOR THE EMERGENCY FEEDS.
LET'S HOPE THEY DON'T NEED US BUT IF THEY DO--
KRSSSHK
--GOT A VISUAL ON SUPERMAN HEADING TOWARD THE BRIDGE. CODE RED.
MOVE OUT!
"BEING THE BOSS IS GREAT. EVERYONE SHOULD DO IT."

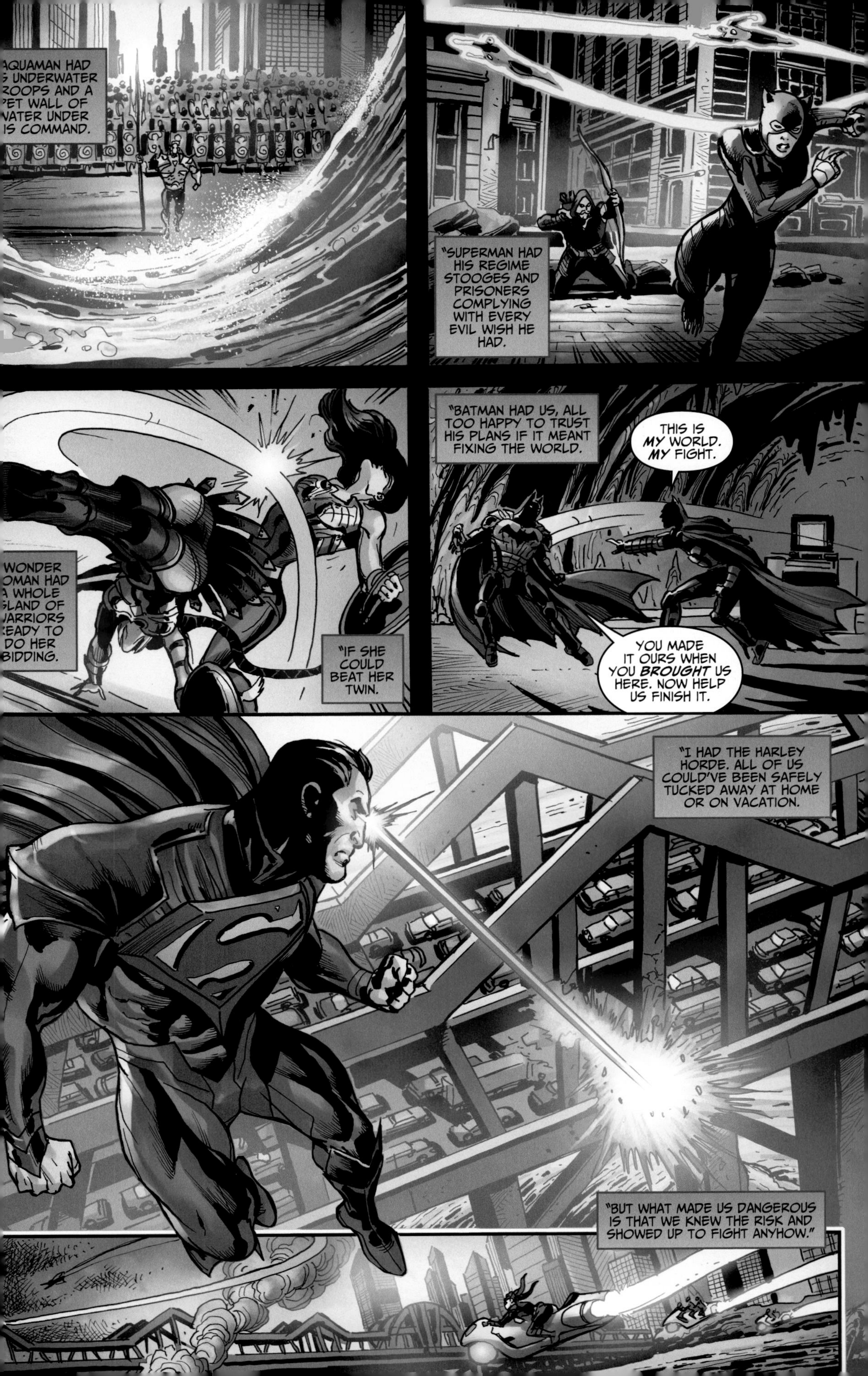

AQUAMAN HAD
S UNDERWATER
ROOPS AND A
PET WALL OF
WATER UNDER
IS COMMAND.
"SUPERMAN HAD HIS REGIME STOOGES AND PRISONERS COMPLYING WITH EVERY EVIL WISH HE HAD.
WONDER
OMAN HAD
A WHOLE
SLAND OF
WARRIORS
READY TO
DO HER
BIDDING.
"IF SHE COULD BEAT HER TWIN.
"BATMAN HAD US, ALL TOO HAPPY TO TRUST HIS PLANS IF IT MEANT FIXING THE WORLD.
THIS IS MY WORLD. MY FIGHT.
YOU MADE IT OURS WHEN YOU BROUGHT US HERE. NOW HELP US FINISH IT.
"I HAD THE HARLEY HORDE. ALL OF US COULD'VE BEEN SAFELY TUCKED AWAY AT HOME OR ON VACATION.
"BUT WHAT MADE US DANGEROUS IS THAT WE KNEW THE RISK AND SHOWED UP TO FIGHT ANYHOW."

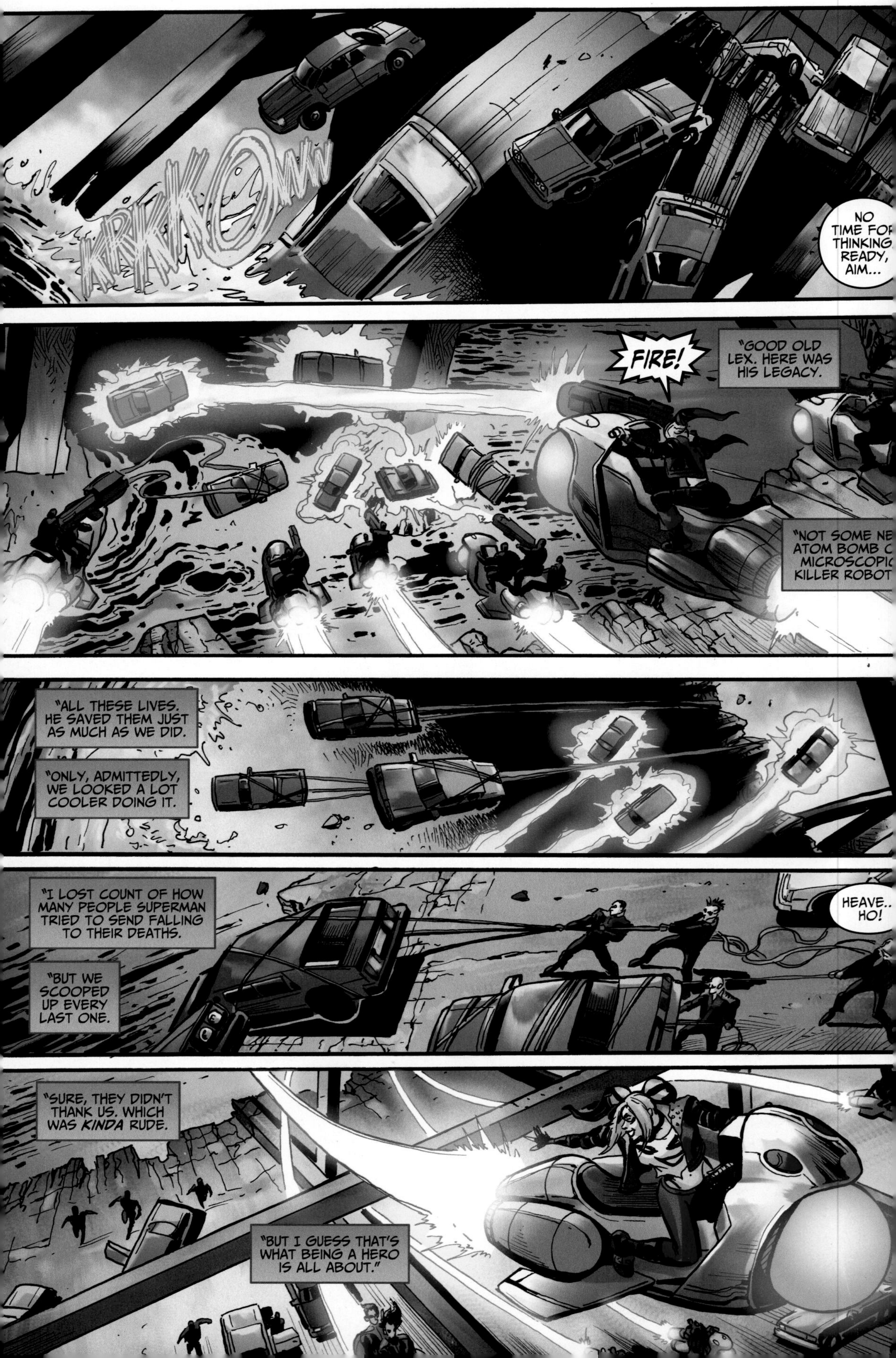
KRKKOWW
NO TIME FOR THINKING READY, AIM...
FIRE!
"GOOD OLD LEX. HERE WAS HIS LEGACY.
"NOT SOME NE ATOM BOMB C MICROSCOPIC KILLER ROBOT
"ALL THESE LIVES. HE SAVED THEM JUST AS MUCH AS WE DID.
"ONLY, ADMITTEDLY, WE LOOKED A LOT COOLER DOING IT.
"I LOST COUNT OF HOW MANY PEOPLE SUPERMAN TRIED TO SEND FALLING TO THEIR DEATHS.
"BUT WE SCOOPED UP EVERY LAST ONE.
HEAVE... HO!
"SURE, THEY DIDN'T THANK US. WHICH WAS *KINDA* RUDE.
"BUT I GUESS THAT'S WHAT BEING A HERO IS ALL ABOUT."

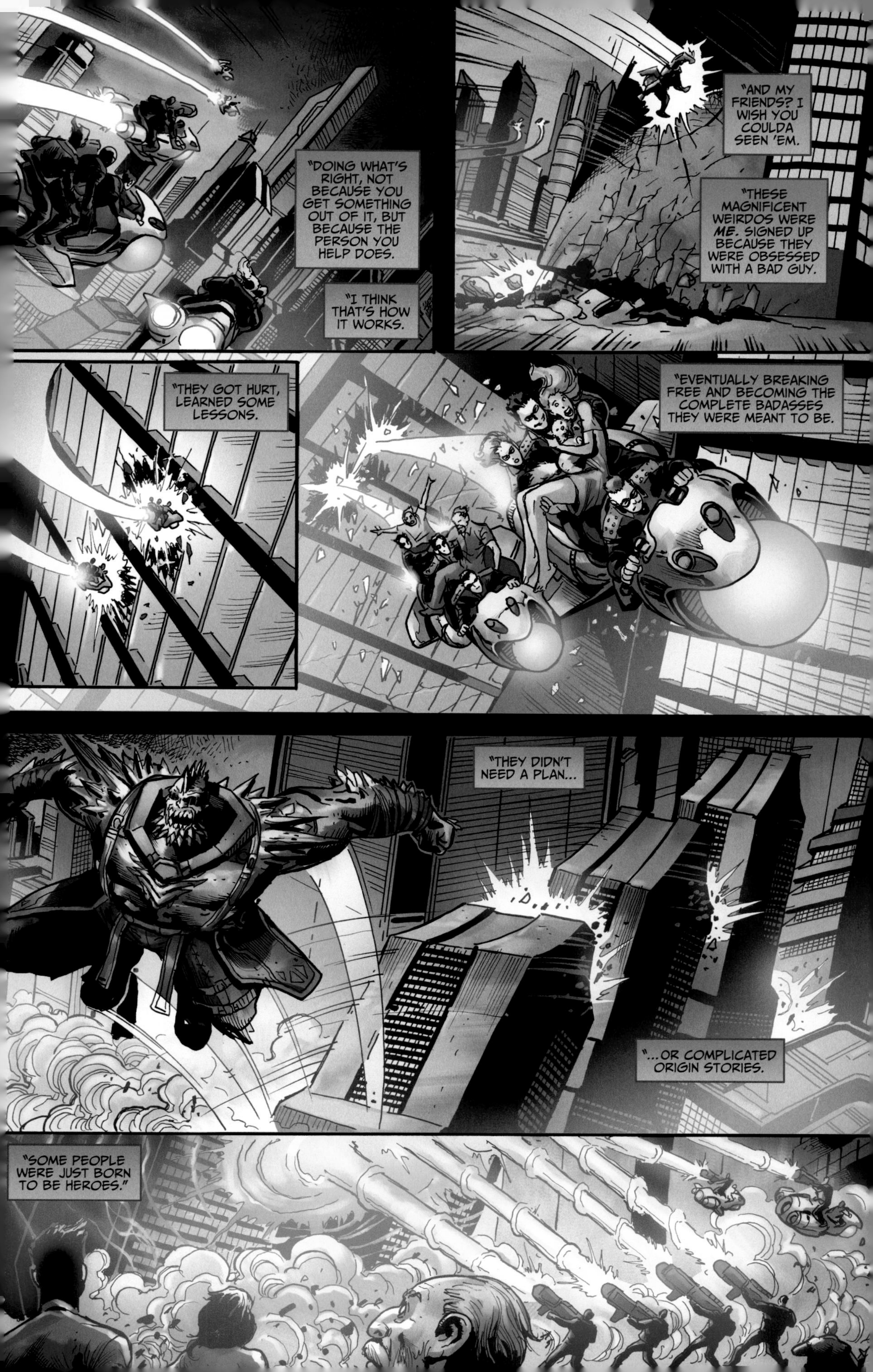
"DOING WHAT'S RIGHT, NOT BECAUSE YOU GET SOMETHING OUT OF IT, BUT BECAUSE THE PERSON YOU HELP DOES.
"I THINK THAT'S HOW IT WORKS.
"AND MY FRIENDS? I WISH YOU COULDA SEEN 'EM.
"THESE MAGNIFICENT WEIRDOS WERE ME. SIGNED UP BECAUSE THEY WERE OBSESSED WITH A BAD GUY.
"THEY GOT HURT, LEARNED SOME LESSONS.
"EVENTUALLY BREAKING FREE AND BECOMING THE COMPLETE BADASSES THEY WERE MEANT TO BE.
"THEY DIDN'T NEED A PLAN...
"...OR COMPLICATED ORIGIN STORIES.
"SOME PEOPLE WERE JUST BORN TO BE HEROES."

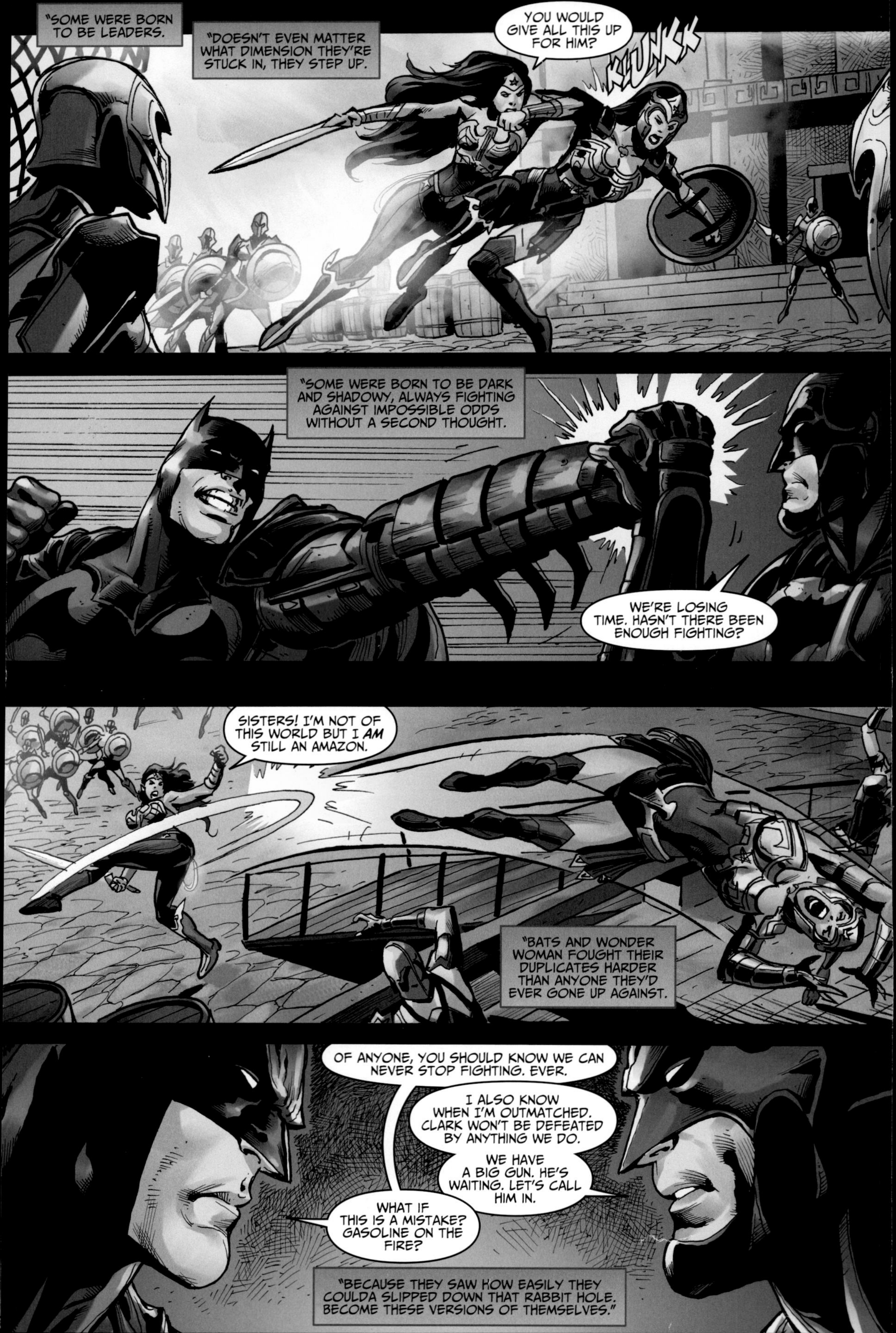
"SOME WERE BORN TO BE LEADERS.
"DOESN'T EVEN MATTER WHAT DIMENSION THEY'RE STUCK IN, THEY STEP UP.
YOU WOULD GIVE ALL THIS UP FOR HIM?
KLUNKK
"SOME WERE BORN TO BE DARK AND SHADOWY, ALWAYS FIGHTING AGAINST IMPOSSIBLE ODDS WITHOUT A SECOND THOUGHT.
WE'RE LOSING TIME. HASN'T THERE BEEN ENOUGH FIGHTING?
SISTERS! I'M NOT OF THIS WORLD BUT I *AM* STILL AN AMAZON.
"BATS AND WONDER WOMAN FOUGHT THEIR DUPLICATES HARDER THAN ANYONE THEY'D EVER GONE UP AGAINST.
OF ANYONE, YOU SHOULD KNOW WE CAN NEVER STOP FIGHTING. EVER.
I ALSO KNOW WHEN I'M OUTMATCHED. CLARK WON'T BE DEFEATED BY ANYTHING WE DO.
WE HAVE A BIG GUN. HE'S WAITING. LET'S CALL HIM IN.
WHAT IF THIS IS A MISTAKE? GASOLINE ON THE FIRE?
"BECAUSE THEY SAW HOW EASILY THEY COULDA SLIPPED DOWN THAT RABBIT HOLE. BECOME THESE VERSIONS OF THEMSELVES."

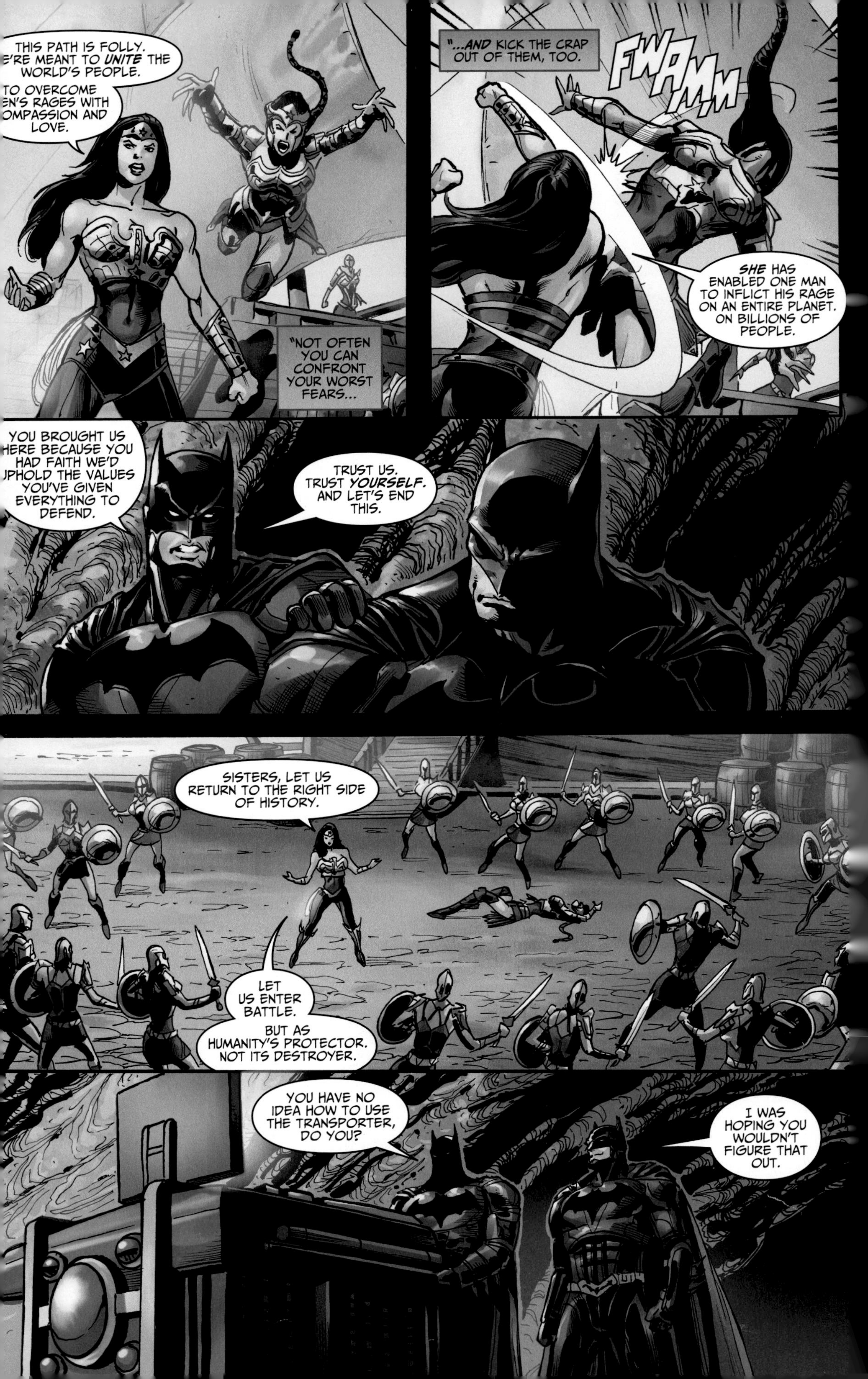

THIS PATH IS FOLLY. WE'RE MEANT TO *UNITE* THE WORLD'S PEOPLE.
TO OVERCOME MEN'S RAGES WITH COMPASSION AND LOVE.
"NOT OFTEN YOU CAN CONFRONT YOUR WORST FEARS...
"...*AND* KICK THE CRAP OUT OF THEM, TOO.
FWAMM
SHE HAS ENABLED ONE MAN TO INFLICT HIS RAGE ON AN ENTIRE PLANET. ON BILLIONS OF PEOPLE.
YOU BROUGHT US HERE BECAUSE YOU HAD FAITH WE'D UPHOLD THE VALUES YOU'VE GIVEN EVERYTHING TO DEFEND.
TRUST US. TRUST *YOURSELF.* AND LET'S END THIS.
SISTERS, LET US RETURN TO THE RIGHT SIDE OF HISTORY.
LET US ENTER BATTLE.
BUT AS HUMANITY'S PROTECTOR. NOT ITS DESTROYER.
YOU HAVE NO IDEA HOW TO USE THE TRANSPORTER, DO YOU?
I WAS HOPING YOU WOULDN'T FIGURE THAT OUT.

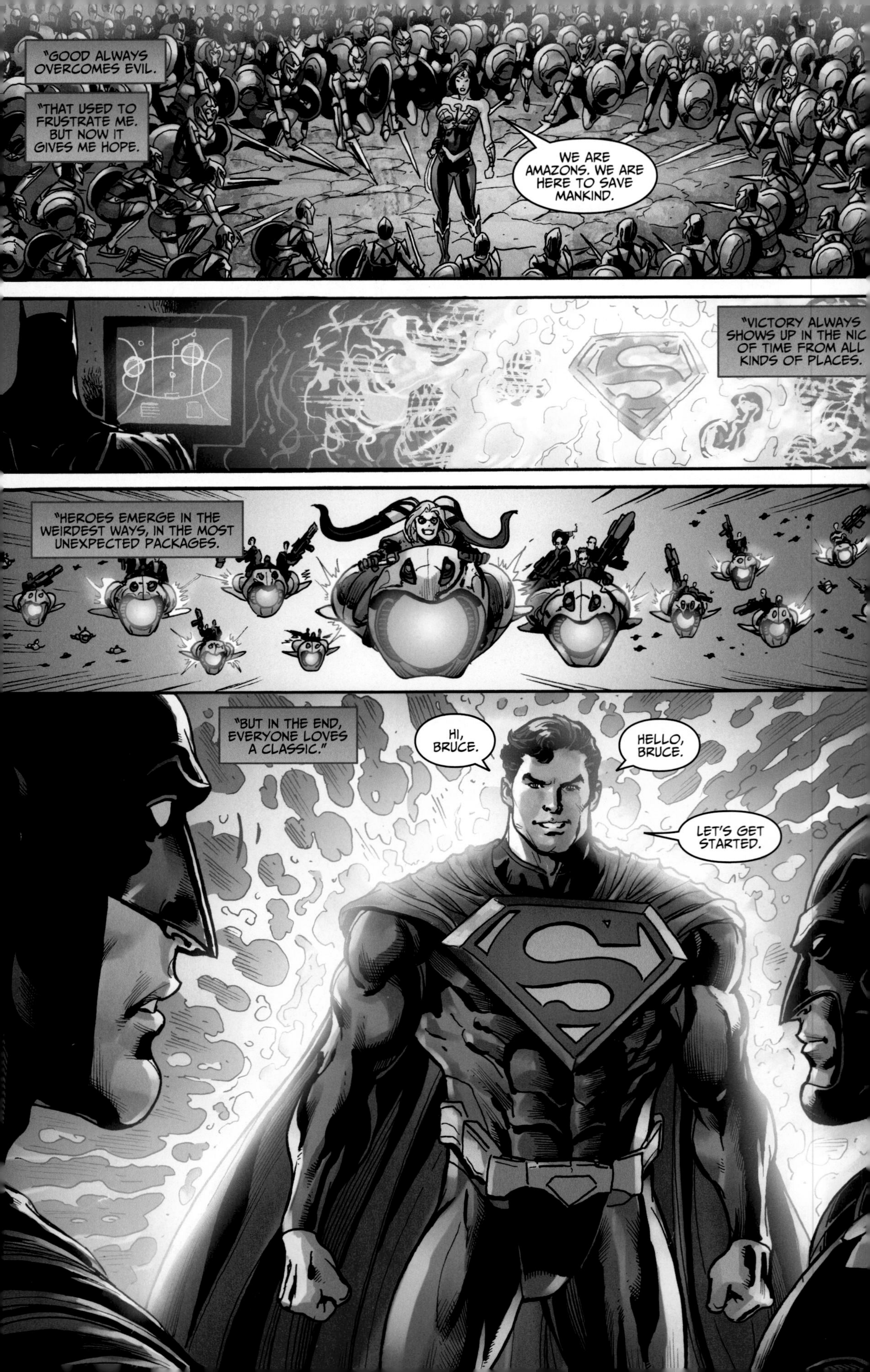
"GOOD ALWAYS OVERCOMES EVIL.
"THAT USED TO FRUSTRATE ME. BUT NOW IT GIVES ME HOPE.
WE ARE AMAZONS. WE ARE HERE TO SAVE MANKIND.
"VICTORY ALWAYS SHOWS UP IN THE NIC OF TIME FROM ALL KINDS OF PLACES.
"HEROES EMERGE IN THE WEIRDEST WAYS, IN THE MOST UNEXPECTED PACKAGES.
"BUT IN THE END, EVERYONE LOVES A CLASSIC."
HI, BRUCE.
HELLO, BRUCE.
LET'S GET STARTED.

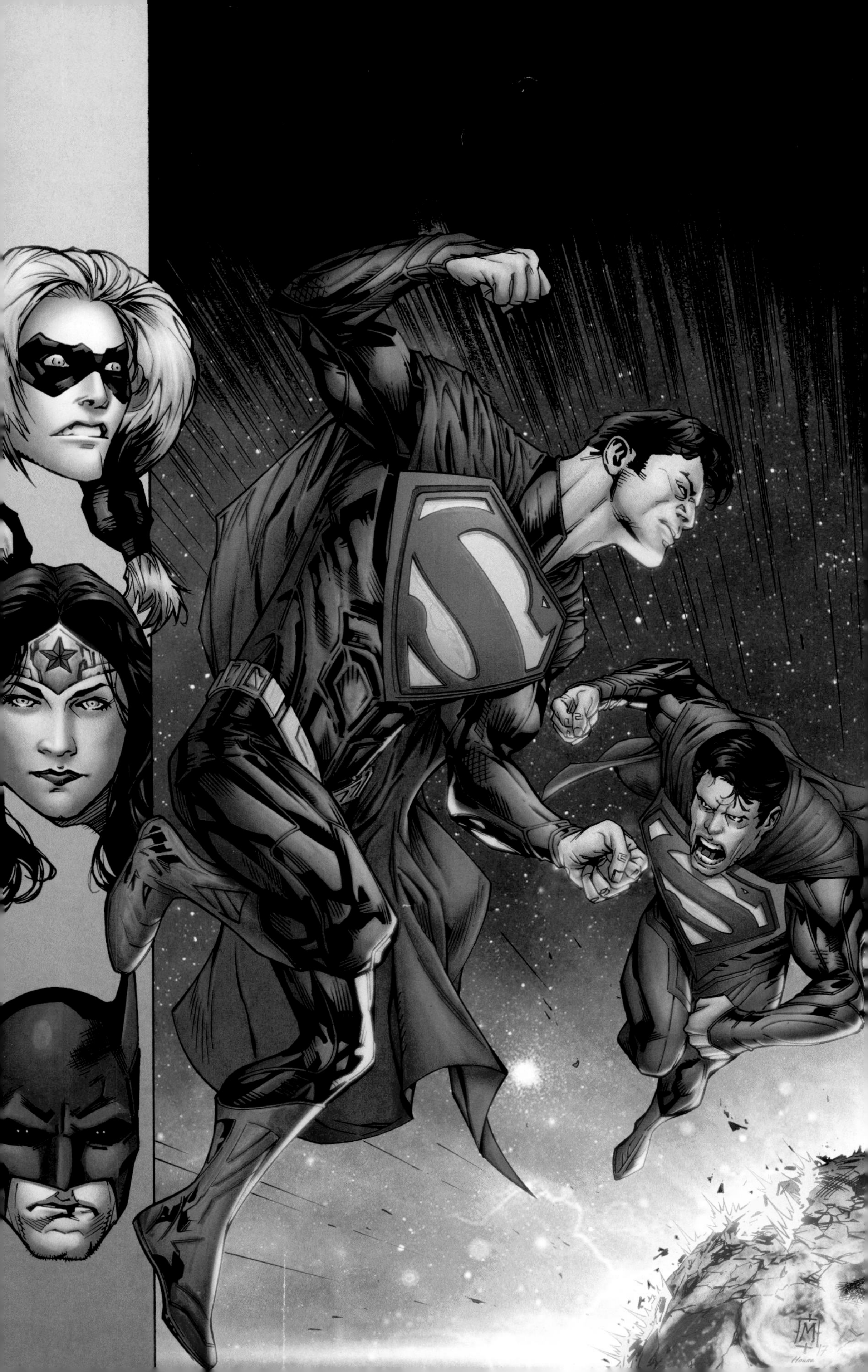

"And Injustice For All" Tom Derenick Daniel Sampere Pencillers Tom Derenick Juan Albarran Inkers
J. Nanjan Colorist Cover art by Matthew Clark and Andrew Dalhouse

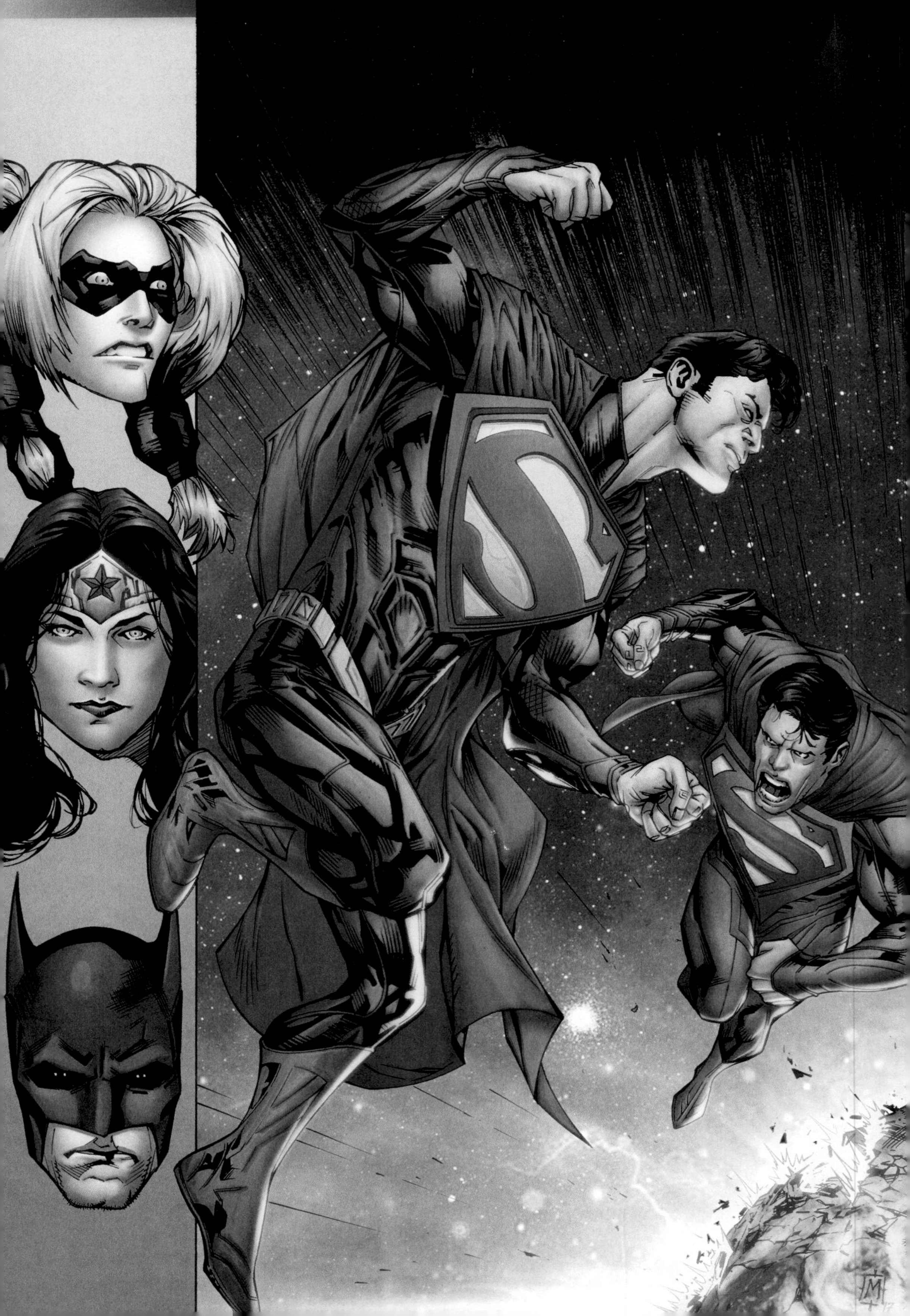

OKAY, ALMOST DONE. JUT GET READY, AUSE THIS LAST PART IS A DOOZY.

THIS IS WHERE I GO FROM FOLK HERO TO ACTUAL LEGEND, MINOR IRRITANT TO DECIDING FACTOR.

THIS IS HOW I BECAME A SUPER-HERO.

"ME AND MY HARLEY HORDE WERE BUSIER THAN WE'D EVER BEEN.

"WITH EVERY CAPED CRUSADER FIGHTING EVERY ARCH-VILLAIN, THERE WAS NO ROOM FOR THEM TO THINK ABOUT THE WORLD THEY WERE ACTUALLY FIGHTING FOR.

"THAT'S WHERE WE CAME IN.

"THERE WAS NO ONE TO TELL US NO. NO ONE TO CRITICIZE OUR METHODS.

"JUST GRATEFUL PEOPLE WHO HUGGED US EXTRA CLOSE WHEN WE PUT THEIR FEET BACK ON SOLID GROUND.

"I LOST COUNT OF HOW MANY. ENOUGH OF THEM THAT WE HAD TO LEAVE THE BAR, BORROW AN AIRPORT HANGAR.

"BUT IF THE WORLD WAS GONNA END? THERE WERE ENOUGH OF THEM THAT WE'D BE ABLE TO START OVER AGAIN."

C'MON IN AND GET COZY! WE'VE GOT COCOA AND BOARD GAMES.

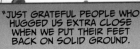

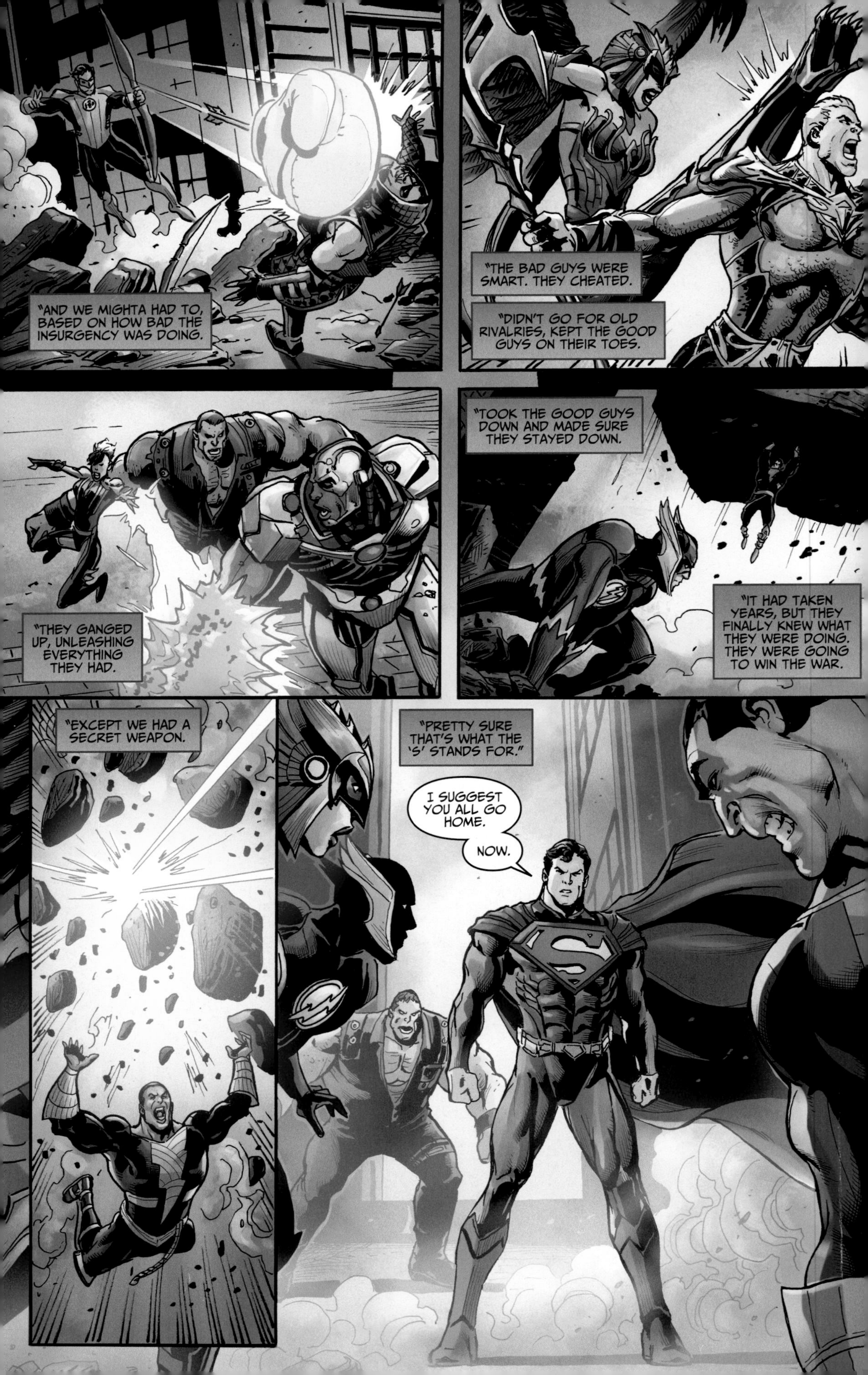
"AND WE MIGHTA HAD TO, BASED ON HOW BAD THE INSURGENCY WAS DOING.
"THE BAD GUYS WERE SMART. THEY CHEATED.
"DIDN'T GO FOR OLD RIVALRIES, KEPT THE GOOD GUYS ON THEIR TOES.
"THEY GANGED UP, UNLEASHING EVERYTHING THEY HAD.
"TOOK THE GOOD GUYS DOWN AND MADE SURE THEY STAYED DOWN.
"IT HAD TAKEN YEARS, BUT THEY FINALLY KNEW WHAT THEY WERE DOING. THEY WERE GOING TO WIN THE WAR.
"EXCEPT WE HAD A SECRET WEAPON.
"PRETTY SURE THAT'S WHAT THE 'S' STANDS FOR."
I SUGGEST YOU ALL GO HOME.
NOW.

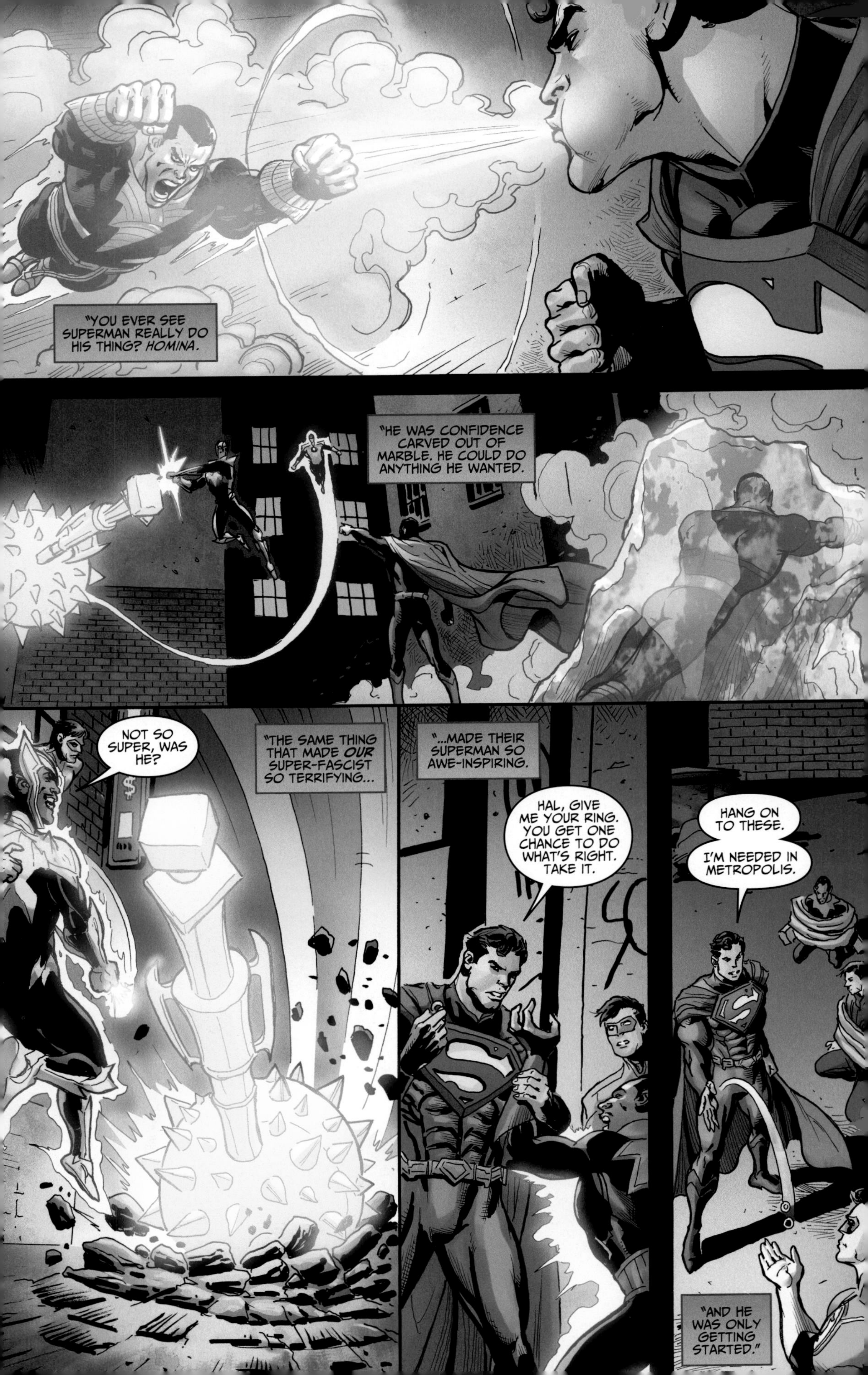
"YOU EVER SEE SUPERMAN REALLY DO HIS THING? *HOMINA*.
"HE WAS CONFIDENCE CARVED OUT OF MARBLE. HE COULD DO ANYTHING HE WANTED.
NOT SO SUPER, WAS HE?
"THE SAME THING THAT MADE *OUR* SUPER-FASCIST SO TERRIFYING...
"...MADE THEIR SUPERMAN SO AWE-INSPIRING.
HAL, GIVE ME YOUR RING. YOU GET ONE CHANCE TO DO WHAT'S RIGHT. TAKE IT.
HANG ON TO THESE.
I'M NEEDED IN METROPOLIS.
"AND HE WAS ONLY GETTING STARTED."

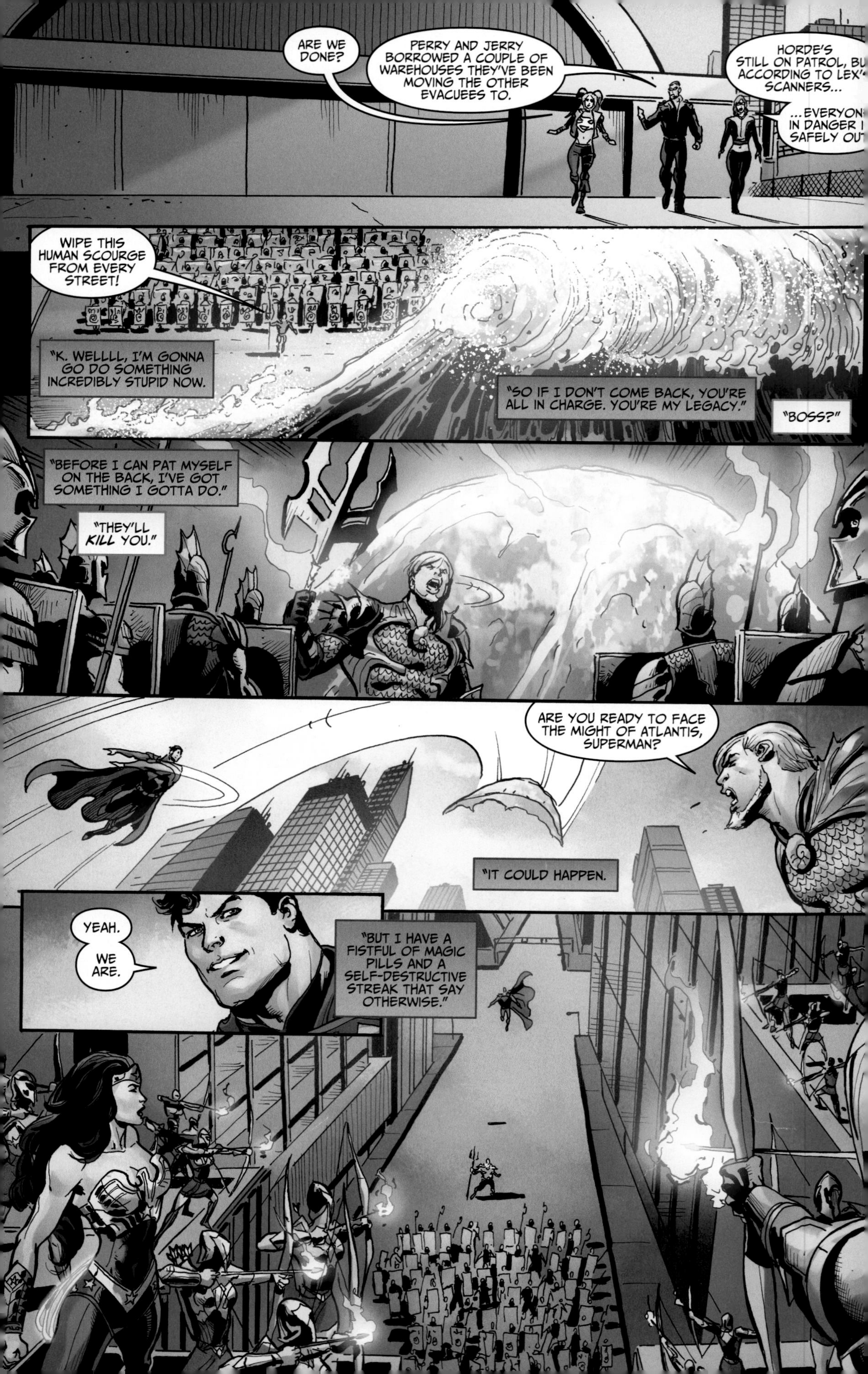
ARE WE DONE?
PERRY AND JERRY BORROWED A COUPLE OF WAREHOUSES THEY'VE BEEN MOVING THE OTHER EVACUEES TO.
HORDE'S STILL ON PATROL, BU ACCORDING TO LEX' SCANNERS...
...EVERYON IN DANGER I SAFELY OUT
WIPE THIS HUMAN SCOURGE FROM EVERY STREET!
"K. WELLLL, I'M GONNA GO DO SOMETHING INCREDIBLY STUPID NOW.
"SO IF I DON'T COME BACK, YOU'RE ALL IN CHARGE. YOU'RE MY LEGACY."
"BOSS?"
"BEFORE I CAN PAT MYSELF ON THE BACK, I'VE GOT SOMETHING I GOTTA DO."
"THEY'LL KILL YOU."
ARE YOU READY TO FACE THE MIGHT OF ATLANTIS, SUPERMAN?
"IT COULD HAPPEN.
YEAH.
WE ARE.
"BUT I HAVE A FISTFUL OF MAGIC PILLS AND A SELF-DESTRUCTIVE STREAK THAT SAY OTHERWISE."

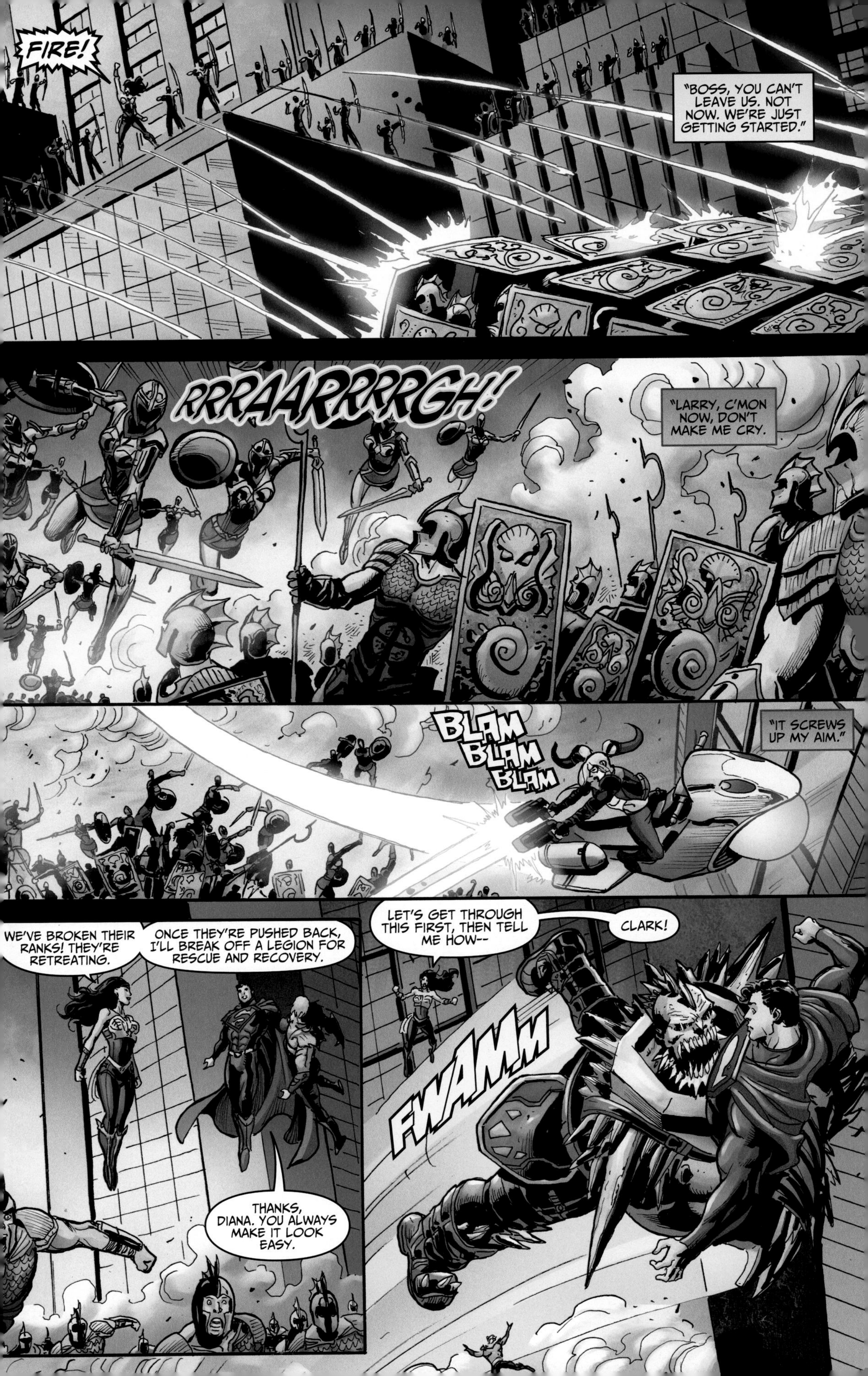
FIRE!
"BOSS, YOU CAN'T LEAVE US. NOT NOW. WE'RE JUST GETTING STARTED."
RRRAARRRRGH!
"LARRY, C'MON NOW, DON'T MAKE ME CRY.
BLAM BLAM BLAM
"IT SCREWS UP MY AIM."
WE'VE BROKEN THEIR RANKS! THEY'RE RETREATING.
ONCE THEY'RE PUSHED BACK, I'LL BREAK OFF A LEGION FOR RESCUE AND RECOVERY.
THANKS, DIANA. YOU ALWAYS MAKE IT LOOK EASY.
LET'S GET THROUGH THIS FIRST, THEN TELL ME HOW--
CLARK!
FWAMM

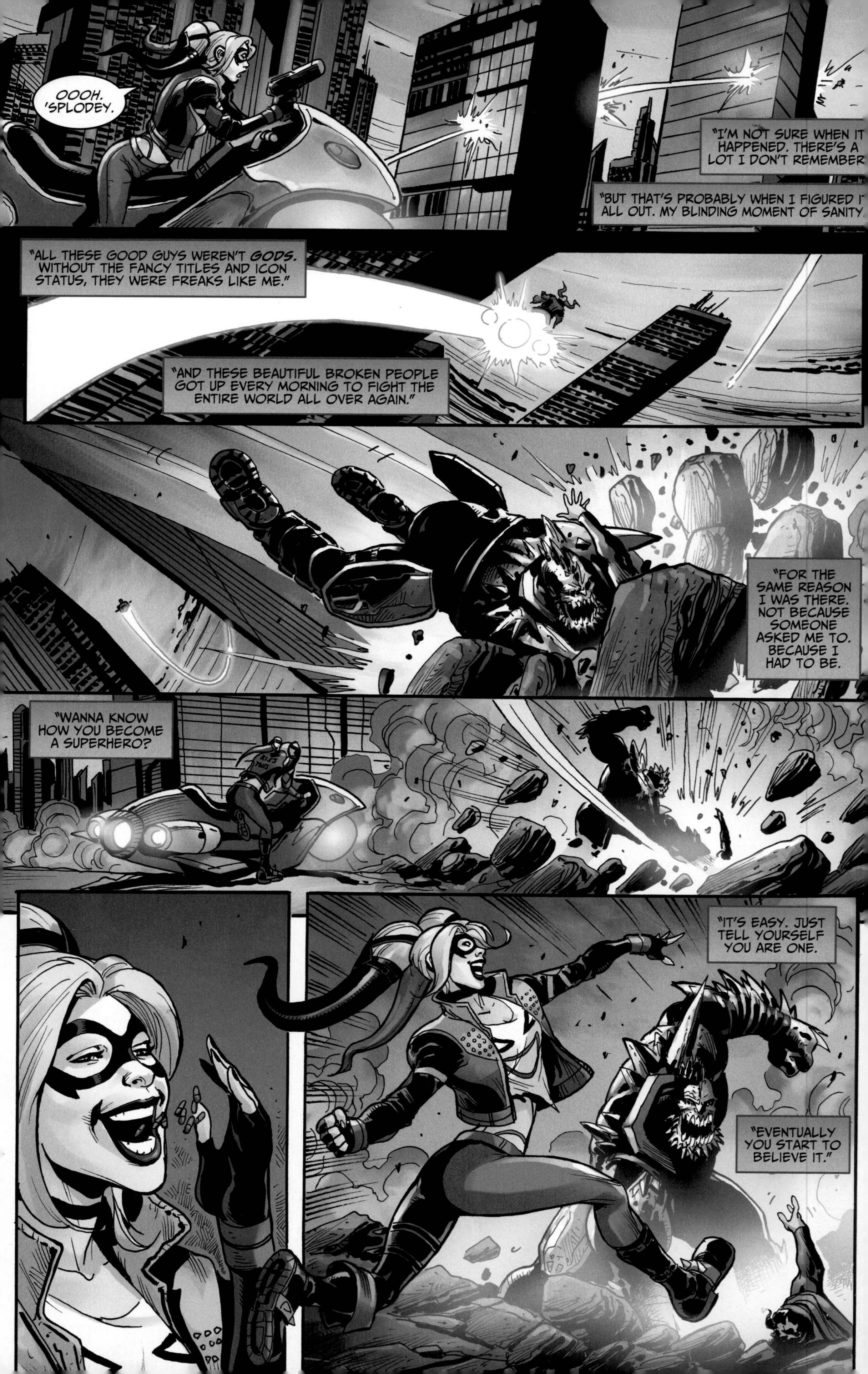
OOOH. 'SPLODEY.
"I'M NOT SURE WHEN IT HAPPENED. THERE'S A LOT I DON'T REMEMBER.
"BUT THAT'S PROBABLY WHEN I FIGURED IT ALL OUT. MY BLINDING MOMENT OF SANITY.
"ALL THESE GOOD GUYS WEREN'T GODS. WITHOUT THE FANCY TITLES AND ICON STATUS, THEY WERE FREAKS LIKE ME."
"AND THESE BEAUTIFUL BROKEN PEOPLE GOT UP EVERY MORNING TO FIGHT THE ENTIRE WORLD ALL OVER AGAIN."
"FOR THE SAME REASON I WAS THERE. NOT BECAUSE SOMEONE ASKED ME TO. BECAUSE I HAD TO BE.
"WANNA KNOW HOW YOU BECOME A SUPERHERO?
"IT'S EASY. JUST TELL YOURSELF YOU ARE ONE.
"EVENTUALLY YOU START TO BELIEVE IT."

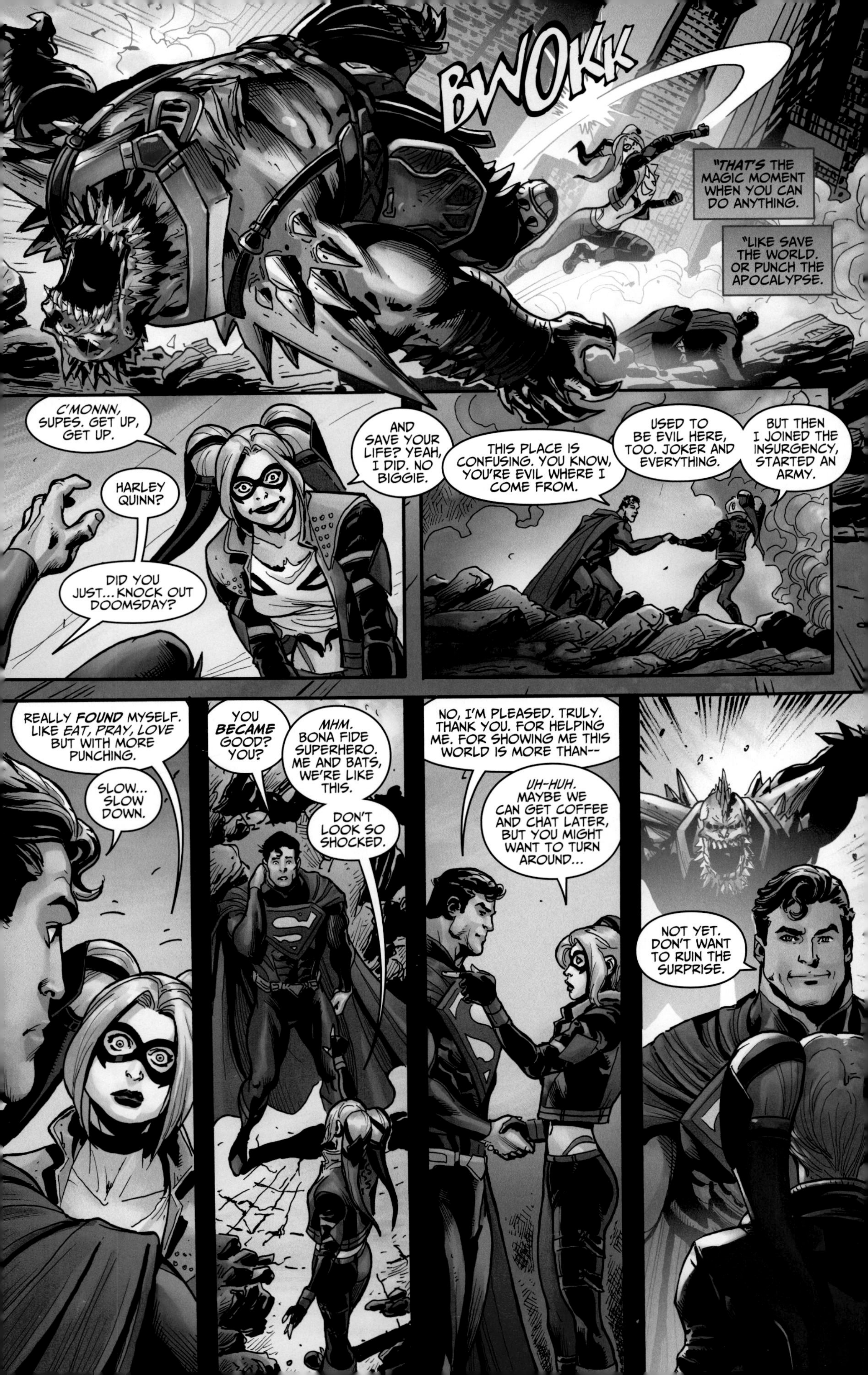
BWOKK
"THAT'S THE MAGIC MOMENT WHEN YOU CAN DO ANYTHING.
"LIKE SAVE THE WORLD. OR PUNCH THE APOCALYPSE.
C'MONNN, SUPES. GET UP, GET UP.
HARLEY QUINN?
DID YOU JUST... KNOCK OUT DOOMSDAY?
AND SAVE YOUR LIFE? YEAH, I DID. NO BIGGIE.
THIS PLACE IS CONFUSING. YOU KNOW, YOU'RE EVIL WHERE I COME FROM.
USED TO BE EVIL HERE, TOO. JOKER AND EVERYTHING.
BUT THEN I JOINED THE INSURGENCY, STARTED AN ARMY.
REALLY FOUND MYSELF. LIKE EAT, PRAY, LOVE BUT WITH MORE PUNCHING.
SLOW... SLOW DOWN.
YOU BECAME GOOD? YOU?
MHM. BONA FIDE SUPERHERO. ME AND BATS, WE'RE LIKE THIS.
DON'T LOOK SO SHOCKED.
NO, I'M PLEASED. TRULY. THANK YOU. FOR HELPING ME. FOR SHOWING ME THIS WORLD IS MORE THAN--
UH-HUH. MAYBE WE CAN GET COFFEE AND CHAT LATER, BUT YOU MIGHT WANT TO TURN AROUND...
NOT YET. DON'T WANT TO RUIN THE SURPRISE.

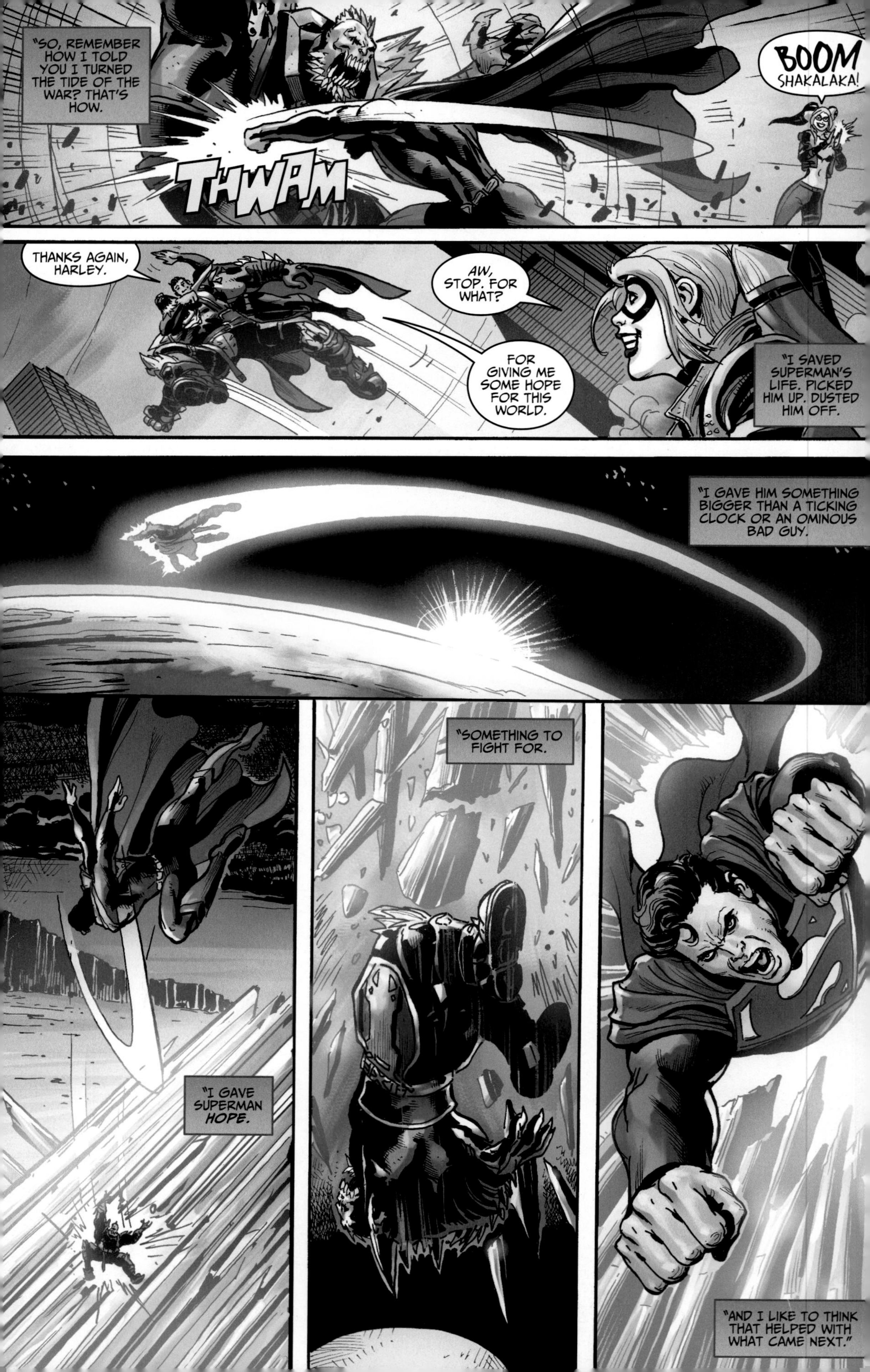
"SO, REMEMBER HOW I TOLD YOU I TURNED THE TIDE OF THE WAR? THAT'S HOW.
BOOM SHAKALAKA!
THWAM
THANKS AGAIN, HARLEY.
AW, STOP. FOR WHAT?
FOR GIVING ME SOME HOPE FOR THIS WORLD.
"I SAVED SUPERMAN'S LIFE. PICKED HIM UP. DUSTED HIM OFF.
"I GAVE HIM SOMETHING BIGGER THAN A TICKING CLOCK OR AN OMINOUS BAD GUY.
"I GAVE SUPERMAN *HOPE*.
"SOMETHING TO FIGHT FOR.
"AND I LIKE TO THINK THAT HELPED WITH WHAT CAME NEXT."

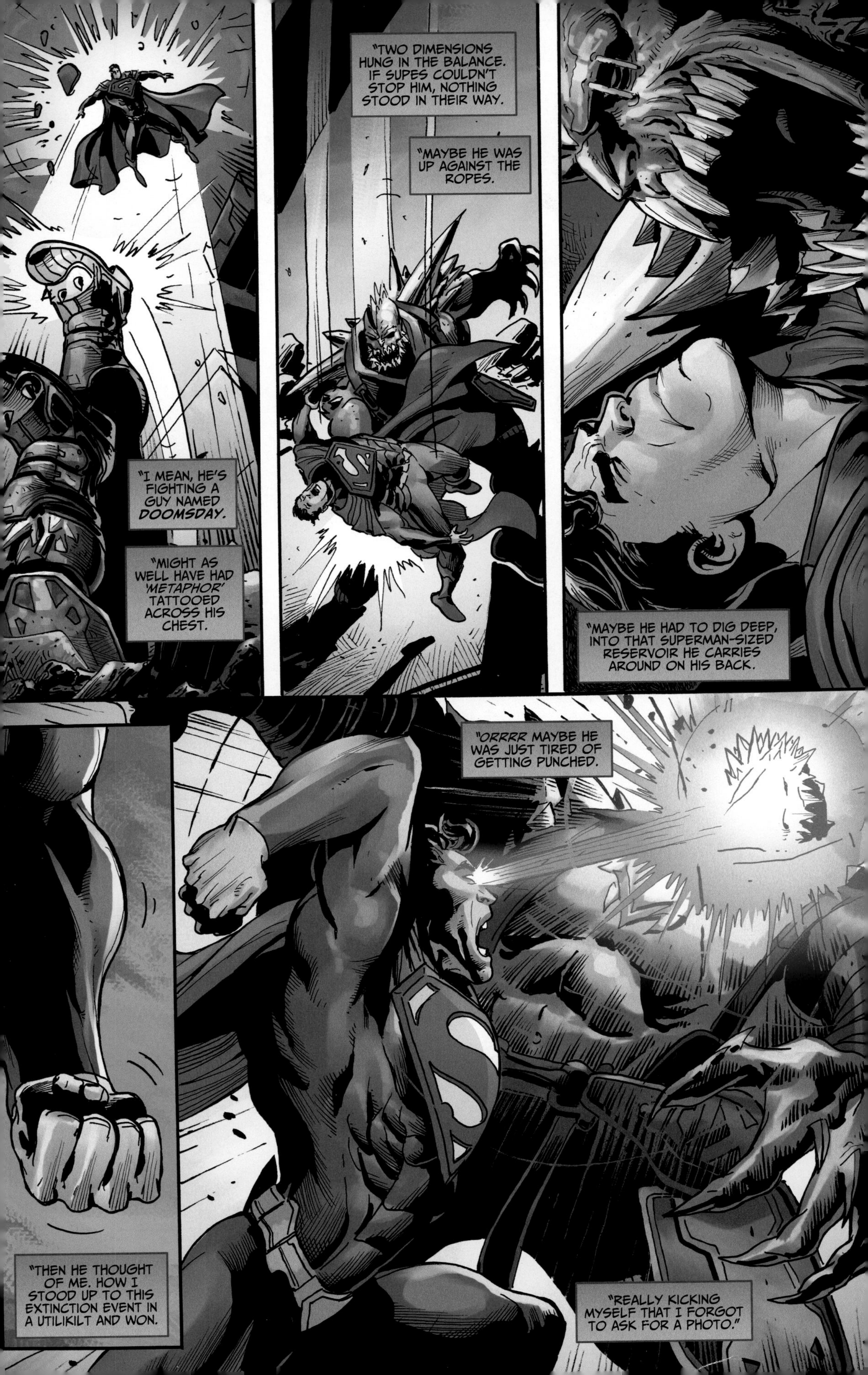
"I MEAN, HE'S FIGHTING A GUY NAMED DOOMSDAY.
"MIGHT AS WELL HAVE HAD 'METAPHOR' TATTOOED ACROSS HIS CHEST.
"TWO DIMENSIONS HUNG IN THE BALANCE. IF SUPES COULDN'T STOP HIM, NOTHING STOOD IN THEIR WAY.
"MAYBE HE WAS UP AGAINST THE ROPES.
"MAYBE HE HAD TO DIG DEEP, INTO THAT SUPERMAN-SIZED RESERVOIR HE CARRIES AROUND ON HIS BACK.
"ORRRR MAYBE HE WAS JUST TIRED OF GETTING PUNCHED.
"THEN HE THOUGHT OF ME. HOW I STOOD UP TO THIS EXTINCTION EVENT IN A UTILIKILT AND WON.
"REALLY KICKING MYSELF THAT I FORGOT TO ASK FOR A PHOTO."

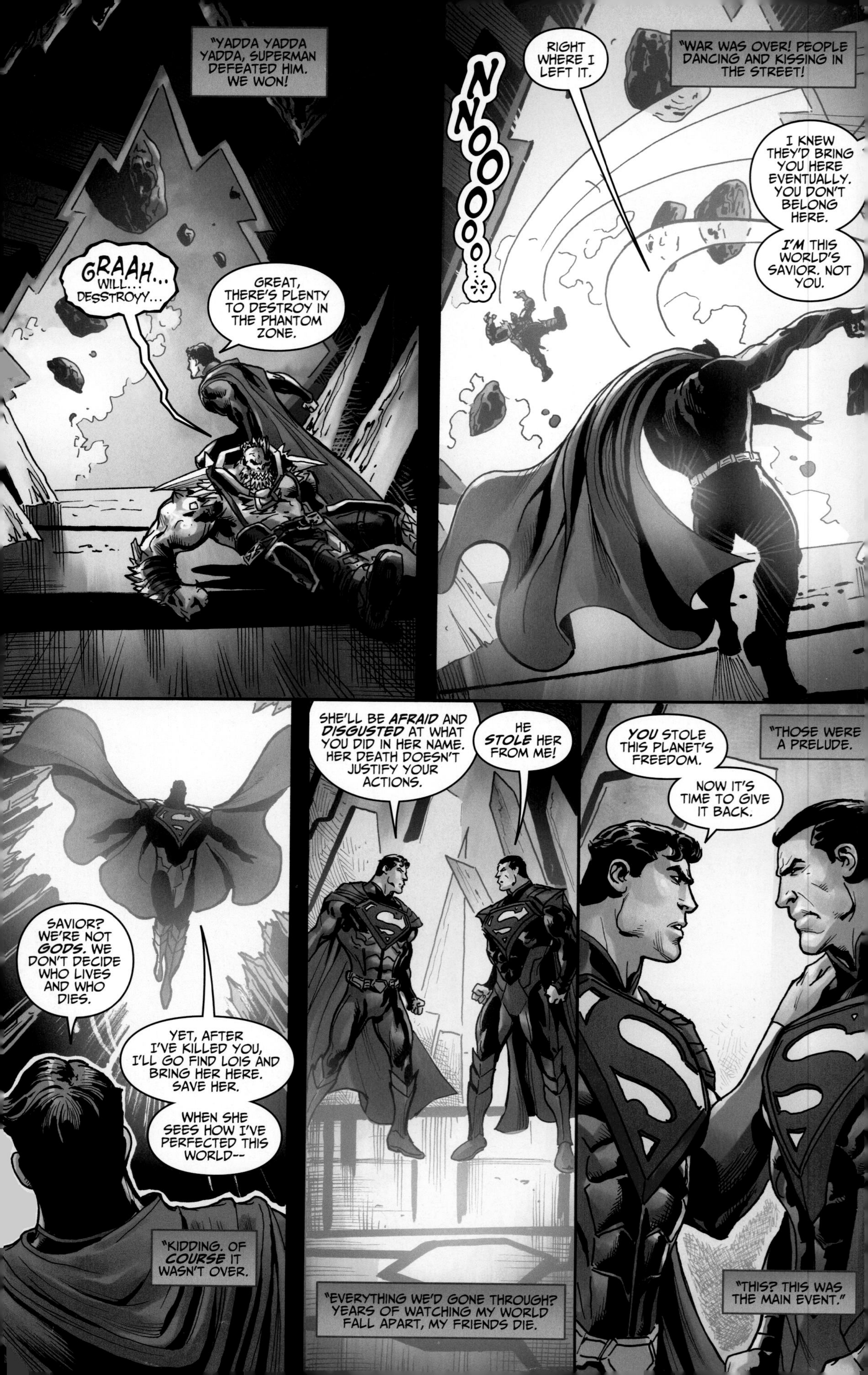
"YADDA YADDA YADDA, SUPERMAN DEFEATED HIM. WE WON!
GRAAH... WILL... DESSTROYY...
GREAT, THERE'S PLENTY TO DESTROY IN THE PHANTOM ZONE.
NNOOOOO...!
RIGHT WHERE I LEFT IT.
"WAR WAS OVER! PEOPLE DANCING AND KISSING IN THE STREET!
I KNEW THEY'D BRING YOU HERE EVENTUALLY. YOU DON'T BELONG HERE.
I'M THIS WORLD'S SAVIOR. NOT YOU.
SAVIOR? WE'RE NOT GODS. WE DON'T DECIDE WHO LIVES AND WHO DIES.
YET, AFTER I'VE KILLED YOU, I'LL GO FIND LOIS AND BRING HER HERE. SAVE HER.
WHEN SHE SEES HOW I'VE PERFECTED THIS WORLD--
"KIDDING. OF COURSE IT WASN'T OVER.
SHE'LL BE AFRAID AND DISGUSTED AT WHAT YOU DID IN HER NAME. HER DEATH DOESN'T JUSTIFY YOUR ACTIONS.
HE STOLE HER FROM ME!
"EVERYTHING WE'D GONE THROUGH? YEARS OF WATCHING MY WORLD FALL APART, MY FRIENDS DIE.
YOU STOLE THIS PLANET'S FREEDOM.
NOW IT'S TIME TO GIVE IT BACK.
"THOSE WERE A PRELUDE.
"THIS? THIS WAS THE MAIN EVENT."

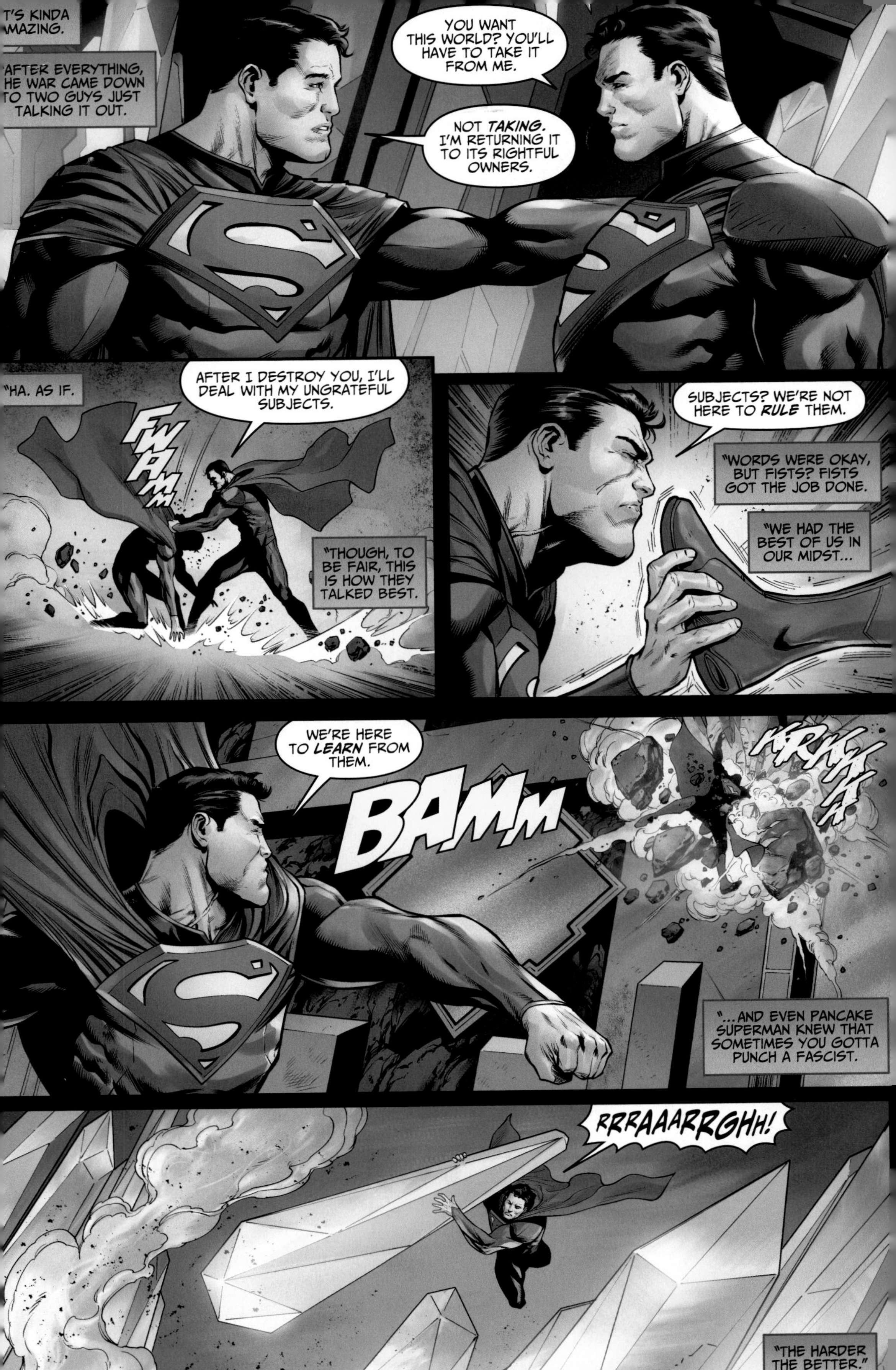
T'S KINDA AMAZING.
AFTER EVERYTHING, HE WAR CAME DOWN TO TWO GUYS JUST TALKING IT OUT.
YOU WANT THIS WORLD? YOU'LL HAVE TO TAKE IT FROM ME.
NOT TAKING. I'M RETURNING IT TO ITS RIGHTFUL OWNERS.
"HA. AS IF.
AFTER I DESTROY YOU, I'LL DEAL WITH MY UNGRATEFUL SUBJECTS.
FWAMM
"THOUGH, TO BE FAIR, THIS IS HOW THEY TALKED BEST.
SUBJECTS? WE'RE NOT HERE TO RULE THEM.
"WORDS WERE OKAY, BUT FISTS? FISTS GOT THE JOB DONE.
"WE HAD THE BEST OF US IN OUR MIDST...
WE'RE HERE TO LEARN FROM THEM.
BAMM
KRKKK
"...AND EVEN PANCAKE SUPERMAN KNEW THAT SOMETIMES YOU GOTTA PUNCH A FASCIST.
RRRAAARRGHH!
"THE HARDER THE BETTER."

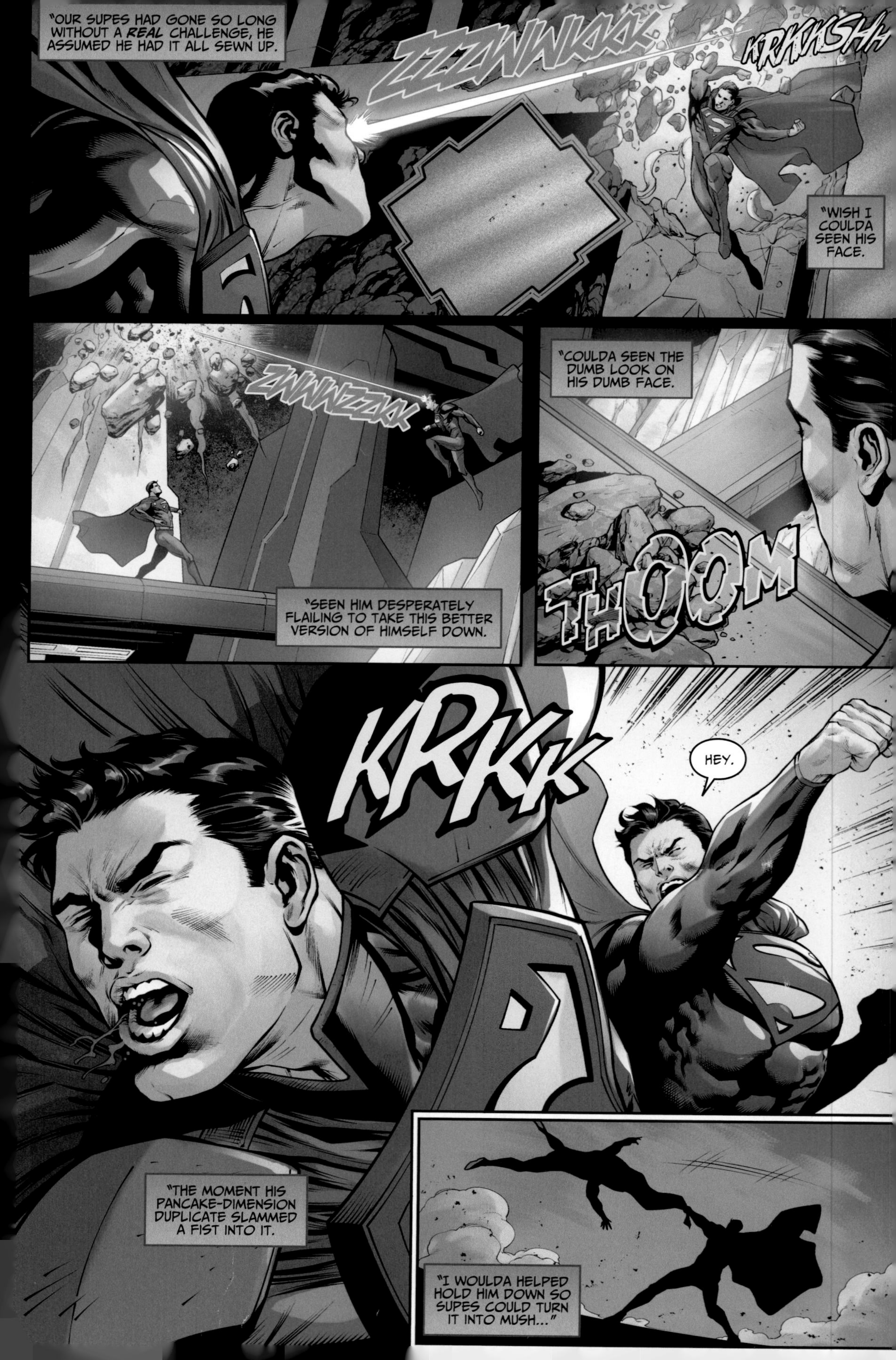
"OUR SUPES HAD GONE SO LONG WITHOUT A *REAL* CHALLENGE, HE ASSUMED HE HAD IT ALL SEWN UP.
ZZZZWWKKKK
KRKKSHH
"WISH I COULDA SEEN HIS FACE.
ZWWWZZAKK
"SEEN HIM DESPERATELY FLAILING TO TAKE THIS BETTER VERSION OF HIMSELF DOWN.
"COULDA SEEN THE DUMB LOOK ON HIS DUMB FACE.
THOOM
KRKK
HEY.
"THE MOMENT HIS PANCAKE-DIMENSION DUPLICATE SLAMMED A FIST INTO IT.
"I WOULDA HELPED HOLD HIM DOWN SO SUPES COULD TURN IT INTO MUSH..."

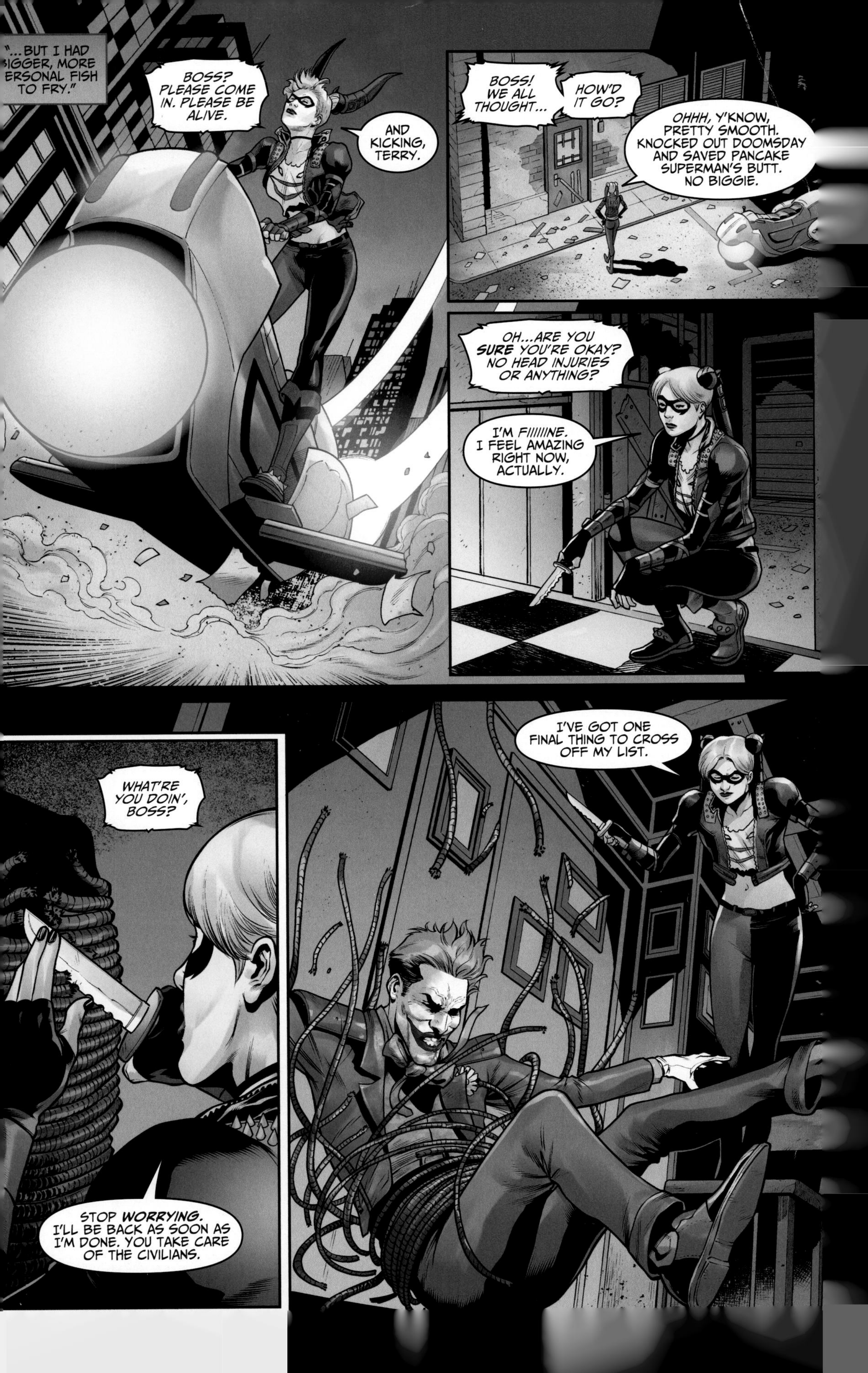
"...BUT I HAD BIGGER, MORE PERSONAL FISH TO FRY."
BOSS? PLEASE COME IN. PLEASE BE ALIVE.
AND KICKING, TERRY.
BOSS! WE ALL THOUGHT...
HOW'D IT GO?
OHHH, Y'KNOW, PRETTY SMOOTH. KNOCKED OUT DOOMSDAY AND SAVED PANCAKE SUPERMAN'S BUTT. NO BIGGIE.
OH...ARE YOU SURE YOU'RE OKAY? NO HEAD INJURIES OR ANYTHING?
I'M FIIIIIINE. I FEEL AMAZING RIGHT NOW, ACTUALLY.
WHAT'RE YOU DOIN', BOSS?
STOP WORRYING. I'LL BE BACK AS SOON AS I'M DONE. YOU TAKE CARE OF THE CIVILIANS.
I'VE GOT ONE FINAL THING TO CROSS OFF MY LIST.

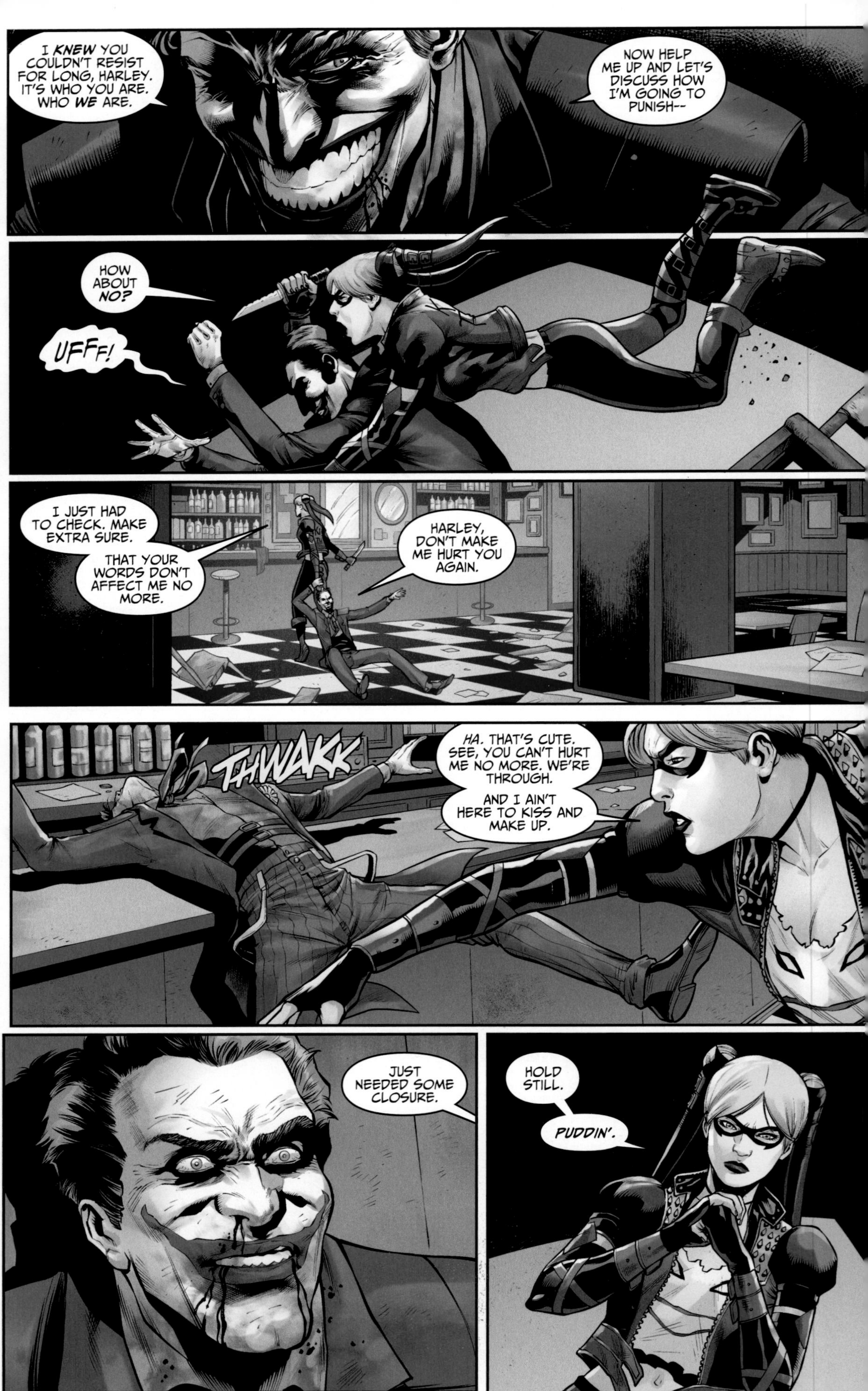
I KNEW YOU COULDN'T RESIST FOR LONG, HARLEY. IT'S WHO YOU ARE. WHO WE ARE.
NOW HELP ME UP AND LET'S DISCUSS HOW I'M GOING TO PUNISH--
HOW ABOUT NO?
UFFF!
I JUST HAD TO CHECK. MAKE EXTRA SURE.
THAT YOUR WORDS DON'T AFFECT ME NO MORE.
HARLEY, DON'T MAKE ME HURT YOU AGAIN.
THWAKK
HA. THAT'S CUTE. SEE, YOU CAN'T HURT ME NO MORE. WE'RE THROUGH.
AND I AIN'T HERE TO KISS AND MAKE UP.
JUST NEEDED SOME CLOSURE.
HOLD STILL.
PUDDIN'.

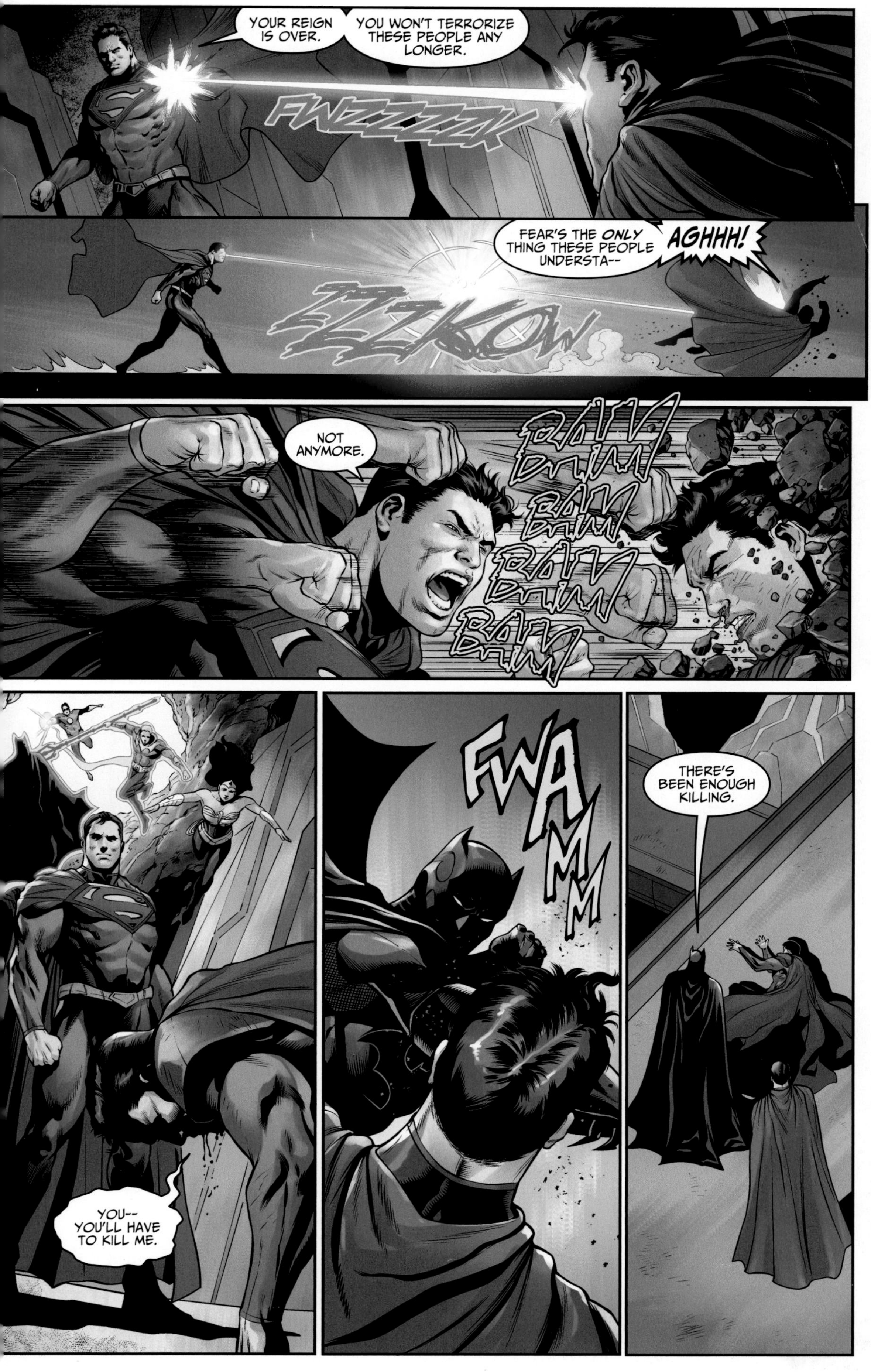
YOUR REIGN IS OVER.
YOU WON'T TERRORIZE THESE PEOPLE ANY LONGER.
FWZZZZK
FEAR'S THE ONLY THING THESE PEOPLE UNDERSTA--
AGHHH!
ZZKOW
NOT ANYMORE.
BAM BAM BAM BAM
YOU-- YOU'LL HAVE TO KILL ME.
FWAMM
THERE'S BEEN ENOUGH KILLING.

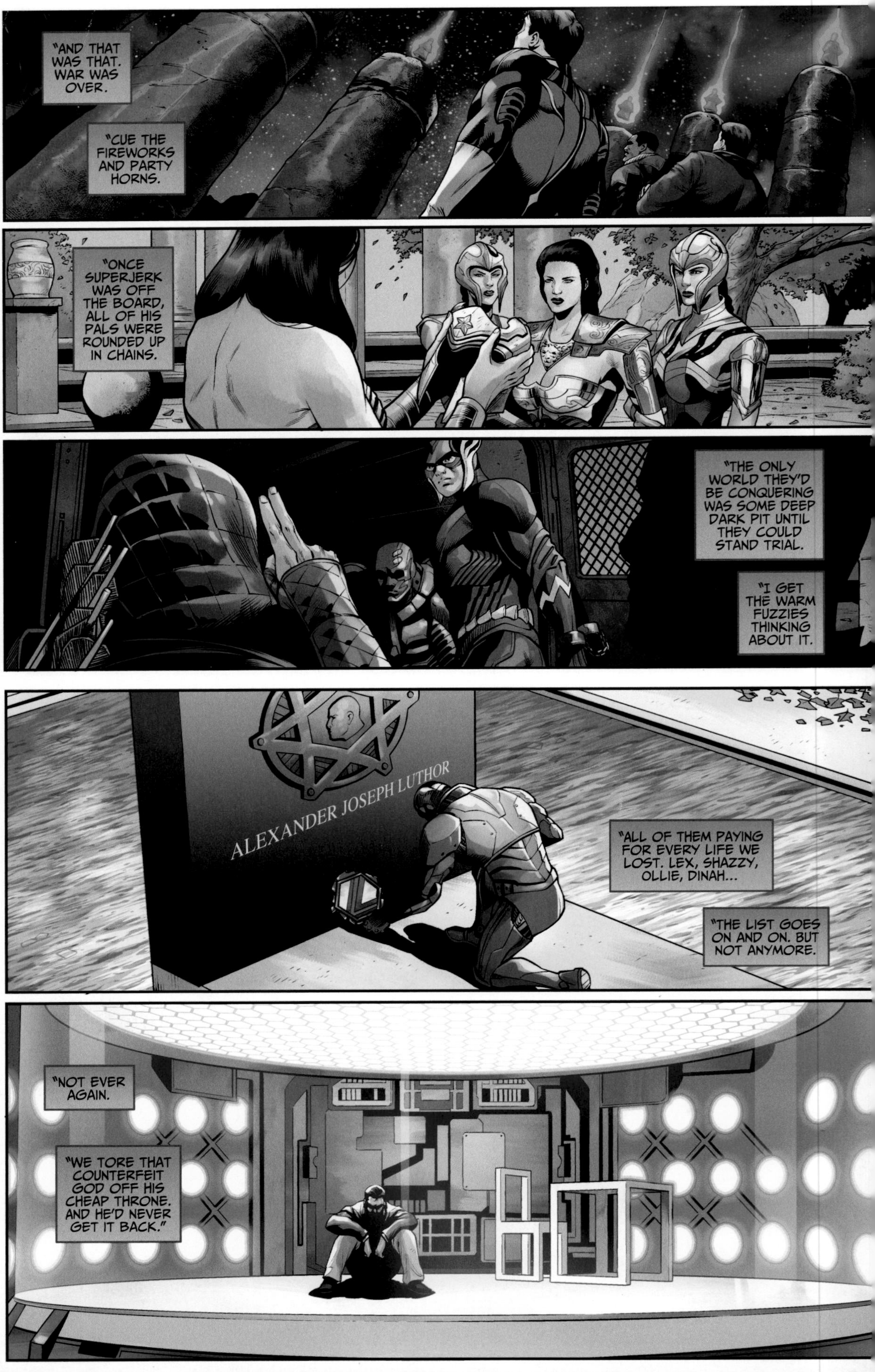
"AND THAT WAS THAT. WAR WAS OVER.
"CUE THE FIREWORKS AND PARTY HORNS.
"ONCE SUPERJERK WAS OFF THE BOARD, ALL OF HIS PALS WERE ROUNDED UP IN CHAINS.
"THE ONLY WORLD THEY'D BE CONQUERING WAS SOME DEEP DARK PIT UNTIL THEY COULD STAND TRIAL.
"I GET THE WARM FUZZIES THINKING ABOUT IT.
ALEXANDER JOSEPH LUTHOR
"ALL OF THEM PAYING FOR EVERY LIFE WE LOST. LEX, SHAZZY, OLLIE, DINAH...
"THE LIST GOES ON AND ON. BUT NOT ANYMORE.
"NOT EVER AGAIN.
"WE TORE THAT COUNTERFEIT GOD OFF HIS CHEAP THRONE. AND HE'D NEVER GET IT BACK."

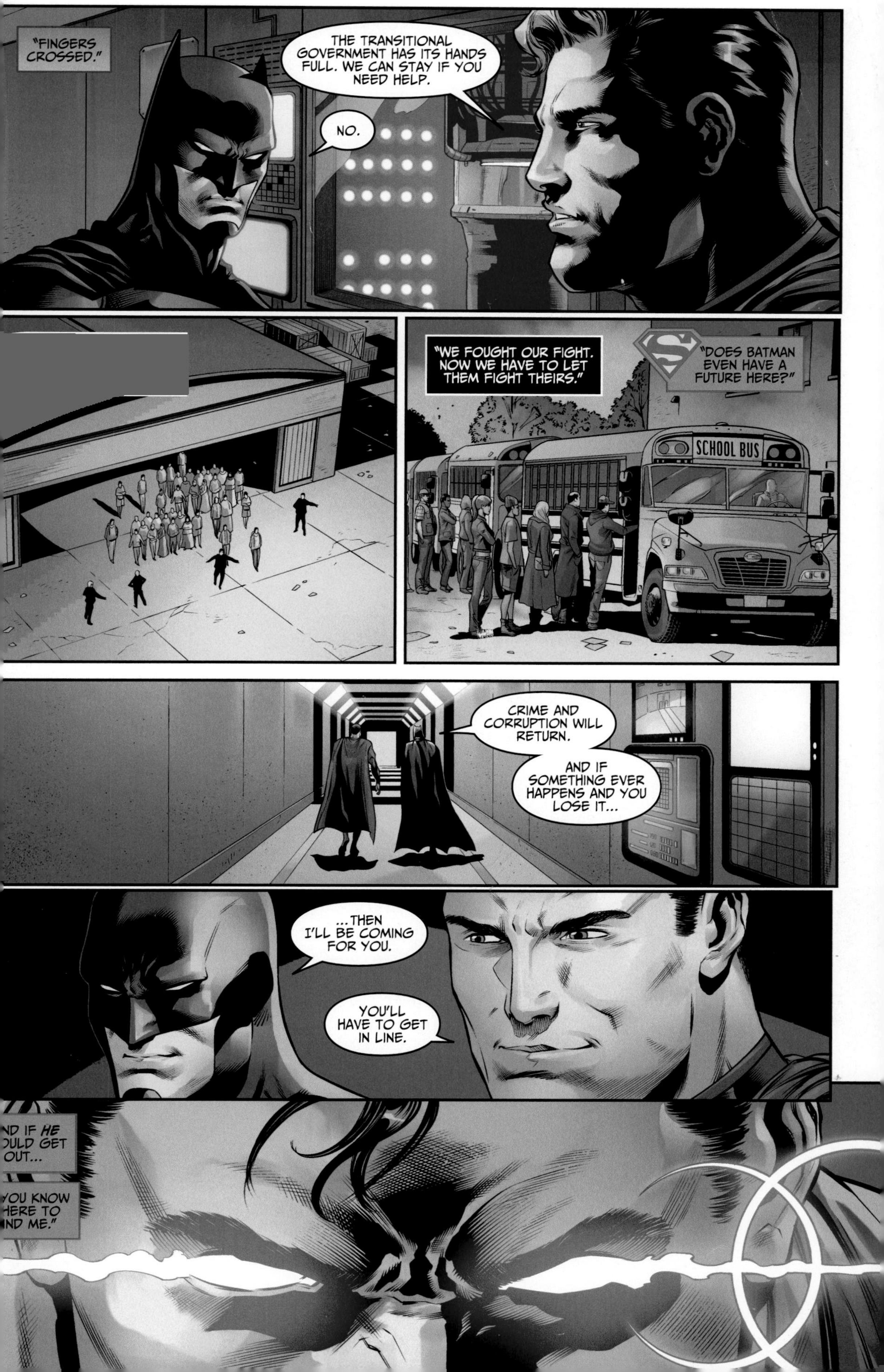
"FINGERS CROSSED."
THE TRANSITIONAL GOVERNMENT HAS ITS HANDS FULL. WE CAN STAY IF YOU NEED HELP.
NO.
"WE FOUGHT OUR FIGHT. NOW WE HAVE TO LET THEM FIGHT THEIRS."
"DOES BATMAN EVEN HAVE A FUTURE HERE?"
SCHOOL BUS
CRIME AND CORRUPTION WILL RETURN.
AND IF SOMETHING EVER HAPPENS AND YOU LOSE IT...
...THEN I'LL BE COMING FOR YOU.
YOU'LL HAVE TO GET IN LINE.
ND IF HE OULD GET OUT...
YOU KNOW HERE TO ND ME."

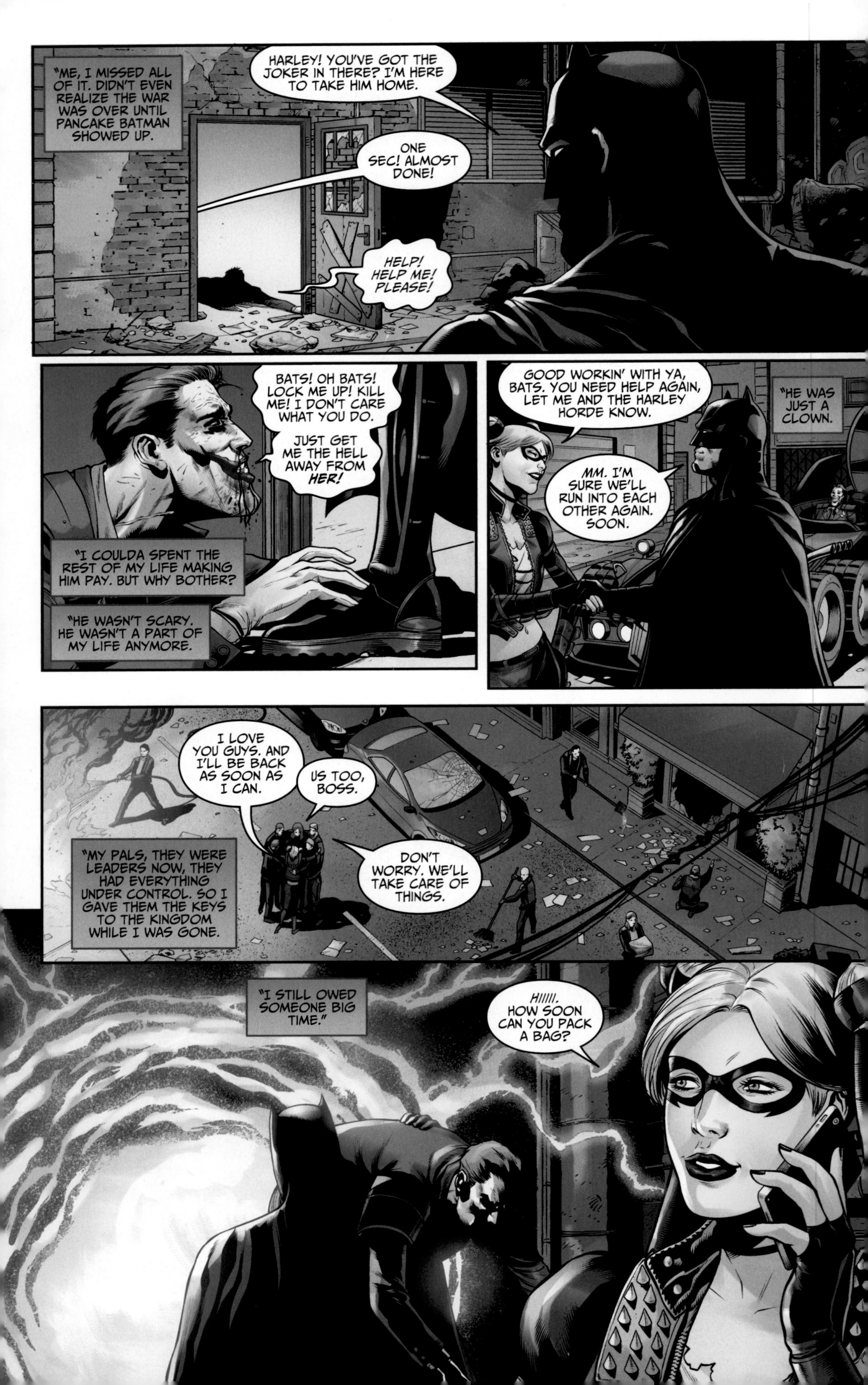
"ME, I MISSED ALL OF IT. DIDN'T EVEN REALIZE THE WAR WAS OVER UNTIL PANCAKE BATMAN SHOWED UP.
HARLEY! YOU'VE GOT THE JOKER IN THERE? I'M HERE TO TAKE HIM HOME.
ONE SEC! ALMOST DONE!
HELP! HELP ME! PLEASE!
BATS! OH BATS! LOCK ME UP! KILL ME! I DON'T CARE WHAT YOU DO.
JUST GET ME THE HELL AWAY FROM HER!
"I COULDA SPENT THE REST OF MY LIFE MAKING HIM PAY. BUT WHY BOTHER?
"HE WASN'T SCARY. HE WASN'T A PART OF MY LIFE ANYMORE.
GOOD WORKIN' WITH YA, BATS. YOU NEED HELP AGAIN, LET ME AND THE HARLEY HORDE KNOW.
"HE WAS JUST A CLOWN.
MM. I'M SURE WE'LL RUN INTO EACH OTHER AGAIN. SOON.
I LOVE YOU GUYS. AND I'LL BE BACK AS SOON AS I CAN.
US TOO, BOSS.
"MY PALS, THEY WERE LEADERS NOW, THEY HAD EVERYTHING UNDER CONTROL. SO I GAVE THEM THE KEYS TO THE KINGDOM WHILE I WAS GONE.
DON'T WORRY. WE'LL TAKE CARE OF THINGS.
"I STILL OWED SOMEONE BIG TIME."
HIIIII. HOW SOON CAN YOU PACK A BAG?

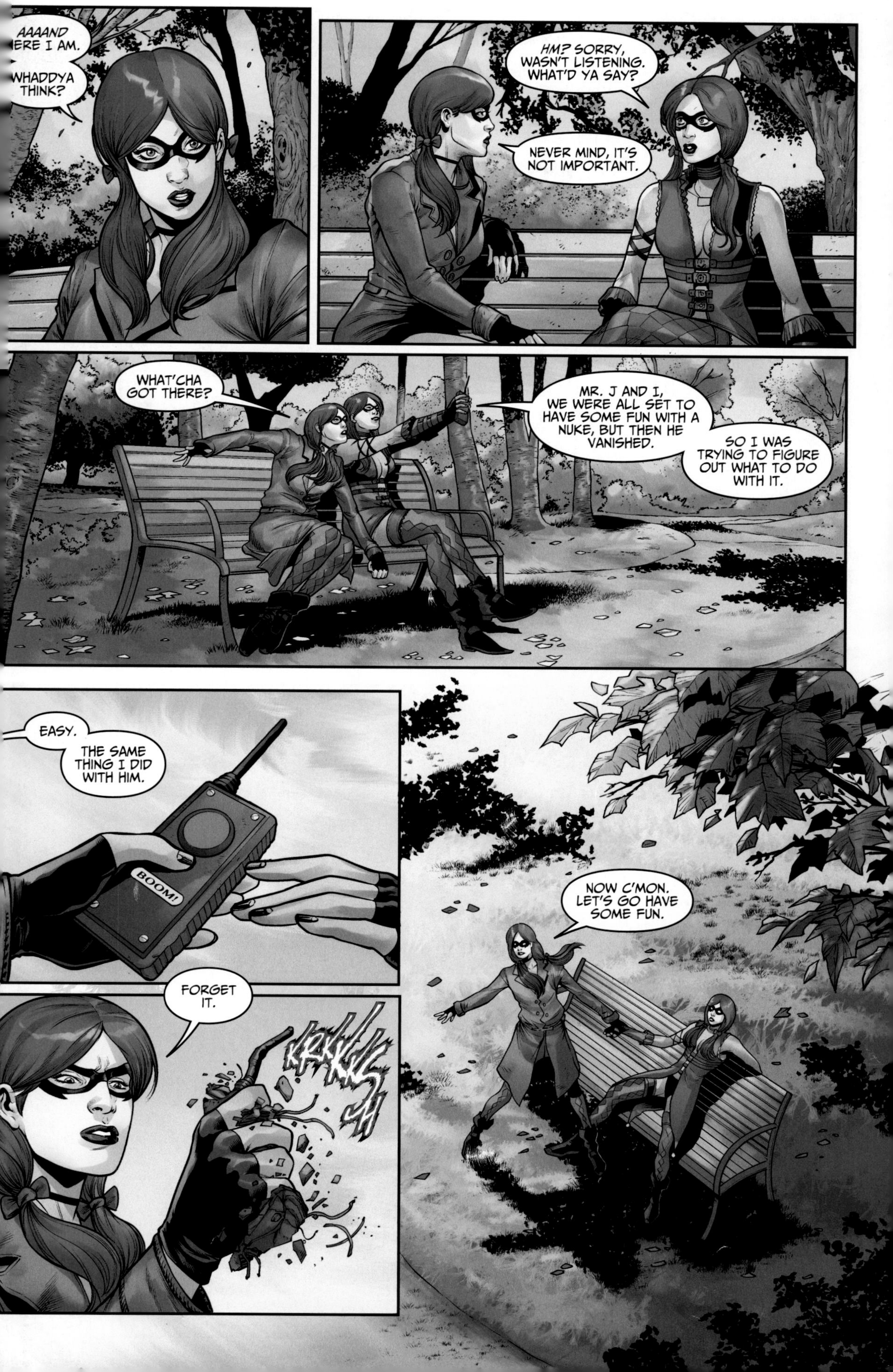

AAAAND ERE I AM.
WHADDYA THINK?
HM? SORRY, WASN'T LISTENING. WHAT'D YA SAY?
NEVER MIND, IT'S NOT IMPORTANT.
WHAT'CHA GOT THERE?
MR. J AND I, WE WERE ALL SET TO HAVE SOME FUN WITH A NUKE, BUT THEN HE VANISHED.
SO I WAS TRYING TO FIGURE OUT WHAT TO DO WITH IT.
EASY.
THE SAME THING I DID WITH HIM.
BOOM!
FORGET IT.
NOW C'MON. LET'S GO HAVE SOME FUN.

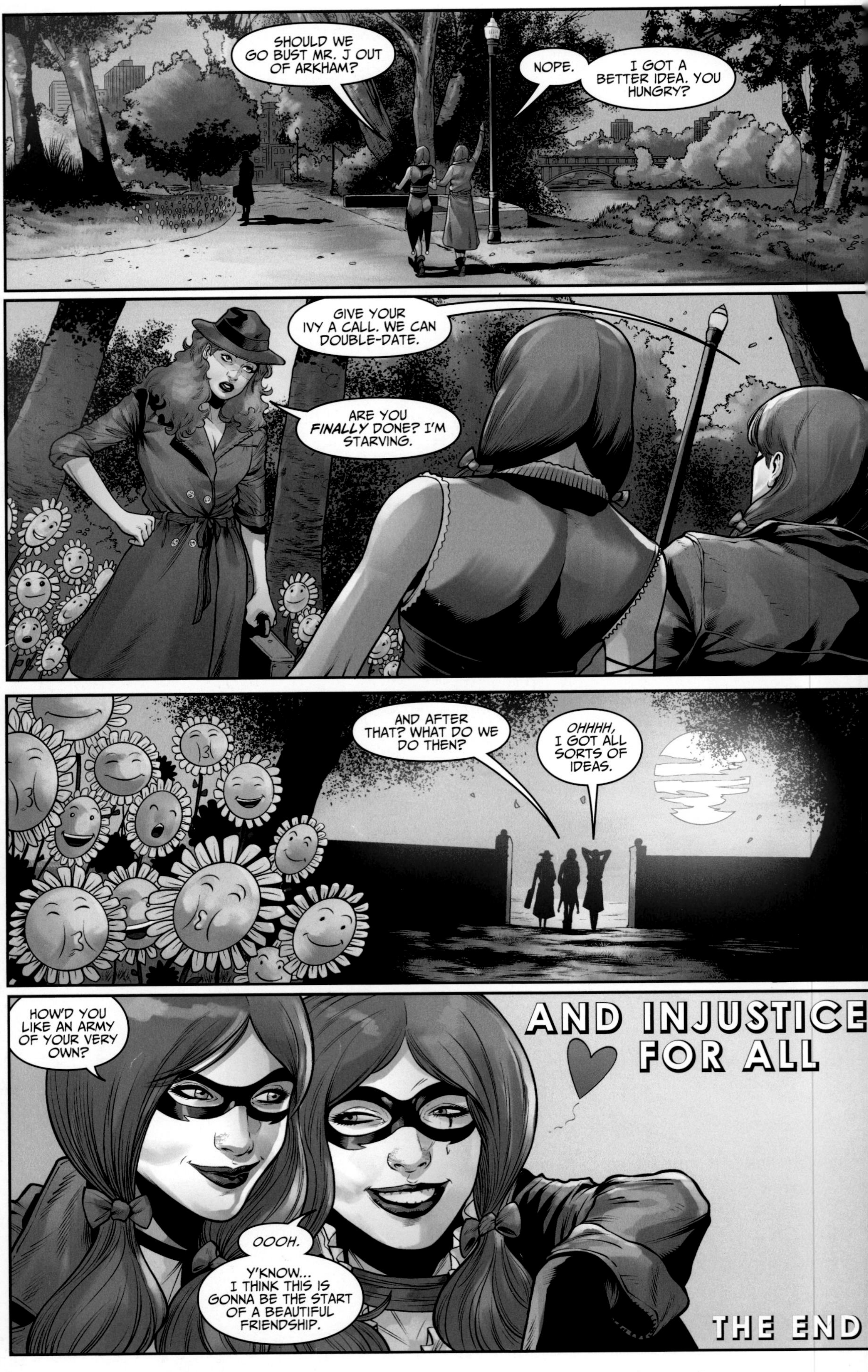
SHOULD WE GO BUST MR. J OUT OF ARKHAM?
NOPE.
I GOT A BETTER IDEA. YOU HUNGRY?
GIVE YOUR IVY A CALL. WE CAN DOUBLE-DATE.
ARE YOU FINALLY DONE? I'M STARVING.
AND AFTER THAT? WHAT DO WE DO THEN?
OHHHH, I GOT ALL SORTS OF IDEAS.
HOW'D YOU LIKE AN ARMY OF YOUR VERY OWN?
AND INJUSTICE FOR ALL
OOOH.
Y'KNOW... I THINK THIS IS GONNA BE THE START OF A BEAUTIFUL FRIENDSHIP.
THE END